Better Business

BETTER BUSINESS

HOW THE B CORP MOVEMENT IS REMAKING CAPITALISM

● ● ●

CHRISTOPHER MARQUIS

Yale

UNIVERSITY PRESS

New Haven and London

Published with assistance from the foundation established in memory of Amasa Stone Mather of the Class of 1907, Yale College

Yale University Press books may be purchased in quantity for educational, business, or promotional use. For information, please e-mail sales. press@yale.edu (U.S. office) or sales@yaleup.co.uk (U.K. office).

Set in Gotham and Adobe Garamond types by IDS Infotech Ltd.
Printed in the United States of America.

Library of Congress Control Number: 2020933181
ISBN 978-0-300-24715-2 (hardcover : alk. paper)

A catalogue record for this book is available from the British Library.

This paper meets the requirements of ANSI/NISO Z39.48-1992 (Permanence of Paper).

10 9 8 7 6 5 4 3 2 1

For Li Ying

Contents

Preface

The B Corp movement is the most important social movement you've never heard of.

If you care about rising inequality and decreasing economic mobility, the climate crisis, the coming soil and water crisis, and the political crisis of tribalism, then you should care about the B Corp movement. If you care about long-term economic growth as well as the future of high-quality jobs and work itself in an age of mass automation, then you need to know more about it.

Founded by a nonprofit called B Lab, the B Corp movement is focused on creating a new kind of company that has a triple bottom line—people, planet, and profits—baked into its DNA. At the center of this work is a rigorous assessment whereby companies' performance is judged not just on earnings but on contribution to society and the environment. Thousands of companies around the globe have undergone this assessment. These B Corporations take responsibility for how they affect every one of their stakeholders, not just those who own shares.

Over the last fifteen years, as a professor of business administration at Harvard and Cornell, I have engaged directly with the next generation of business and civic leaders, the people who will shape the economy of tomorrow. At Harvard Business School (HBS), I taught courses on social innovation and institutional change. When I was out giving talks or consulting with companies, I would frequently be asked to name the most impressive example of business innovation I had seen. I always had a few choice answers, things that had recently caught my interest or impressed me. But since 2009, my answer to this question has consistently been the B Corp movement.

At first most of the people I talked to would reply, "Huh?" Now I am more likely to get nods of recognition. The B Corp movement is picking up steam, and business leaders, particularly those concerned about sustainability, are taking notice. Firms in the food and beverage industry might have heard that the Paris-based multinational food products company Danone committed to becoming a B Corp. In the apparel world, well-known brands like Patagonia and EILEEN FISHER have long been certified B Corps and active supporters of the movement. But the full scope of the movement and its potential impact are still not fully appreciated. Most business leaders still regard B Corp companies as occupying a niche at the fringe of their industries—as "cute" social enterprises that could never truly succeed.

Those assumptions are wrong—the B Corp movement has grown exponentially in just its first decade, and I believe that it and associated ideas are poised to be a catalyst for reforming our capitalist economy. To understand this shift, we need to have a systematic understanding of the movement's breadth and scope, including its dynamics and history. The stories of B Corporations in this book illustrate how and why their certification can make a fundamental difference to their business operations and the future.

But it's important to note that the movement is about much more than the number of certified B Corporations. In the last decade, the team at B Lab has created innovative tools for assessing companies and built networks to encourage the growth of the movement. In addition to Danone, B Lab has grabbed the attention of multinational corporations such as Unilever, Procter & Gamble, Nestlé, and Gap, as well as many of the most innovative companies founded in the last decade, including Kickstarter, Allbirds, Casper, and Bombas. In inter-acting with hundreds of executives at scores of social businesses like these, I have found that they are spearheading a social movement: they are interested in promoting not just their own business ideas but the broader notion of creating businesses that are better for all stakeholders.

B Lab has also crafted a legal innovation called the benefit corpo-ration that places social benefits and the rights of workers, the com-munity, and the environment on an equal footing with the financial interests of shareholders. Political figures on both sides of the party aisle have supported the passage of legislation that establishes benefit corporations in most U.S. states. This innovation is sweeping the globe—similar legislation has been passed in Italy, Colombia, Ecua-dor, and the Canadian province of British Columbia, and is under discussion in many other countries.

This book tracks the way all of these different pieces have come together to create an ongoing revolution.

My interest in the movement was sparked in the spring of 2009, when I was teaching a course at HBS on how large companies such as IBM, Goldman Sachs, and Timberland could be strategic in their corporate social responsibility (CSR) programs. One day a student commented that if we wanted to learn about true innovation in the area, we should not study the CSR programs of large companies but examine how social values can be more fundamentally embedded in a company's DNA. Unclear on what she meant, I asked her to elaborate and she described what a B Corp was and listed several certified B Corporations that I knew well, including Method Home Products, King Arthur Flour, and the Boston-based social investment pioneer Trillium Asset Management. I was a bit embarrassed that I had never heard of B Corps until that day, so I spent some time researching the movement. The information I found online reeled me in, but I still wanted to know more. I got in touch with the founders of B Lab, and in 2010 I published the first in-depth case study of their work.

Since then, my colleagues and I have researched and published more than fifty Harvard case studies on social innovation, increasingly focused on B Corporations and the movement they are creating. My earliest accounts of B Corporations were written before I had grasped the full breadth of the movement. In 2011, a student class project introduced me to sweetriot—an all-natural, women-owned chocolate company with innovative supplier practices that produces delicious nibs, small pieces of crushed cacao beans covered in chocolate. When I visited the company's headquarters in Greenwich Village to interview its leaders, I was surprised to see a B Corp certificate hanging on the wall. A year later, a research assistant's passion about Warby Parker's eyewear and its buy-one, give-one donation model convinced me that it was an important company to study. Again, a visit to its corporate headquarters revealed to me that Warby Parker was a certified B Corp (for reasons that I will describe later, it no longer is). Clearly my millennial students and researchers were seeing a bigger picture that had not yet come into focus for me.

The change I've witnessed over just a decade has been incredible. In 2009, just a handful of pioneering students knew about B Corps. Today, when I begin the first class of the course I teach on social entrepreneurship at Cornell, I ask my students to raise their hands if they've heard of the movement—and nearly everyone's hand shoots up. More important, however, is how deeply passionate they are about the project and how much they want to be involved. Every year since 2010, I've invited B Lab leaders to visit my classes and sponsored campus events to discuss their work. Disappointingly, the first such event attracted only a handful of students. Since 2016, however, some of these events have been standing room only in spaces that hold more than a hundred people. Students sit on the steps and crowd in the doorways to hear what the B Lab founders have to say.

I have learned as much from my students about the importance of developing this new way of doing business as I have taught them. Millennials make up approximately half of the workforce already, and over the next few decades, as their boomer parents pass on, it is estimated that they will inherit $30 trillion.[1] They have a significant desire to create positive change through their purchases and work, and the B Corp movement is capable of delivering this. As consumers, voters, and future leaders, they will be the vanguard that drives it forward, though it will take all generations—all people—to really make it happen.

It is important to recognize that this movement is truly global. More than 50 percent of B Corps are outside the United States. My first personal experience with how widespread this movement had become was in China in 2014. I had been invited to give a presentation on corporate social responsibility to the inaugural class of the Peking University Master of Social Enterprise Management program. I assumed that these students would want to see recognizable names, so I reverted to my examples of Goldman Sachs and IBM, while also adding a few Chinese examples. After my presentation, a student leader politely let me know that many of them were disappointed that I hadn't discussed B Corporations; they had seen from my résumé that I had been researching this subject and hoped I'd be presenting on it. Impressed, I told her to ask the program advisor to invite me to return to give a presentation on B Corps. A few months later, I returned to Beijing to deliver a public lecture on the B Corp movement attended by local Chinese entrepreneurs as well as interested students. This brought my work to the attention of social enterprise leaders in Hong Kong, and in November 2017 I was a keynote speaker at the

Hong Kong Social Enterprise Summit, which had over four thousand attendees; I had been invited specifically because of my focus on B Corps. I spoke right after Hong Kong's chief executive Carrie Lam. In 2017, I researched and published a Harvard Kennedy School case study on First Respond, the first certified B Corp in Mainland China.

Then, in February 2018, I was one of twelve global academics (including Nobel Prize–winning economist Edmund Phelps) who were chosen to brief Chinese prime minister Li Keqiang on key changes in the world that China should understand and adapt to. While I was asked to speak on social entrepreneurship and innovation generally, I spent about a third of my twenty minutes on the potential of the B Corp movement for China. China's B Corp movement is still in its infancy, but the drive and passion are there. The organizers must have found the topic interesting, as I was invited to participate in this gathering in 2019 and 2020. In January 2020, right before China's coronavirus lockdown, I met the prime minister in Beijing again and presented to his team on many of the key ideas in this book. Little did I know that, only months later, the world would be in a different place and the ideas in this book would be even more important.

In addition to my students and the social entrepreneurs who are founding B Corps, I have also been energized by growing enthusiasm from a third set of actors: regular people who believe that there should be change in this country and want to know more about the B Corp movement. When I teach executives or talk with friends and colleagues about B Corps, many express surprise that they had not already heard of it. Once awareness kicks in, they begin to see such companies everywhere.

Even a decade into my work on this topic, I am surprised and inspired almost every day by the number of B Corporations I come across. Not long ago as I was having dinner in a restaurant a few blocks from my apartment in New York City, I ordered a bottle of wine from the biodynamic French vintner Chateau Maris. The wine was delicious, but I wasn't expecting the B Corp logo prominently displayed on the back of the bottle. Chateau Maris became certified in 2016—the first winery in Europe to do so. Robert Eden, founder of Chateau Maris, explained why a French winery would want to receive a U.S.-based certification: "B Corp is a great roadmap to entice us and encourage us to take steps within our company to open up more to social and environmental aspects. It also allows us to put in place certain management tools, so we become more precise and more accurate in achieving our goals. . . . It opens up many doors that we didn't know were there."[2] The vineyard works at improving its supplier chain, using biodynamic methods in agriculture, and improving the local community—while also making great-tasting wine.

All of these experiences tell me that the B Corp movement is poised to break out. Tipping points typically occur after a change has been percolating under the surface for a while and has not yet been fully recognized. At some point, an event connects the dots and leads to greater awareness and a steeper growth trajectory. I sincerely hope that this book will play a part in that.

Better Business

Introduction

Many people, especially young people, deeply distrust our current system of capitalism. They have good reason to. Despite the astounding technological innovations it has enabled, only some people have benefited. Though a host of indicators tell us that the economy is strong, vast numbers of people struggle to pay for basic provisions such as food and shelter. When the economy falters, average people see that the rich stay rich and the rest bear the brunt. Lots of smart young people are unable to find jobs that suit their talents. Further education might help them, but many can't afford it.

If that isn't enough, they can see that the climate is changing and that much of the business world is loath to admit and address its culpability in that phenomenon. Hurricanes Irma, Maria, and Harvey physically devastated parts of North America, creating long-term economic damage. Heat waves in Pakistan and tsunamis in Indonesia, among many other natural disasters, have left thousands dead and homeless.

California businessman Paul Hawken, the cofounder of the gardening retailer Smith and Hawken, put it this way: "We are stealing the future, selling it in the present, and calling it GDP."[1] What does that mean? It means that the industrial world is built by sleight of hand. Companies don't have to pay for the damage their pollution creates, but if those costs were factored into their operations, they would be losing money. In fact, research has shown that if we took their environmental impacts into account, none of the top industry sectors would be profitable.[2]

Furthermore, the corporate world has been rife with scandals; companies have been exposed for the ways in which they disregard not only environmental but also human costs. Uber and the Weinstein Company, among many others, have been called out for allowing a culture of sexism and harassment to thrive at their companies.[3] HSBC bank in the United Kingdom was exposed for paying men twice as much as women, and pay inequality exists in virtually every industry across the globe.[4] It isn't hard to figure out how companies benefit from ignoring a culture of harassment, or from offering less pay to those who have been conditioned not to ask for more than they're given. These are direct consequences of *shareholder primacy*, a focus on maximizing profits and share values to the exclusion of equity and fairness.

Under the banner of serving shareholders first, businesses have compartmentalized their liabilities. Typically costs that are outside of a company's immediate purview—for example, the quality of the air in the towns in which they operate, the healthcare costs of their employees— are considered *externalities*. Economic theory based on shareholder primacy says that corporations should limit the cost of externalities to return more money to shareholders. But this has led us to the crucial tipping point that we find ourselves at today.

This is brought into relief by the US health care industry response to the coronavirus pandemic. To reduce costs, vital equipment such as facial masks and ventilators are produced "just in time," and offshoring and outsourcing is rampant. The result is a fragile system that can't deal well with crises. It is key, now, for us to think not about externalities but about interdependencies—to understand that companies, communities, consumers, employees, and the planet itself are all intimately connected. Every decision made by one actor in this web directly affects all of the others.

Historically, governments addressed these issues, developing policies and programs to hold companies accountable. Today, they are not only pulling back from regulation, they are enacting destructive policies themselves. The Trump administration's environmental irresponsibility and tax cutting dominate the headlines, but this has been happening all over the world.

At some point, someone will have to pay. It may not be the generation in power today, but it will likely be the next one. And they aren't happy about it. Capitalism, as we've known it for the last half century, with its overwhelming focus on shareholder primacy, must become a thing of the past.

Luckily, not all businesses are motivated by unchecked greed. A growing number of companies are working to secure a higher quality of life for everyone, not just the rich, to steer us away from our impending fall off the environmental and societal cliff. More than three thousand of them all over the world, including many that make products we consume and use every day, have been certified by B Lab. The B Corp movement that they are creating is one in which businesses recognize that they can only truly thrive when they benefit everyone who is affected by their operations.

The B Corp movement is, in large part, a direct response to the toxic workplace cultures, poor environmental standards, and profit-centered mindsets that have long dominated the corporate world. It is a grassroots movement that began from the bottom and is working its way to the top alongside a number of other movements and organizations that share a similar spirit, among them Virgin Group founder Richard Branson's B Team and Whole Foods CEO John Mackey's Conscious Capitalism. B Corps have also been actively involved in Pope Francis's Economy of Francesco, which aims to "make the economy of today and tomorrow fair, sustainable and inclusive, with no one left behind."[5] In December 2019, over five hundred B Corps publicly committed at the UN Climate Change Conference, COP25, to accelerate the reduction of their greenhouse gas emissions to reach net zero by the year 2030, a full twenty years ahead of the 2050 targets set in the Paris Agreement.[6] B Lab also recently joined forces with the United Nations to help operationalize its seventeen Sustainable Development Goals (SDGs) for business.

Among the thousands of certified B Corporations are independent firms like Patagonia, business units of multinational corporations like Campbell Soup and Gap, and start-ups such as Kickstarter. In the United Kingdom, leading media company the Guardian Media Group, publisher of the *Guardian* and the *Observer,* was certified in 2019. And in South America, Natura, a publicly traded $3 billion cosmetics company that recently acquired U.S. beauty industry pioneer Avon, and TriCiclos, a recycling company, are also driving changes in the mindsets of employees, investors, consumers, and governments.

In addition to its certification process, B Lab has been working to create a new corporate form that formalizes social responsibility in companies' governance. Thirty-five American states have passed benefit corporation legislation as of early 2020, and more than ten thousand U.S. companies have incorporated using the benefit corporation form. Benefit corporation legislation has already passed in Italy, Colombia, Ecuador, and British Columbia; Argentina, Australia, Brazil, Canada, Chile, and France are among the countries that are currently working to enact it.

This book is about much more than just the B Corp movement. It tracks the evolution of the principles and practices developed by B Lab and others in order to understand why they are necessary, to highlight how they work in practice, and to encourage others to join this movement to reform capitalism. While individually, what are known as "social businesses" create important impacts, the traditional conception of them as a "fourth sector" assumes that the rest of capitalism should maintain its current way of thinking. What's needed—and what the B Corp movement represents—is a fundamentally new way of doing business.

B Lab got the movement going, but to transform capitalism, we all need to be completely on board. Companies must adhere to higher standards and work to increase their positive impacts. Consumers must use their everyday purchases to choose the type of world they want to live in. Employees must demand more of their employers and, in turn, be passionate and dedicated themselves to sustainable practices. Investors, especially those in the public markets, must hold companies to a rigorous and all-encompassing standard. Policy makers must actively enact change through the policies and statutes they support. Citizens must speak up with their votes. The system cannot change itself—only we can.

Although it is not usually thought of as a social business, Paris-based Danone has been a pioneer in this space. Its global CEO Emmanuel Faber saw the B Corp movement as revolutionary and jumped on board; as of early 2020, Danone has seventeen certified B Corps in its corporate portfolio, including its North American subsidiary. As Faber told me, becoming a B Corporation gave Danone "an ability to say, 'This is the kind of company we are. More and more companies should be like that.' "

Founded in 1973 by Fred Keller, Cascade Engineering, a large plastics manufacturing company headquartered in Grand Rapids, Michigan, has been an equal opportunity employer since its very first day and worked with other companies in Michigan to combat racism. Christina Keller, Fred Keller's daughter and Cascade's current CEO, describes the company's triple bottom line: "We don't take a hierarchical approach to people; everybody has value." She emphasizes, "It's not good enough to say, 'Hey, you're valued' "; the company actively helps formerly incarcerated and people on welfare to reestablish careers. She continues, "Care for the planet was a big part of our upbringing. . . . And now that translates into recycled materials, zero waste-to-landfill, etc. in the facility. And then on the profit side: How can we be the most effective that we can be? How can we figure out how to solve problems?"[7]

Fred Keller teaches a course at Cornell University on sustainable business, and when he met the B Lab founders, he knew he wanted to support the movement. As Christina Keller explains, "Our values have always been there. We became a B Corp to help push the movement forward, and push it in a new way, and attract or come together with others that have similar values. [It's not as if] we put the B on and started doing anything differently. This was kind of an additional certification to help us look at how we can get better and connect with a greater community."[8]

There is an important distinction between being a B Corporation and other forms of socially focused corporate activities, such as donating to nonprofits and implementing recycling plans. Corporate social responsibility (CSR), a business approach that encourages sustainability in the behaviors of corporations, has been around for quite some time. On the surface, these ideas are certainly laudable. However, many companies and their leaders have been accused of "greenwashing"— that is, of being all talk and no action. They publicize their "green" work—whether that be environmental initiatives or social ones—while hiding the true costs of their business.

For instance, for many years, BP was investing in alternative energy and claiming its two-letter name stood for "Beyond Petroleum." In 2000, to reflect this new image, the company changed its logo from the traditional shield with BP in the middle to a green and yellow sunflower design.[9] Then in 2010 the *Deepwater Horizon* oil spill occurred, and the public learned that BP's internal practices did not match its public relations. The environmental and human cost of the oil spill was devastating. The explosion itself cost eleven people their lives, and direct exposure to the fumes that arose when the platform exploded or from the spill itself could lead to long-term skin and respiratory issues. The animal life in the area has yet to recover. In 2017, seven years after the spill occurred, a local fisherman described the long-term effects: "I saw a fish this summer . . . that still had spinal deformities. Speckled trout born with kinks in their spines. I've seen bottlenose dolphins with big blotches on them. That's not normal." For a long time, seafood from this area was toxic. Perhaps the most considerable human cost was economic—many industries were affected, from fishing to tourism.[10]

How can consumers, employees, and others tell the difference between companies that are truly doing good and those that are all talk? If we are ever to trust corporations again, their first step must be toward greater transparency and accountability. Those issues cut to the core of the BP case. In 2018, BP announced a renewed focus on cutting emissions from its oil and gas rigs, certainly a laudable goal at first glance. However, it continued to ignore the much bigger contributions to global warming that its actual products—oil and gas— make. Critics such as Tom Burke, the chairman of environmental think tank E3G and a former BP advisor, labeled this a "20th century response to a 21st century problem."[11] Consumers need to be able to look behind the logo and understand how green and well run a company's operations actually are at the core, not just through side projects or public relations.

I witnessed this confusion firsthand on a recent trip with family and friends in Boulder, Colorado. I had explained my research on the B Corporation movement, which most of them had never heard of. That evening, as we walked in an outdoor retail area, they were amazed as I pointed out the B Corps companies, including Patagonia, Ben & Jerry's, Athleta (an athletic wear brand owned by Gap that had the B Corp logo prominently displayed on its front window), and locally owned Newton Running.

Interestingly, one of my friends asked about Lush Cosmetics, expecting it to be on the list of B Corps that I was rattling off. Why have some brands that portray a socially responsible image not joined the movement? Although I couldn't be sure, I suspected that Lush's use of chemicals at the time, which the company had been criticized for, might be one of the reasons.[12] The company's use of plastic packaging, despite the "farmers' market" look of the store, might also be holding it back from meeting B Lab's standards. At the bottom of Lush's website, where many companies feature certification badges attesting that their products are Fair Trade, organic, and/or cruelty free, Lush lists a series of terms that bear a striking resemblance to certification badges: "fighting animal testing," "ethical buying," "100% vegetarian," "handmade," and "naked! Packaging." Exploring these various claims leads to stories from the company itself, but not much in terms of third-party certifications or audits.[13] While recent press releases do suggest that Lush may be doing a lot of good work in eliminating chemicals and wasteful packaging, without a rigorous third-party assessment, it is difficult to judge the veracity of the company's claims. My friends and family realized that the B Corp brand is an incredibly powerful tool to easily and reliably identify socially responsible businesses.

Two important features set companies like Danone North America and Cascade Engineering apart from other "responsible" or "conscious" businesses. First, as noted, is that they have undergone a rigorous assessment of their activities and are transparent to the public about the results. People can "see" and judge for themselves the company's actions. Second is that they have changed their governance, incorporating a social mission into the legal foundation of the company, recognizing that the company is deeply interdependent with society. This new version of business and the economy can provide the foundation for a better, more equitable and sustainable form of capitalism.

This movement has become international—it has spread to all four corners of the world, is embraced by local entrepreneurs, and has been met with excitement and passion in every country it's made landfall in. Truly, full global expansion is the only way for this movement to push our economy past the tipping point to a more sustainable form of capitalism.

While businesses can't solve every problem we face, they have a big role to play in a capitalist society; they can continue to tip the scales toward the benefit of the few, with toxic side effects for all, or they can guide us toward better, more equitable long-term solutions. In today's political and social environment, such a shift is more important than ever, and it *is* happening. Millennials are largely driving this change through their preference—as consumers and as workers—for companies that challenge the mainstream and are socially and environmentally responsible. The B Corp movement not only provides a framework to do this but is also a rallying point for others to get behind.

In 2017, the business world was taken aback when the UK-based consumer goods company Unilever rejected a $143 billion bid by Kraft Heinz. The bid was backed by the major shareholders of Kraft Heinz: Berkshire Hathaway—owned by the world's best-known capitalist, Warren Buffett—and the Brazilian private equity firm 3G Capital. According to everything we know about capitalism, the bid should have been accepted because it would have enriched Unilever shareholders. But it wasn't. Why? Because the battle between the power of traditional capitalism, focused solely on business profit to the exclusion of all else, and the need to recognize that companies and society are deeply linked had come to a head.[14]

Unilever's CEO at the time, Paul Polman, described the failed bid as "a clash between people who think about billions of people in the world and some people that think about a few billionaires."[15] On one side stood Buffett, whose many famous investments include the classic American brands Coca-Cola, Dairy Queen, and McDonald's. While Buffett's down-to-earth lifestyle is as lauded as his investment acumen—he still lives in the Omaha house he bought in 1958 and eats breakfast every day at McDonald's, despite his constantly increasing wealth—his choice to associate himself with fast food companies appears increasingly inconsistent with the sustainability-focused values of today's young consumers.[16] On the other side stood Polman, a self-effacing corporate statesman who preferred to make investments in socially responsible businesses, including such well-known brands as Seventh Generation and Ben & Jerry's, and lesser-known ones such as Pukka Herbs, Mae Terra, Sir Kensington's, and Sundial, all of them certified B Corporations that develop natural and organic products.

Polman is not a naïve man; he understood the strategic value of positioning his company to better meet the needs and interests of the next generation. Under his leadership, Unilever's guiding mission was to follow responsible business practices and to prioritize the needs of all stakeholders—which includes you, me, and everyone else on the planet. As Polman put it, "I don't think our fiduciary duty is to put shareholders first. I say the opposite." Unilever strives to focus on "improving the lives of the world's citizens and come up with genuine sustainable solutions," and this mindset is rooted in the company's belief that being "in sync with consumers and society" will ultimately lead to favorable shareholder returns.[17]

A stronger reputation among consumers, better employee retention, environmentally sound practices, *and* healthy profits: this is a new capitalism built on interdependencies. This new way of doing business is evolving capitalism from a twentieth-century model of wealth maximization for shareholders to a new system that maximizes value for society. Many people questioned the wisdom of Unilever's decision when it rejected the Kraft Heinz bid, and the company may continue to face risks because of it. But so far, the numbers are on Unilever's side. The company's "sustainable living" brands have been outperforming its other brands for several years: they grew 46 percent faster than the rest of its business in 2017, fueling most of its sales growth. Polman knew that Berkshire Hathaway and 3G Capital focus on generating short-term value and often implement intensive cost-cutting measures in the companies they acquire. That might mean employees losing their jobs, environmental programs facing the chopping block, and long-term sustainability initiatives getting stuck in neutral—the potential loss of anything and everything that doesn't translate into short-term profit.[18]

Rejecting the bid was a not-so-quiet moment of revolt against shareholder primacy. However, I see this this example mainly as a leading indicator that there is another way to do business. Buffett and Polman personify the fundamental difference between two types of corporate cultures that are now very clearly opposing each other. On one side is traditional business, with its exclusive focus on shareholders' profit and short-term returns. On the other is business with a triple bottom line: people, planet, and profit. Companies like Unilever are at the forefront of redefining capitalism, and young people—and their day-to-day choices—are helping them do it. But creating a sustainable business model is only the first step. Without concomitant legal changes, those well-intentioned changes could wither over time as companies take on new management and investors. Indeed, Polman has since retired from Unilever. It remains to be seen whether the company will continue on the course he set for it.

Across many industries, "challenger brands" that have embraced the triple bottom line are redefining what it means to be a company in the twenty-first century. Method and Seventh Generation, for example, have challenged the chemical-based cleaning and home product industry by providing natural, nontoxic, and biodegradable products. The success of both brands can be attributed to the growing consumer consciousness of toxic chemicals and their effects on the environment, as well as the companies' risk-taking attitude in standing up to traditional, mainstream corporations.

As we've seen, people feel that the current system is flawed and is failing them. Forty percent of America's wealth is in the hands of just 1 percent of the population.[19] Carbon in our atmosphere has surpassed the four hundred parts per million that is widely considered dangerous.[20] Legal structures hinder long-term value creation for shareholders and stakeholders alike, while a lack of standards makes it difficult for consumers, investors, policy makers, and workers to distinguish good companies from good marketing. The growing movement of people who seek to use business to address these challenges is one of the most important social trends of our time. Tens of millions of consumers, investors, and workers are seeking to align their purchases, investments, and employment decisions with their values.

Millennials want more than just a paycheck—studies show they want a higher purpose and a connection to the social values of the companies they choose to work for, and that they generally reject the traditional, singular goal of capitalism—maximizing profits.[21] The rise of B Corps is a clear indication of this trend. Two-thirds of millennials shared that the reason they accepted a job offer was the mission of their company. Many B Corps have stated that they noticed an uptick in recruitment post-certification and that many new applicants credit their B Corp certification as the reason they're applying.[22] A 2019 Deloitte study showed that most college-educated millennials believe that the primary purpose of business should be to act as a force for good, to improve the world. However, fewer than half of the millennials surveyed said that businesses behave ethically. Millennials and Gen Zers are losing faith in the current system and its leadership for a myriad of reasons, and they are attracted to socially responsible businesses that take care of their employees.[23]

Market research confirms that millennials are much more conscious than older generations about the products and businesses they endorse through their consumption. A recent survey conducted by the Harvard Kennedy School found that more than 50 percent of people between the ages of eighteen and twenty-nine reject capitalism.[24] They want transparency and a clear understanding of the brands they consume. A Brookings Institution report found that 90 percent of millennials are more likely to buy from companies that support solutions to social issues than from other companies.[25] Larry Fink, CEO of the world's largest investment firm, BlackRock, wrote in his 2019 annual letter that millennials "will drive not only their decisions as employees but also as investors, with the world undergoing the largest transfer of wealth in history: $24 trillion from baby boomers to millennials. As this wealth shifts and investing preferences change, environmental, social, and governance issues will be increasingly material to corporate valuations."[26]

Though a new belief system is on the rise, the status quo is still protected by the old guard, men and women who do not welcome change. The first decade of the B Corp movement has not been easy, and the challenges will continue to grow until we reach the day that the movement becomes the all-encompassing success that it must. Our future is at stake—not just millennials' but everyone's. While the current global political landscape is deeply polarized (as attested by the election and subsequent years in office of President Trump and the vote leading to Brexit, among many other examples), there are also suggestions that there is significant support for progressive economic policies and a greater focus on the natural environment, even among more traditionalist and conservative segments of the U.S. population. These include a leaning toward policies for higher taxes on the rich and greater control of corporations. For instance, a 2017 Pew study showed that 94 percent of "Market Skeptic Republicans" (about 30 percent of registered Republican voters) believe that the economy unfairly favors powerful interests, and that taxes on corporations and large businesses should be raised; this view places them closer on the spectrum to liberals than conservatives.[27] Further, a majority of the population disapproves of Trump's 2017 tax overhaul bill, which saw an incredible cut in taxes on the wealthy and on large corporations, with little relief offered to the lower and middle classes.[28] Many self-described conservatives are taking stands on social and cultural issues (immigration, reproductive rights, LGBTQ+ rights) and fiscal issues that are more "liberal" than not.

Awareness of the B Corp movement will grow exponentially in the coming years. Almost every day I see news reports that show its pervasiveness. For example, on one day in August 2018, a number of articles in the *New York Times* and other media caught my attention. One was an op-ed first published a number of months ago entitled "No Wonder Millennials Hate Capitalism," which hardly came as a surprise to me.[29] Indra Nooyi, the CEO of Pepsi, was stepping down from her position, and the focus of the coverage was on how she had reoriented Pepsi around healthier foods.[30] A key example was its purchase of Bare Foods, which is a certified B Corp. Then there was a story about Massachusetts governor Deval Patrick, who had just said that President Trump should be impeached, and who at the time was rumored to be interested in running for president in 2020. Before entering the race, Patrick worked for Bain's impact investing arm. His first investment was in Sundial Brands, a B Corp, and he is a vocal supporter of B Lab's analytics platform for evaluating social investments.[31]

Around the same time, Senator Elizabeth Warren wrote an op-ed in the *Wall Street Journal* announcing her Accountable Capitalism Act, which would require all corporations with more than $1 billion in revenues to become federally chartered (currently corporate charters are at the state level in the United States) and adopt a model of governance in which directors must consider the interests of all major stakeholders—not just shareholders—in company decisions. Its headline was "Companies Shouldn't Be Accountable Only to Shareholders."[32] As Warren acknowledges, her proposed legislation is based on the benefit corporation model pioneered by B Lab, which is already in use in Delaware, legal home to two-thirds of the Fortune 500.

Before dismissing Warren's ideas as massive government overreach, as some have done, you might be interested to know that there are only about thirty-eight hundred businesses in the United States with revenues greater than $1 billion. Is it unreasonable to require them to put the interests of their workers, their customers, and their communities on par with the interests of their shareholders? Given the multiple crises we face, not least the crisis of trust (corporations are among the least trusted institutions in the United States), this doesn't seem like an irrational conversation to have as we enter into the 2020 presidential campaign, and contemplate the economic forces behind such social-political movements as Brexit, the Yellow Vests, and the Extinction Rebellion.

On the other side of the aisle, Senator Marco Rubio recently released a forty-page report entitled "American Investment in the 21st Century" in which he made the case that the American economy is suffering from an unhealthy focus on short-term financial returns. The report specifically implicates shareholder primacy theory as the main reason for the "shift of American business away from the traditional role expected of it in our economy," as the "theory tilts business decision-making towards returning money quickly and predictably to investors rather than building long-term corporate capabilities, reduces investment in research and innovation, and undervalues American workers' contribution to production." The Rubio report concludes: "We need to build an economy that can see past the pressure to understand value-creation in narrow and short-run financial terms, and instead envision a future worth investing in for the long-term."[33]

Senators Elizabeth Warren and Marco Rubio don't agree on much, but they agree on their diagnosis of the cancer that's killing American competitiveness, American communities, and American workers—shareholder primacy. Republican governors, including Nikki Haley, Mike Pence, and Scott Walker, have signed benefit corporation legislation. It is rare today to see Democrats and Republicans agree on anything, which suggests that other policies that put people rather than profits at the center of our economic decision making could gain bipartisan support.

Even CEOs of the largest American companies are starting to come to this conclusion. On August 19, 2019, the Business Roundtable, an influential trade group that represents two hundred of America's largest companies, changed its "Statement on the Purpose of a Corporation" to reflect that corporations should meet the needs not just of shareholders but also those of its stakeholders such as employees, consumers, and society.[34] While this is an exciting development and may represent the fundamental shift in corporate ideology the world needs, the statement has come under significant critique because few details have been offered on how companies will be held accountable for implementing this new purpose. Unless these CEOs put actions behind their words, this will be just another example of business leaders giving lip service to making the world a better place while continuing to operate in the same old way.

For instance, to make such statements a reality, they need to support holding companies accountable to stakeholders, begin aligning performance standards inside the firm with stakeholder-oriented objectives and, most important, begin discussing these objectives with investors and government leaders. For wide-scale change to occur, it is essential for these leaders to convince the capital markets and policy makers of the importance of stakeholder-aligned governance structures.

We are at the dawn of a new age of interdependence, but there is still much work to be done to overthrow shareholder primacy. Based on more than a decade of research and featuring interviews with leaders of dozens of leading global companies, this book explores how and why the change led by B Lab is working. B Lab's model focuses on accountability, performance standards, and stakeholder governance and, as we will see, strongly resonates with employees even as it is gaining interest from and helping to foster the growing impact investing movement. The entrepreneurs involved are creating this change by promoting deep local networks, and the movement is rapidly spreading around the globe.

As I will also show you, there are three key areas of work that are needed to help it diffuse further. First is moving from a focus on growing the number of B Corps to creating systems whereby all companies can be like B Corps. Partnering with important international initiatives such as the United Nation's Sustainable Development Goals is an important step in this direction. Furthermore, B Lab must continue attracting larger multinationals to take their CSR to a deeper level, and provide a way to change public markets to a longer-term orientation. Finally, all people—including you, the reader—need to become a part of this critical movement. Only through understanding the power and importance of our consumption choices can we change the world for the better.

1

Focusing on Interdependencies, Not Externalities

Capitalism as it is practiced today is at the root of many serious problems. But the message of this book is not altogether grim—when it is properly regulated by governments, capitalism can also be a tremendous force for good. The technological innovations and economic development it has spurred have lifted hundreds of millions of people out of poverty. The challenge is to harness capitalism's positive elements while also protecting individuals and society from its negative aspects.

To reform our economy to meet the needs of all stakeholders, governments, companies, and consumers must take every aspect of a company's performance into account, ensuring that its social and environmental costs are kept to a minimum. An interdependent economy would not allow businesses to ignore their externalities, to shrug their shoulders and look the other way when their nonrecyclable products end up in landfills and oceans, or when their low wages require employees to take on additional employment to keep afloat. This sense of accountability, essentially, is what the B Corp movement has begun to create.

The B Corp movement was started by three friends who met at Stanford University, pursued successful business careers, and recognized that the business world they were operating in needed to change. Jay Coen Gilbert was the cofounder of a successful basketball footwear and apparel company, AND 1. Bart Houlahan was an investment banker who later joined AND 1 and became its president. Andrew Kassoy managed investments for Michael Dell's private investment company before diving into the world of social entrepreneurship and sustainable businesses. Their personal styles reflect their backgrounds. Though almost always sharply dressed, Kassoy is humble and empathetic. Coen Gilbert provides a big-picture vision delivered through humor and an off-the-cuff approach. Houlahan's passionate energy—reflected in his constant smile—is more deliberate and methodical.

Each questioned the relentless pursuit of short-term profits. Why couldn't businesses also protect and enrich the lives of their employees? Why couldn't they focus on helping their local communities? Why couldn't they commit to environmental responsibility as a core principle? Together, they arrived at two key conclusions:

- Businesses can have a tremendous positive impact on society.
- The institutions that currently support businesses do not allow them to capitalize on that potential—both legal and cultural restrictions focused on shareholder primacy constrain what even well-intentioned business leaders can do.

So they decided to create a remedy—to find a way to scale a business, raise outside capital, and maintain liquidity while remaining true to a social mission. In 2006, they unveiled B Lab: a nonprofit organization dedicated to redefining business as a competition to be not only the "best in the world, but best *for* the world."[1]

To combat issues with how the current system is designed, the B Lab team developed an approach centering on companies' social and environmental transparency and accountability. After all, it's all well and good to *say* that your company is invested in all stakeholders, but if you aren't transparent about your actual performance and held accountable, how can consumers or employees believe you and trust your intentions?

Fundamental to their mission's success was the creation of the benefit corporation—a new form of incorporation that *legally* places social benefits and the rights of workers, the community, and the environment on an equal footing with the interests of shareholders. Without such a legal obligation, the B Lab trio realized, companies risk being pulled away from their mission over time, especially when they need to bring in outside capital. Coen Gilbert and Houlahan had dealt with this problem in their own business venture: "I helped build AND 1 with two purposes: to create private wealth, but also to create broader impact," Houlahan recalled, but they found it impossible to "scale and sell and still hold onto mission over time."[2] The B Lab cofounders envisioned a legal framework that would make higher purpose a competitive advantage.

Why do we need this added focus on accountability and corporate governance? In recent years, as capitalism has increasingly focused on shareholder primacy, companies have shifted to exploiting externalities—that is, the large incentives that exist for companies to offload their environmental and human costs to society, even if doing so is hurting others, whether it be through environmental damage, worker exploitation, or other means. The accountability and corporate governance innovations profiled below provide a platform for companies to put other stakeholders—such as employees, the environment, and communities—on par with financial stockholders.

The Myths of Shareholder Primacy

Incorporation is a powerful technology that can be used to transform society in positive ways. Major economic and innovation breakthroughs, from the industrial revolution to the information revolution, happened in part because incorporation allowed individuals to pool their wealth into collective enterprises. Features such as limited liability encouraged investment by reducing risks, while unlimited duration allowed companies to enter long-term contracts. This unique legal structure was initially created to help develop large commercial ventures such as railroads and banks. In those ventures, the investors *were* the customers—they were fundamentally interdependent with the rest of society. Therefore, unlike what is commonly thought of as the raison d'être of the corporation today—maximizing investment returns—early corporations focused on providing goods and services that served the public interest. Investing in these early corporations meant that you were investing in keeping costs low and service high both for yourself and for your community.

But over time, the original purposes of corporations was obscured. Eventually, the legal concept of shareholder primacy came to dominate corporate law and industry. But there are a number of myths underlying this perspective that need to be exposed.

Myth 1: Shareholder Primacy Is Natural

Our understanding of the corporation underwent a dramatic change in the second half of the twentieth century. Profit in the form of the maximization of shareholder wealth was increasingly seen as its sole purpose. The idea that shareholder capitalism is the natural way markets should operate has since seeped into our collective unconscious. Yet looking at how this concept developed proves that it clearly is not the result of a natural progression toward the most efficient system, but stems from a very specific historical legacy that can be traced back to a number of influential American economists in the 1970s and 1980s. An intellectual revolution asserting that shareholders' interests should be paramount began. In 1970, Milton Friedman, the best-known member of the famous Chicago School, which vigorously promoted free market economics, wrote an article for *New York Times Magazine* denouncing corporate "social responsibility" as irresponsible since it was potentially a misuse of shareholder resources.

Friedman believed that "there is one and only one social responsibility of business—to use its resources and engage in activities designed to increase its profits."[3]

But in the early history of business in the United States, profit maximization was not the sole purpose. As sociologist William Roy shows in his award-winning book *Socializing Capital,* the modern model of a for-profit corporation emerged out of a series of inadvertent choices and circumstances. Corporations were originally created to build infrastructure, support education, and operate markets. State governments created the first corporations, which were accountable to them. But by the end of the nineteenth century, laws of incorporation allowing for the privatization of companies began to pass. In the early 1900s, Roy explains, small manufacturers began to merge in order to protect themselves from the government and banks, and especially their larger competitors. Thus, the beginnings of our current capitalist model began out of a desire to overturn socially focused mandates, exert power, and achieve market control.[4]

The ideas and revolution created by Friedman and his intellectual successors were a direct response to an era where stakeholder ideas held more sway. As discussed in the groundbreaking 1932 book by Adolf A. Berle and Gardiner C. Means, *The Modern Corporation and Private Property,* the U.S. business environment during the first part of the twentieth century was characterized by dispersed owners, leaving managers insulated from shareholder pressures. Thus, they could address issues brought by labor, provide excellent benefits for their employees, invest in their communities, and be generous in their philanthropy. However, at the same time, such structures led to bloated corporations and many examples of managers who were more interested in securing their own position than serving corporate interests.[5]

To correct these downsides, Friedman and others emphasized that managers and executives were only "agents" who served shareholders' interests, and that structures needed to be created to align managers with those interests. This theory and associated practices evolved for the next two decades, becoming what we recognize today as shareholder capitalism. The consensus, both in society and the law, held that the board of directors and executives had to act solely in a way that increased shareholders' wealth, or they could be sued for not fulfilling their "fiduciary duty" to protect shareholders' interests above all else. This philosophy also pervades practices such as share-based incentive compensation packages. Proponents of this theory argue that this is the most efficient form of capitalism.

Eventually, this idea that a company is primarily responsible to its shareholders became encoded in our laws, institutionalized in investment markets, and entrenched in our minds and culture. James Perry, CEO of COOK, a manufacturer and retailer of ready meals with a natural focus, says, "It is like a Jedi mind trick that has been played on the human race." B-Lab's Jay Coen Gilbert likens it to a "source code error" at the core of capitalism.[6] Fifty years after Friedman's article appeared, the global economy continues to follow his plan of action, despite the fact that the world has changed quite dramatically. As we will see throughout this book, dire consequences have arisen from focusing primarily on serving shareholders. Serving a broader set of stakeholders is not only more consistent with how capitalism was practiced for most of its history; it is in fact a much more sustainable system.

Myth 2: Shareholder Primacy Is Better for Investors

In 2012, the late Lynn Stout, a renowned legal scholar at Cornell Law School, published *The Shareholder Value Myth: How Putting Shareholders First Harms Investors, Corporations, and the Public*, a no-holds-barred exposé of the lies the corporate world tells itself about shareholder primacy and an explanation of why following that path will lead to disaster. Stout sharply questioned the supposed efficiency of the system, pointing out the inherent conflict posed by the fact that there is no single shareholder value: the strategies and values that work for one shareholder at a specific point in time may offer dismal results to other shareholders over a longer length of time. We see this very clearly in the behaviors of short-term and long-term investors. Short-term investors often push strategies that temporarily cause a market price to increase; then they sell, and the company pays the price. Without some type of unity among shareholders—a corporate purpose embedded in the corporation's governing documents, for example—long-term impact and improvement cannot happen.[7]

Such an effect is even more pronounced in capital markets that are dominated by institutions, as is the case in the United States and most other developed countries. Institutional investors—pensions, retirement funds, mutual funds—all hold highly diversified long-term portfolios that encompass the global market. It is important to recognize that these institutional investors are, in reality, all of us. It is *our* retirement plans and pensions that make up these investments, and we are the beneficiaries of the gains. Every decision they make regarding where to invest the nation's money affects all of our lives— what type of policies are pushed forward, what type of issues are brought to the forefront of the world's attention, how the country's social and environmental issues are addressed, and more.

Because of their massive size, these investors are essentially "universal owners": their holdings represent the economy in general as opposed to one specific investment, and so they require the entirety of the market to be healthy, not just one company. Research tells us that for universal owners, more than 80 percent of financial returns come from the performance of the market itself, not the fluctuations of one particular investment. Because of that, the most important things affecting investment performance for the vast majority of Americans—

these universal owners—are big-picture ("macro") characteristics such as levels of pollution, societal unrest, and other broader social and environmental trends that are frequently thought of as externalities. These issues affect the economy as a whole, and therefore their portfolios. Meanwhile, people who invest for short-term gains are much less interested in macro issues and, in fact, may consider it wasteful for a company to invest in employee training, pollution abatement, or any environmentally conscious work—the kind of spending that would minimize their short-term returns.[8]

Rick Alexander, who has been recognized as one of the top ten corporate lawyers in the world but who now calls himself a "recovering corporate lawyer," describes it this way: "I think that there needs to be public engagement where there is a cultural mind shift to explain that what's good for GM specifically, for example, might not be good for America." Alexander until recently headed legal policy at B Lab, and in 2019 founded the Shareholder Commons, an organization dedicated to working with the capital markets more broadly to overthrow shareholder primacy. He explains that, because shareholders of GM also own companies like Apple and Alphabet (the parent company of Google), the notion of doing what is "good for GM" should not be narrowly focused on shareholder monetary returns; instead, people need to start considering what can lead to "a thriving world and economy where everybody can do well."

Myth 3: Shareholder Primacy Is Better for All

The importance of universal ownership becomes even more significant when we consider the extent to which shareholder primacy affects the collective good. Alexander recalls that when he read Lynn Stout's book he realized "these things I've assumed for 25 years are just bad assumptions." He was particularly affected by the argument that if a person acted the way corporations are allowed to, if they "did everything possible to maximize their own value and, as long as they follow the law, without caring how much they hurt other people or the environment, we would call that person a sociopath. And yet this is what we expect boards of directors to do." We consider a company successful as long as it provides a return on our capital. Instead, Alexander argues, we should consider a company successful if it provides a return on our capital *without* depleting other capitals on which we depend, be they human, natural, or social.[9]

To truly assess corporate performance, we need to incorporate externalities into the equation. For example, if the economic damage caused by pollution were factored into a company's cost, it would likely be losing money. Research from environmental data collection firm Trucost illustrates just how significant these issues are. Examining the one hundred biggest environmental hazards caused by companies, Trucost concluded that they cost the global economy $4.7 *trillion* a year. The sectors causing the most damage are coal power generation in East Asia and North America, and global agriculture, particularly in areas where water is scarce. The environmental and societal costs in these sectors far outweigh their overall revenue. In other words, "No high impact region-sectors generate sufficient profit to cover their environmental impacts. . . . If unpriced natural capital costs are internalized, a large proportion would have to be passed on to consumers."[10] But herein lies a problem—consumers, understandably, don't want to be burdened with these costs either. But if we can understand the important effects of internalizing externalities, we can at least have an open debate about how to best manage the costs.

At the root of the issue is the fact that our current system sees wealth entirely in terms of value generated through exchange. Factors outside of the specific exchange, the "externalities," have no price and so are essentially considered free. Such "free gifts" to corporations in their pursuit of profit have traditionally included natural environmental factors such as water and air. While the way that externalities impact the natural environment is becoming better known, less understood is the impact on employees, communities, and consumers. For example, the "gig economy," much heralded when it first emerged, seemed to be a good thing for many people. It offered flexibility and additional opportunities for people with lower incomes. But most businesses that operate in this way recognize no obligation to most of the people who work for them. For instance, in 2017 it was estimated that Uber had over 2 million "driver-partners" worldwide but recognized only about ten thousand of them as actual employees. In that way, the company is able to ruthlessly focus on its own growth. By not actually employing the vast majority of its labor force, it is passing the bulk of the associated costs of doing business, such as healthcare, retirement benefits, and insurance, onto society. Furthermore, this trend has led to people needing to work multiple gig jobs, at the cost of their health—more Americans today are working multiple jobs than ever before.[11]

One important way companies have shifted externalities to society is the widespread replacement of defined benefit pension plans, which guarantee a specific retirement income, with defined contribution plans such as 401(k)s, which transfer a large share of risk and responsibility to employees. Since these plans don't guarantee a retirement income amount, this has led not only to a rising retirement crisis but has exposed everyday Americans to "the market" in unprecedented ways. For many employees, particularly those who started their careers in the 1970s or 1980s, landing a job at a big, well-known corporation was a boon. "You'll always have a job," people would say. "The benefits will be amazing." But in the last two to three decades, these same companies have been slashing pensions and shifting employees who'd worked with them for decades to other types of plans or freezing their pensions altogether.[12] Sears, once the country's largest employer, ended its pension plans in 2006, though employees and retirees are still entitled to the benefits they accrued prior to that. Rather than being happy that the company is able to do as much as it is doing for its older employees and existing retirees, executives at Sears complain about it: CEO Edward Lampert has said that the retirement plans are a burden that hobbled Sears in competing with other retailers, "many of which don't have large pension plans, and thus have not been required to allocate billions of dollars to these liabilities."[13] By liabilities, of course, Sears means its own employees, who built the business over decades. While this sounds reasonable from today's logic of profit maximization, at a deeper level it resonates with Alexander's likening of a corporation to a sociopath.

For universal owners, these environmental and social externalities are unavoidable: they are reflected in higher insurance costs due to pollution, natural disasters and public health crises like the coronavirus pandemic, instability that stem from inequality, and other social and environmental phenomena. If someone invests in a specific company, that person might look at such factors as short-term risks or costs. But the effects of one company's actions (or inactions) on issues such as pollution or economic inequality for its workers inevitably spill over, affecting individuals and other companies in their community, region, or country. Depending on the company's size, these decisions to shortchange the environment or their workers could affect the entire global economy. Universal owners recognize the fundamental interdependence between business and society and thus the value of investments to mitigate the damages caused to the environment and to the global community. Externalities should be acknowledged, at the very least, and ideally they should be internalized. While public policies to protect the most vulnerable among the population and within the environment are essential, the B Corp model also allows us to have open, direct, and engaging public conversations about who should bear these costs—it requires that corporations make these externalities, and the ways that they affect the average person transparent, which in turn forces accountability.

Some companies have learned the problems with shareholder primacy the hard way. Consider John Mackey, the CEO of Whole Foods. Now a household name in North America, Whole Foods grew out of a dream that college dropout Mackey had when he was twenty-three years old. For over three decades, Mackey propelled the Whole Foods mission to provide natural food options to communities forward— through rejections from venture capitalists, stigma against "hippies," and an initial public offering in 1992. But by the 2010s, just as Whole Foods hit its peak stock price, competitors had risen up everywhere and things started to take a turn.[14]

Mackey was an early detractor of the B Corp movement, even though his business's mission and values seem naturally aligned with it. Mackey has been at the forefront of "conscious capitalism," a movement founded on the belief that "free enterprise capitalism is the most powerful economic system for social cooperation and human progress ever conceived." The key differences between conscious capitalism and related ideas such as CSR, sustainability, impact initiatives, and the B Corp movement are verified performance, legal accountability, and public transparency. While agreeing that it is a good idea to "take care of stakeholders," Mackey asked, "What do you need this legal form for?" He dedicated a section of his book *Conscious Capitalism,* published in 2013, to explaining the flaws of the B Corp movement. As long as your social purpose is clear and your company continues to make money, he said, there is no reason to upend the principle of shareholder value maximization.[15]

However, his views changed when his own company came under attack from some powerful shareholders. In the spring of 2017, Whole

Foods' second-largest shareholder, the investment management firm Jana Partners, signaled its intention to sell the company, and many other shareholders followed suit. In June 2017, Mackey instead sold Whole Foods to Amazon for $13.7 billion—a move that shocked most people, given the seemingly different values of the two companies. The global behemoth that values efficiency over social values seemed like a strange home for this counterculture company focused on organic food and environmentalism. In a live, onstage interview with B Lab founder Coen Gilbert at the 2017 B Corp Champions Retreat, Mackey explained his thinking. "They wanted to take over the company, take over our board, and force us into a sale," he said. "Boy, did I wish we were a B Corp." Mackey reiterated his evolved views of the B Corp movement at his own Conscious Capitalism CEO Summit in 2018.[16]

Rick Alexander explains how being a benefit corporation protects companies from the type of situation Whole Foods faced: "If someone is looking to take shares in a corporation and work as an activist shareholder, then whether the company [has adopted] benefit corporation [governance] would likely factor into the decision. It's harder to wrestle with this company than one that hasn't declared its purpose outside of increasing share price. It should be a powerful deterrent; a CEO with a long-term plan to include sustainability would mean the legal argument an activist shareholder would be making wouldn't resonate."[17]

After the sale, Mackey reflected that B Corps were the "tip of a reform movement that capitalism needs as a whole." While current systems are set up to prioritize the market, increasingly consumers and employees are interested in how a company acts in the marketplace instead. He remarked, "I know the part of capitalism that is the most diseased. It's the financial sector. It's almost lost its gyroscope of values, it has become just about money and profits." Mackey and others like him have learned the hard way that once shareholder activists come into play, the values and mission of the company don't matter anymore. What does matter is how they can maximize their profits more, even if it means taking apart and destroying the whole company. As Mackey sees it, "That's a very sick part of capitalism."[18] The B Corporation movement, to match Mackey's metaphor, offers a cure for the sickness.

Overthrowing Shareholder Primacy

Overthrowing shareholder primacy and focusing attention on a business's interdependencies is easier said than done; it requires systematic changes in legal systems, the way investors assess companies, and even the way we think about the purpose of business. Some people believe we have to start with cultural change: shifting our assumptions and norms as a society. This is in keeping with the spirit of Mackey's "conscious capitalism," which proposes that if the company makes a conscious decision to work toward all stakeholder interests and establish a higher purpose—a social mission—then it will *do good* and be a good company. But as Mackey learned, this is not enough. Voluntary CSR programs, while potentially laudable individually, are not enough to overcome the problems inherent in the existing system either. While Unilever's Polman was admirably able to focus on investing in long-term sustainability, one wonders what would happen if Unilever did not also deliver financially.

The laws governing corporations must be overhauled for this shift to truly take hold. Leo E. Strine Jr., the former chief justice of the Supreme Court of Delaware, wrote in an essay entitled "The Dangers of Denial" that "lecturing others to do the right thing without acknowledging the rules that apply to their behavior and the power dynamics to which they are subject is not a responsible path to social progress."[19] Confronting the difficult challenges that arise because of corporate governance laws may be the essential first step toward making for-profit corporations responsible and sustainable.

Soon after its founding, the B Lab team worked with lawyers and government officials to draft legislation that would encode a triple bottom line, one that recognizes not just financial but also social and environmental factors, into the foundations of a new type of company called a benefit corporation. Benefit corporations are required *by law* to consider the interests of employees, customers, communities, and the environment as well as the interests of shareholders. This is a legally binding shift in the traditional power structure of the corporation.

In most states and countries that have passed this type of legislation, benefit corporations must be completely transparent about their impacts and undergo periodic evaluation against a credible third-party standard of the company's overall social and environmental performance. This emphasis on transparency puts more power back into the hands of the people: workers, customers, and other stakeholders, including investors who care about managing systemic risk and/or creating positive impact alongside positive returns. It also is an essential remedy for influential and very sensible critiques of shareholder governance. In its public response to the Business Roundtable statement, the Council of Institutional Investors argued that "accountability to everyone means accountability to no one," and "if 'stakeholder governance' and 'sustainability' become hiding places for poor management, or for stalling needed change, the economy more generally will lose out."[20]

Thus, as Chief Justice Leo E. Strine comments, it is the system that needs to be changed; companies or CEOs can't just say they believe in shareholder governance. "If we wish to make the corporation more socially responsible, we must do it the proper way. If we believe that other constituencies should be given more protection within corporation law itself, then statutes should be adopted giving those constituencies enforceable rights that they can wield. But a more effective and direct way to protect interests such as the environment, workers, and consumers would be to revive externality regulation. We must also address the incentives and duties of institutional investors—who act as the direct stockholders of most public companies—so that these investors behave in a manner more consistent with the longer-term investment horizon of the human beings whose capital they control."[21]

Yvon Chouinard, an avid rock climber, developed a new type of piton as a teenager in the 1970s and Patagonia grew from there—from his parents' garage into the globally recognizable brand that it is today. The piton side of the business was eventually discontinued when it became clear that the product was damaging the natural rock landscapes that climbers loved—a testament to Chouinard's deep commitment to environmentalism.[22] In 2018, the company decided to buckle down and make its mission much more direct: "Patagonia is in business to save our home planet." Chouinard even gave new guidelines to the human resources department: if everything else is equal, hire the person who is the most passionate about saving the planet. This commitment also led to Patagonia becoming one of California's first benefit corporations. In 2011, on the first morning that companies could register as benefit corporations, Chouinard said: "I hope that five years from now, ten years from now, we'll look back and say this was the start of the revolution. The existing paradigm isn't working anymore—this is the future."[23]

Today, Chouinard spends his summers fly-fishing in Wyoming. When he comes into work, he sits at an old wooden desk with just a landline on it, across from CEO Rose Marcario.[24] Chouinard's description of why his company reincorporated as a benefit corporation shows he takes a very long view: "Patagonia is trying to build a company that could last 100 years. . . . Benefit corporation legislation creates the legal framework to enable mission-driven companies like Patagonia to stay mission-driven through succession, capital raises, and even changes in ownership, by institutionalizing the values, culture, processes, and high standards put in place by founding entrepreneurs."[25] Patagonia is still at the vanguard of the B Corp movement. Marcario is quoted in Patagonia's Benefit Report as stating, "The B Corp movement is one of the most important of our lifetime, built on the simple fact that business impacts and serves more than just shareholders—it has an equal responsibility to the community and to the planet."[26]

Prioritizing Accountability through Corporate Governance

It's reasonable to ask why changing business and capitalism more broadly is the key solution to delivering a more sustainable and equitable society. Isn't this just letting the fox guard the henhouse? Shouldn't even more power be shifted to other sectors of society such as the government and nongovernmental actors? Why not focus on a more radical change built on these alternative systems?

Nonprofit organizations or nongovernmental organizations (NGOs) offer a lot of flexibility when it comes to social impact, and they don't have to unravel the intricacies of modern-day capitalism and our current market system. In many ways, NGOs have always been the go-to organizations for delivering social good and advocating for societal change. But these types of organizations have important limitations, among them how they can generate revenue. The cofounders of She Geeks Out, a consulting and training organization dedicated to educating and supporting diverse, inclusive companies and organizations, told me about the difficulties they had in finding the right organizational form to register as. They first applied to be a nonprofit organization, but they weren't allowed to incorporate as an NGO because they generated revenue. They were told they could be a 501(c)(6), but found that there were limited benefits for them under that status. Instead, they became a certified B Corporation. For many organizations that want to make a social or environmental impact, the time needed to raise funds and apply for grants as a nonprofit could be better used. The need to focus on meeting their funders' needs and/or showing their impact means that they are less able to address the social issues they were founded to address.

My focus in this book is on how the key issues underlying inequality and decreasing sustainability can be—and need to be—addressed directly. The economy can be far more inclusive if we change how the capitalist system is practiced at a fundamental level. A vibrant NGO sector is necessary for a healthy society, but as our current situation shows, NGOs often lack sufficient resources to make a continual impact, and they cannot effectively counteract the ill effects of a market that's gone mad for profits.

Benefit corporation status allows companies with a social purpose more flexibility in how they can deliver on that purpose. For instance, Practice Makes Perfect, a certified B Corp focused on providing summer school and academic summer programming, changed from a 501(c)3 nonprofit to a benefit corporation a couple of years after it began. Karim Abouelnaga, its founder, explained that since nonprofits are funded by tax deductions, money that would otherwise have gone to the government, board members are meant to act in the best interests of the government. However, Abouelnaga found that as Practice Makes Perfect grew, these interests didn't always line up with the company's mission. He also felt limited in what he could do: "There were times where I found myself wanting to take bigger risks and make larger leaps to serve more students only to be told I needed to be 'more realistic' or 'not take on that level of risk.' "[27] The company decided that converting to a benefit corporation would address all of those concerns while helping it stay true to its mission.

Why not start with government-led solutions, then? As I've noted, making changes to the laws governing corporations is an essential step in the change that's happening. But public policies and legal protections, although necessary components of a fair and equitable economy, can't solve every global crisis and social problem. What's needed is a combination of work by governments and by corporations.

The Green New Deal introduced by Representative Alexandria Ocasio-Cortez and Senator Ed Markey in early 2019 may appear to offer promise. The resolution calls for a transformation of the American economy by developing policies and incentives to reduce emissions and making all power clean and renewable by 2030, and it focuses on the underserved groups that are the most directly affected by climate change—people of color, the poor, migrants, and indigenous peoples—by demanding the creation of more jobs and easy access to clean water, healthy food, unpolluted air, and more. As a direction without policy specifics, it is commendable and certainly necessary, given the state of the environment and the country.[28]

But for some, the Green New Deal feels like an old-school solution, another twentieth-century response to a twenty-first-century problem. While evocative, its name recalls an earlier era of "big government" before corporations came to dominate the economy and society. While I support the goals of the plan, I would argue that the root causes of the problems also need to be addressed, and those roots can be found in our current model of corporate governance. Fundamental change requires a focus on shifting corporations' actions and mindsets. These shifts can be supported and accelerated by smart public policies.

A promising step in this direction is the aforementioned Accountable Capitalism Act proposed by Senator Elizabeth Warren. Along with its requirement that all corporations with more than $1 billion in revenues adopt the benefit corporation model, it would go further: requiring employees to elect 40 percent of the company's board, mandating public disclosure of all political contributions, and allowing the federal government to revoke corporate status if the company engages in illegal conduct. Changes that fundamentally shift the underlying objectives of corporations are needed to address the systemic root causes of the problems that corporations created in the first place.

Furthermore, since the *Citizens United v. Federal Election Commission* decision that guarantees free speech to organizations such as corporations, labor unions, and other associations, large corporations and special interests have held increasing sway over policy making. And politicians have to appeal to multiple stakeholders simultaneously, so the solutions they create are often suboptimal. In the tobacco industry, for example, large manufacturers are well known for their interference with government policy making: an investigation by Reuters in 2017 found evidence that Philip Morris has formed giant lobbying campaigns to minimize and delay tobacco controls around the world.[29] To depend solely on the government to advance the interests of a movement to reform capitalism would be to overlook the intimate relationship between policy makers and corporate special interests, particularly in the United States.

Protecting against "All Talk, No Action"

Many big businesses pay lip service to the idea of the "social impact" of capitalism, but they've often done so to legitimize and protect their market positions and the systems that created them. Saying the right words and taking the right actions are very different things. Words simply aren't enough. We have followed this recipe over the last few decades, with the rising focus on "CSR" and ideas like "shared value," but we are in a worse place now than when we started. Consumers were at first pacified by these ideas but have now, understandably, grown skeptical.

Anand Giridharadas's 2019 book *Winners Take All: The Elite Charade of Changing the World* accuses elite business leaders and corporations of talking about making the world a better place while upholding the same old damaging capitalist values. He uses the term *Market-World* to refer to a belief system that is focused on using the tools of capitalism to change the world, arguing that it ignores the possibility that capitalism itself is the problem. To look to business for a solution is futile, he says—we should look to public sector solutions instead. Giridharadas is critical of B Lab as potentially another elite-led attempt to change the system, although he acknowledges that B Corporations are a useful innovation. But he believes they can be scaled quickly only with the help of public policy.[30]

Giridharadas isn't wrong. Many have noticed business elites' emphasis on programs that look and sound good but don't do good. Coen Gilbert quotes Joseph Stiglitz, the Nobel Prize–winning economist, on this point: "They would fund a million of these buzzwordy programs rather than fundamentally question the rules of the game— or even alter their own behavior to reduce the harm of the existing distorted, inefficient and unfair rules."[31]

Just Capital, a nonprofit spearheaded by hedge fund billionaire Paul Tudor Jones II with multimillionaire celebrities, including Deepak Chopra and Ariana Huffington, listed as cofounders, has been subject to this type of critique. The mission of Just Capital is identified as investing in companies that do good in ways that reflect Americans' priorities.[32] Yet a quick look at their top companies left me a bit confused—it's clear that there's a weakness in Just Capital's crowd-sourced methodology to identify what qualifies as a good company. While I respect their democratic intentions, a concern is that since shareholder primacy has become so entrenched in our society, it is not clear that aggregating individuals' opinions is a valid way to identify what is responsible corporate behavior.

For instance, the first time I looked at the Just Capital list, in 2018, one of their lauded companies was Pepsi, which markets soft drinks and snack foods.[33] While there is nothing in principle wrong with these products if they are consumed moderately, Pepsi's high reliance on the sweetener high fructose corn syrup (which has been specifically linked to obesity), potentially carcinogenic chemicals, and other additives that make its products addictive raises significant questions about the social value of its core products.[34] Pepsi has initiated programs or campaigns focused on social and environmental good; it even purchased a B Corp. But the way the company formulates its products poses health risks to large portions of the world's population. Until its leaders are able to shift their company in a fundamental way, I question whether they should be lauded for undertaking CSR programs that merely compensate for the fundamental problems their own products are creating.

Many of Just Capital's top twenty companies over the years are semiconductor firms—an industry that has come under attack for its use of toxic chemicals.[35] A quick look at Texas Instruments' Glassdoor reviews by employees shows that its profit-sharing plan is advantageous. And the firm was ranked as one of the top five most just companies in 2018 and 2019. But, more tellingly, the critiques provided by current and past employees highlight its disregard for work/life balance and its unfair hierarchy.[36] And there is a very high proportion of high-tech firms in Just Capital's lists over the years, which suggests that the criteria are tilted to certain types of firms. The one hundred companies on Just Capital's list of "most just companies" may have impressive employee volunteer programs, offer an extra week of maternity leave, or perhaps even try to be as environmentally sustainable as possible, given their industry—admirable initiatives all. But are they really doing enough to offset the damage they cause to people, the planet, and the economy?[37] Are they factoring in the health and environmental externalities that are at the root of their profits?

To confidently answer these questions, the social and environmental performances of Just Capital's one hundred top companies must be disclosed and assessed against a credible third-party standard—like the B Impact Assessment (BIA)—and verified by a disinterested third party, like B Lab. Until then, the only information that consumers have is the information that the company is willing to provide to them, and given companies' tendencies to disclose only information that makes them look good, there isn't much reason to trust them.

Compensatory Good versus Intrinsic Good

In his critique of Just Capital, media theorist Douglas Rushkoff makes an important distinction between compensatory good and intrinsic good.[38] These companies—*most* large corporations, in fact—often undertake large-scale actions so that they can appear to compensate for the overall harm they might be causing. Pepsi, for example, built a zero-emissions potato chip factory. Yet the core problems don't change—Pepsi is still a junk food company that through its choices fundamentally contributes to our serious health and obesity problems, creating healthcare externalities that must be borne by society. Giridharadas hit the nail on the head in his aforementioned book—too many business leaders and corporations are all talk, no action. They paint a picture of the ways in which they're working toward making the world a better place, but in reality they just keep chugging along, using the same practices that have already done so much damage.

Similar critiques were made in 2018 when Larry Fink, the CEO of the multinational investment management corporation BlackRock, shocked much of the business world by calling for companies to "show how [they] make a positive contribution to society," saying that "companies must benefit all of their stakeholders, including shareholders, employees, customers, and the communities in which they operate."[39] Some reacted to Fink's statement with surprise and delight. But many others accused Fink of jumping on the greenwashing bandwagon. In his 2019 annual letter Fink doubled down, expressing many of the themes of this book—corporate social purpose matters, millennials will drive companies to be more responsible, and, crucially, accountability is at the root of how we need to redesign the system.[40]

I don't necessarily think Fink is being disingenuous. But it is true that often when investors consider something like a company's environmental or social factors, they do so out of self-interest. The increasing presence of social issues on the media stage—from #MeToo to rallies against gun violence to debates on climate change—is increasing their importance in the public's consciousness. By taking steps to be more environmentally sustainable, BlackRock can achieve better returns. As I mentioned regarding the CEOs of the Business Roundtable, for Fink's actions to begin matching his words, he would have to explicitly state his support for replacing shareholder primacy with stakeholder governance, acknowledging that corporations need to focus more on accounting for interdependencies and less on exploiting externalities. He must acknowledge that CEOs can lead with purpose and long-term benefits in mind only when their company's governance aligns with their objectives. Currently, corporations' legal foundations are so steeped in shareholder primacy that it is difficult for CEOs to work toward the changes that Fink calls for. Fink's call to action was addressed to CEOs, but he should also direct his attention to his fellow investors and the investment community. If he were to answer his own call to action and support the adoption of new corporate governance models, like the benefit corporation, then he really could say that he stands for fundamental changes in our economy.

Companies must do more than create compensatory goods; they need to fundamentally shift their perspective on externalities. The argument in this book is that B Corps offer transparent accountability, and they create intrinsic goods. Intrinsic goods occur when the core aspects of a business are oriented around creating positive impact in the world—not as an afterthought or as the side effect of a marketing ploy to improve the company's reputation. Intrinsic goods must be a focal point of the company, tied directly to its mission. If a company shifts its focus to creating intrinsic goods for the world, then it truly is being a business for good.

It doesn't take much searching to find certified B Corporations that are creating intrinsic good every single day. Greyston Bakery in Yonkers, New York, which makes gourmet brownies, cookies, and those wonderful chunky bits in fellow B Corp Ben & Jerry's ice cream, comes to mind. Greyston has an open hiring policy, which means that anyone can apply for a job and be hired as soon as there is an opening. This includes immigrants and refugees, the economically disadvantaged, people of all faiths and sexual orientations, and the formerly incarcerated. Here's the big-picture mission behind the policy: "Open Hiring creates opportunities for individuals who have been excluded from the mainstream workforce. Complemented by community programs that provide employees and their neighbors with additional services that help people keep a job, Open Hiring provides people with the opportunity to experience the dignity of work and improve their lives and their community."[41]

It is hard to overstate the impact of these policies. Unemployment rates among the formerly incarcerated are at a staggering 27 percent, largely because of the stigma surrounding these men and women.[42] This, of course, contributes to recidivism and other costs for society, such as an increased strain on social welfare programs. Currently, there are over 2 million people in prison or jail in this country.[43]

Further, refugee and immigrant populations have proven time and again that they are essential to the American economy. And the economically disadvantaged are rarely given the opportunity to get back on their feet. These populations have difficulty finding employment because of the stigmas they bear, not because they aren't capable workers. If Greyston's open hiring policy could be scaled up and take effect nationwide, this could have positive long-term effects on not only the individuals concerned but on their families and local communities.

On a smaller but equally intrinsically good scale, Boloco, a B Corp burrito chain that operates in New England, offers its mostly Spanish-speaking employees English-language and leadership training as part of its mission to help low-skilled, marginalized employees advance in society. In an industry that predominantly employs people of color and immigrants, Boloco has made it the company's mission to provide every employee with a living wage. Every year, the minimum wage at Boloco increases, as does the average wage per employee—in 2019, it was about $15.25 an hour. Today, close to 90 percent of certified B Corps pay their employees a living wage. If every company across the nation did this, there would be 15 million more people earning a living wage. The benefits of this mass societal shift would be incredible.[44]

Normally the costs of disadvantaged populations would be passed on to taxpayers. But Boloco and Greyston Bakery are creating fundamental human capital through the work they do—in fact, this is the reason why both companies exist. Greyston Bakery's slogan states, "We don't hire people to bake brownies, we bake brownies to hire people."[45] Boloco states, "Our mission is to better the lives and futures of our people. We use ridiculously delicious burritos to do it."[46]

Not all intrinsic goods are focused on employees, of course. Consumer goods producers can create intrinsic goods by offering high-quality products that have gone through a conscious production process instead of encouraging undiscerning consumption. Unique among apparel companies, Patagonia encourages customers to "buy less"; the company placed ads in the *New York Times* on Black Friday saying, "Don't buy this jacket" or "Don't buy this shirt" to discourage customers from overconsumption. The company also donates 100 percent of its Black Friday in-store sales profits to grassroots environmental organizations.[47] To reduce waste and keep its clothing products out of landfills, Patagonia's return and repair program, "Worn Wear," upholds the company motto "If it's broke, fix it!" The company operates America's biggest gear-repairing store in Reno. In addition to a no-questions-asked return and repair policy, Patagonia organizes workshops and tours ("The Worn Wear Tour") around the country to teach people how to repair their own apparel at home. It also buys back used clothes that are in good condition for resale. Its customers recognize the company's values and are willing to pay for the quality and service they receive. "They don't mind paying more as long as it's high quality," founder Yvon Chouinard said. "What they do is what we should all be doing, which is consuming less and consuming better."[48] In 2019, Patagonia announced it would produce branded logo wear—popular swag at many companies, and a highly profitable business—only for B Corporations, companies that share its vision of responsible capitalism.[49]

Allbirds, a start-up shoe manufacturer, was founded as an alternative to industry giants that pay scant attention to the environmental costs of their products. Allbirds creates two types of very comfortable and fashionable shoes—one out of merino wool and one out of trees. Yes, that's right, trees. As cofounder Joey Zwillinger told me, "We [wanted] to make a shoe like a tree. What I mean by that is that the shoe actually provides more to the Earth than it takes away, from an environmental perspective, and particularly on a carbon emission basis." Allbirds' focus on creating sustainable shoes out of natural materials led the company to research and launch a sole material called

"SweetFoam," which is made out of sugarcane, a completely renew-able resource. Production of SweetFoam's base resin is carbon nega-tive, which means that it cleans the atmosphere, much as a tree does.[50] Instead of maintaining proprietary use of this material, as many com-panies would, Allbirds' founders opened its use up to everyone. "If everyone uses it, the planet's way better off," explains Zwillinger, add-ing, "As more people use it, the cost comes down." Allbirds' work doesn't end there, though—recently, the company announced it would become completely carbon neutral in 2019 by purchasing car-bon offsets while also imposing an internal carbon tax on itself set at 10 cents per shoe to financially recognize what is usually an unac-counted for externality.[51] In 2018, Allbirds raised $50 million from leading mainstream investment firms, including T. Rowe, Fidelity, and Tiger Global. It was valued at $1.4 billion.[52]

Roshan, the largest telecommunications provider in Afghanistan, serves nearly 6 million consumers annually. It has been a certified B Corp since 2012 and consistently ranks in the top 10 percent of the world's certified B Corporations. Located in a war-torn and fragmented economy, Roshan, the country's largest employer, aims to contribute to the social and economic redevelopment of Afghanistan by improving its communications grid. The company has improved healthcare ser-vices in Afghanistan by training doctors and providing telecommuni-cations solutions to hospitals. It has built playgrounds and schools for children, and it encourages sports programs and youth-development initiatives. Importantly, Roshan has made women a specific focus of its efforts, providing them with job and educational opportunities.[53]

The End of Traditional Capitalism as We Know It

In June 2006, the three cofounders of B Lab began reaching out to social entrepreneurs, investors, and thought leaders for guidance and insight into how they could harness their collective interests and skills. From these conversations, the trio came to the conclusion that three fundamental pieces of infrastructure are required to develop capitalism into a positive force in the world: objective standards on what a "good business" is, a legal framework that recognizes stakeholders, and a collective voice to spread those ideas throughout the world. Thus was the B Corp movement set into motion.

2

Interdependence Day

In May 2005, the founders of basketball footwear and apparel company AND 1 finalized the sale of their company to American Sporting Goods. This moment was a turning point for the company's leaders, Jay Coen Gilbert and Bart Houlahan, and their college friend and early AND 1 investor, Andrew Kassoy.

AND 1 is a bit of a Cinderella story. Coen Gilbert had worked as an analyst for McKinsey in New York City for a few years after graduating from Stanford before deciding to pursue his public service interests working for Mayor David Dinkins's Office of Drug Abuse Policy. In 1993, when he was twenty-five, he partnered with his high school friend Seth Berger and Tom Austin on a business idea that Berger had begun hatching toward the end of his second year at Wharton Business School: selling T-shirts with clever slogans out of the back of a car. It quickly evolved into a business venture when they realized that there was significant demand for their products. By their second year, they were a multimillion-dollar basketball apparel brand sold in fifteen hundred stores nationwide.[1]

AND 1, named after the basketball phrase for the additional free throw a player gets when he makes a basket while being fouled, was known for its punchy taglines and streetwise attitude. Its first products were T-shirts with trash-talk slogans like "I'm the bus driver. I take everyone to school"; "Is it hot in here, or is it just me?"; and "Pass. Save yourself the embarrassment." The founders still have the napkins on which they had scribbled some of the first slogans that graced those brand-defining T-shirts.[2]

Six months into the venture, Coen Gilbert attended a wedding where he ran into his old Stanford friend Bart Houlahan, who was working at a small investment bank. As he puts it, "I loved the work I was doing, but I hated the people." While they were catching up, Coen Gilbert mentioned that the fledgling company needed a chief financial officer to turn the brand into a business. Houlahan recalls, "I couldn't believe he hadn't called me, and if I remember correctly, I think I called him a variety of four-letter words. I was about six months from starting Harvard Business School, but after the wedding, I called Harvard and told them to keep their deposit; I was going to join a half-million-dollar t-shirt company."[3]

Over the next twelve years, they scaled the company up to about $250 million in revenue. Houlahan served as CFO and then president of AND 1, while Coen Gilbert was head of product and marketing and then CEO. Having worked so closely together, Houlahan and Coen Gilbert have an easy relationship and understand each other well. "Bart is the most complete business person with whom I have ever worked," Coen Gilbert says. "He's a strategic thinker, a strong leader, a gifted manager, and, most of all, a phenomenal operator who sees how all the pieces need to fit together in what sequence given this budget and that time frame."[4]

AND 1 thrived on the culture of street basketball—local players perfecting their skills on blacktops from dawn to dusk. Its products and unique marketing campaigns were legendary. AND 1 mixtapes, for example—grainy videos taken on handheld cameras and produced with minor editing—became a cultural phenomenon among basketball junkies. Within a few years, street players AND 1 had recruited were going on "mixtape tours" around the country, showing off their talents and their AND 1 gear while gaining huge followings.[5]

In the late 1990s and early 2000s, AND 1 was the second-largest basketball footwear and apparel company in the world (after Nike).

The work environment at AND 1 reflected the company's ethos and, in hindsight, was a clear example of the philosophy of interdependence on which B Lab would later be founded. Houlahan recalls that they were "just trying to create a place that people wanted to be." It developed into a family of coworkers as well as coworkers who were family. Houlahan's wife Chrissy Houlahan, a Stanford-trained engineer, career naval officer, and now U.S. congresswoman, was COO. As Houlahan recalled, they had "eight dogs running through the office, we had a kids' room and a full hoops court at the back of the office where there were [basketball games at lunch and], yoga classes every morning, and childcare . . . it was employee-centric." Coen Gilbert and Houlahan were modeling what they felt was the right way to do business—with more than profit in mind.

AND 1 was also heavily involved in the local community, committing at least 5 percent of its profits to charity annually and installing a "vibrant direct service program," as Houlahan put it. The only aspect of the current B Corp philosophy that the company didn't fully embrace at first was the environmental side: "We were new to green and the environmental elements, we were just kind of waking up to it while organizations like Timberland and Patagonia had already blazed trails in footwear and apparel. But it became an important element of what we were trying to do in making sure we were good to the planet as well as to the people engaged in our business and in our community."

AND 1's service-oriented mission came out of a dark passage in Coen Gilbert's life. Two close friends of his were working in the World Trade Center on September 11, 2001, and his sister, who worked in local TV news, was on the scene before the second tower fell. All of them survived, but the terror of that day lingered. Three days later, Coen Gilbert's father passed away from lung cancer. Two weeks after that, a team member at AND 1, Jean Bernard (J. B.) Jouthe, was killed in a car accident on his way to work. This devastating loss was felt across the whole company. Experiencing these three tragic incidents in quick succession sent Coen Gilbert reeling.[6]

To aid in his recuperation, he attended a weekend retreat in Lenox, Massachusetts, with his wife, Randi, a longtime yogini. She knew that this meditation and yoga retreat was what her husband needed at the time, but she couldn't have suspected how much it would shape their paths moving forward. During the retreat, Coen Gilbert thought about his company's overall business mission—to become the number one basketball company in the world, yes, but what *more* it could be? Thus was born the AND 1 service mission. After much deliberation, the leadership team fine-tuned it; AND 1's main ethos was to become a leader in "compassionate business practices."[7] The company defined this as a commitment not only to do no harm but also to do good—to consider every part of business as an opportunity to serve the community, expecting nothing in return. In a way, this was the birth of the B Corp movement as well, though no one knew it yet. AND 1's service mindset eventually extended to its factories overseas. "We had ten-thousand-plus people working for us in factories in Taiwan and in China," Houlahan says, "so we had a pretty rigorous code of conduct that we enforced with third-party audits twice a year." The workers in those factories were just as important to the company's leaders as the employees sitting in the AND 1 offices in suburban Philadelphia.

AND 1 also made community engagement an important point of focus. "We recognized that we were selling basketball shoes and basketball apparel to eighteen-year-old kids, the vast majority of whom would never be NBA players, and therefore we gave back to that community through donations to educational nonprofits," recalls Houlahan. The company also gave forty hours of paid time off for direct service to each employee every year, encouraging everyone to take advantage of the opportunity. AND 1 held "service fairs at the office, where people would come in and take over the gym and tell us how we could get engaged and do leveraged service, where we used our talents to actually help a local nonprofit," Houlahan said.

But a decade into their venture, the values that Coen Gilbert and Houlahan had cultivated and instilled in their business were put into jeopardy. Relentless competition from Nike, Adidas, and Reebok, the increase of market consolidation in their industry, and some management mistakes led to a decline in sales. Houlahan recalled that at a Nike national sales meeting, a target attached to a key chain was distributed. Its bull's-eye was the AND 1 logo.[8]

To meet the competition, AND 1 took on a sizable outside investment from the private equity firm TA Associates. As Houlahan tells it, "They were terrific investors, but honestly, but we were not playing with our own money anymore. . . . We had $35 million from them that was invested into the company, and we knew we had a fiduciary obligation to them." AND 1 peaked at $220 million in direct revenues and then the bottom dropped out; in eighteen months it lost $100 million. As Houlahan says, "This isn't a Ben & Jerry's or Stonyfield story. Our equity partners were not Unilever or Danone, which truly valued social commitment. [When we took on a financial partner], we knew what we were doing."

Jerry Turner, the CEO of the company that ultimately bought AND 1, was married to the daughter of a factory owner in Shanghai. From the beginning, the AND 1 team had a sense of who they were dealing with. "It was not a factory we would have done business with," explains Coen Gilbert. "Both the quality of the shoes they produced and their labor standards were below par."[9] Turner had been in the business for years—he knew how to make shoes for less while selling them for the same price for as long as he could. He was sure that the consumer wouldn't notice the difference and that his profit margins would be wider.

About a month after the sale, AND 1 had a global sales meeting in Vancouver. Houlahan and Coen Gilbert saw it as an opportunity to thank their employees, say good-bye to them, and hand the company off to its new owner. Houlahan recalls that when Turner held a Q&A session, somebody from the audience asked him, "AND 1, since inception, has had a policy of giving 5 percent of its profits to charity. What is your intention for that program moving forward?" Turner replied, "There's a new charity in town. His name is Jerry Turner."

Within the next few months, the company culture AND 1 had built was systematically dismantled. Turner "dismantled all of AND 1's responsible business practices. We were able to negotiate more generous severance packages for those employees who would be let go, but everything else was wiped out," Coen Gilbert recalls. None of this came as a surprise, but the founders had felt they had no alternative. "Every other potential strategic buyer except one had fallen away and we were doing our best simply to finesse the best deal we could get across the finish line with only two horses left in the race" Coen Gilbert continues. "[Turner] had a particular contempt for 'high-priced' sales people and money that was 'wasted' on marketing." Within a couple of years, Turner had "milked all the equity out of the brand." The quality of the product decreased exponentially and AND 1 went from a premium to a discount brand.[10]

Andrew Kassoy met Coen Gilbert and Houlahan at Stanford University in the late 1980s. "[Kassoy] was two years behind me in school, but ahead of me in most other ways," Coen Gilbert reflected. "He was a fraternity brother of mine and Bart's, and he succeeded me as its president. He was a Boulder-born athlete and a near-concert violinist, a Truman Scholar and wanna-be public servant, maybe an elected official, who, like me with my first job as a consultant for McKinsey, was busy acquiring the private sector skills and relationships on Wall Street that would be of use to the world 'eventually.' "[11] A first-round investor in AND 1, Kassoy eventually cofounded and for many years the managing partner of DLJ Real Estate Capital Partners. He then became a partner at MSD Real Estate Capital, an affiliate of MSD Capital, Michael Dell's private investment firm.

The terrorist attacks of 9/11 were a personal tipping point for Kassoy too; they made him think back to his roots. Public policy was no longer an option, he recalls; he "was pretty turned off at that point by politics." But he was struggling to reconcile what he was doing in his career with what he was personally interested in. Around this time, Kassoy was introduced to the idea of social entrepreneurship through a nonprofit called Echoing Green, which provides seed money to emerging social entrepreneurs. He began to work with and mentor those entrepreneurs to help them develop their business models. But he didn't have an overnight epiphany. He knew for a while that something wasn't right, that he didn't feel fulfilled. "I accidentally started to realize that there was something else that I could be doing that I was really passionate about," he says. "I was spending more of my day at MSD trying to help people figure out how to structure their social enterprise and feeling more satisfied with that than I felt doing my day job."

Kassoy didn't have answers to all the questions the social entrepreneurs asked him, but he knew that they were important. One of their primary questions was where they could find the right investors. According to Kassoy, "That really meant trying to figure out how to build a capital market that could serve them, to put the different pieces of infrastructure that you need together, whether it was a ratings agency or a market maker, a set of private equity invention capital-type funds, or an LBO [leveraged buyout]–type fund that could actually buy these businesses while allowing them to maintain their mission." As these ideas began to emerge in Kassoy's mind, he reconnected with his friends Coen Gilbert and Houlahan.

Kassoy visited them in 2005 while they were in the midst of the AND 1 sale. As Kassoy put it, the two were "distraught."[12] They knew that Turner would destroy their company's mission, but they had no other options. If they didn't sell, they would need to recommit for another ten years, and that would require sacrifices they weren't willing to make in terms of buyouts and difficult negotiations among friends. As Coen Gilbert put it, "We decided we wanted to maximize our friendships more than we wanted to maximize our long-term value."[13]

As the sale was going through, Coen Gilbert and Houlahan increasingly found themselves asking fundamental questions about how businesses that put people first could be better supported. Coen Gilbert had already started on this journey by attending Investors' Circle (IC) and Social Venture Network (SVN) events focused on impact investing and triple bottom line businesses. Increasingly, Kassoy joined their conversations.

After the sale, Coen Gilbert went on sabbatical for a year, spending most of it in Costa Rica, but he kept in regular contact with Houlahan and Kassoy. "We realized two things," Houlahan recalls, "First, that there's a lever that could be pulled with business that has the potential for tremendous force. Second, that the institutions that have been created to support business don't necessarily allow you to pull that lever. You have certain legal and cultural restrictions on how you can run a business. Still, there had to be a way that you could scale a business, raise outside capital, have a little liquidity, and still maintain mission."

Out of these conversations, the group concluded that three things were needed to allow the market to work better: a set of standards that would give consumers, investors, and policy makers the information required to tell the difference between good companies and good marketing; a legal framework that permitted companies to embrace sustainability and social enterprise as core purposes and responsibilities of the business, not just as a competitive advantage; and a collective voice to define what it means to be a good business.

Establishing these three foundational blocks led to the creation of B Lab and the B Corp movement. Often, the trio has wondered if the outcome of AND 1's sale would have been different if the company had been a B Corp. Negotiation relies on positions of power and, as Coen Gilbert puts it, AND 1's wasn't great: "Had our business fundamentals been stronger, had our partner relationships been stronger, had there been other viable buyers, or had the AND 1 Service Mission—or a particular 'non-negotiable' part of it—been baked into the legal DNA of our business, and had AND 1 been using the certified B Corp logo and had retailers or consumers who cared about that, then perhaps our negotiating position would have been strong enough to extract a little more value for our stakeholders."[14] But the more important thing to keep in mind is that AND 1 was a values-led business and, as Houlahan points out, "a better company because of having this mission."

Coen Gilbert noticed another key aspect of running a values-led business—it helped the company recruit great employees: "We were able to attract amazing talent and enjoy very low turnover not just because we were a sexy, fast-growing, insurgent brand, but also because we ran the business with care for people as a core value. People were excited to work at AND 1 not only because it was a great place to work and we shared the financial wealth that we created together, but also because they felt pride that more than 10,000 young women in our factories were treated fairly as members of our extended family, and that we contributed a couple of million dollars to support youth and education programs, and the families impacted by 9/11."[15] Until the bottom dropped out, they could count on their community standing by them—from their vendors to their licensees—by extending the date on payables or allowing for some leeway. That was the clearest indication that they had created a business that people truly felt part of.

Soon, the conversations among the three friends came together into a plan. Houlahan and Coen Gilbert had discussed at length how they could drive more money into good businesses, emphasizing those with strong missions. Kassoy had his own ideas about good business cultivated from his work with social entrepreneurs and the types of holes he had uncovered within that sector. Putting it together, they began with "Let's create a brand for good business and start a company that does something great, that upholds all these things, and can be a shining light." Ultimately, they realized that even if they created a business that could be a force for good, it would be unable to address the world's pressing problems, no matter how big it became. Kassoy explains, "The world didn't need another social business . . . there were tons of them. What we realized as we started to talk to a lot of them was they could all scale to a certain point, but then they needed outside capital, or they needed succession planning." The responsible business sector was sorely lacking those foundational pieces of infrastructure—standards, a legal framework, and a collective voice—that the trio had begun to outline.

At first, they considered creating a fund modeled after Paul Newman's commitment to donate all of his companies' profits to charity. This Newman Venture Fund would invest only in companies that do good and donate all their profits. Coen Gilbert attended many gatherings, events, and conferences as this idea began to take shape. He presented it at an Investors Circle members-only gathering, and a month later the IC organized and cohosted with the Social Venture Network a meeting with Newman Venture–like entrepreneurs.

These meetings foreshadowed many aspects of the journey that Coen Gilbert and his partners were about to embark on. They came to recognize that while investors are the slowest to move from interest to action, entrepreneurs are the quickest. They also saw that entrepreneurs will take opportunities that are presented to them and really *lead*. While exploring passion-driven networks like IC and SVN, Coen Gilbert realized another thing about entrepreneurs: they embrace collaboration and collective action. He recognized their ability to understand systems and networks, and their desire to build these into communities by investing in relationships rooted in shared purpose. The positive reactions he received when he presented the idea of the Newman Venture Fund to these entrepreneurs was a clear indication that he had found a network whose members would support one another and build out from their shared experiences and resources.[16]

Eventually they realized that a venture fund could not upend shareholder primacy in the same way that a holding company might. Venture funds are structured so that a liquidity event is eventually required; to generate the returns needed to attract capital, there must be a sale or change of control fairly quickly. If they were a holding company, they wouldn't have to worry about that because a holding company buys to hold, not to sell. "It takes the view that it wants to own the business for the long term," Kassoy explains. "That long-term view drives short-term decisions in many ways, including in ways that can prioritize long-term mission and value creation over short-term margin and liquidity." If they went with "a holding company instead of a fund that has this short-term perspective; we could create a long-term entity that can create liquidity for entrepreneurs through the shares of the holding company but that can continue to help grow those great businesses."

So B Holdings was born. But when Kassoy connected with his old investors, they had a common set of questions: "How are you going to decide what to invest in?" How could they know the difference between "good companies" and "good marketing"? The trio thought that surely there was some kind of rating system or set standards that went above and beyond the financial impact of a business. But as they soon discovered, no such system existed. Although companies often used words like *green* and *sustainable,* the lack of objective standards meant that every consumer and business had a different understanding of what those words promised. It also meant that companies could claim that something was "green" or "sustainable" whether it was or not. While other industry-specific or product-specific certifications tapped socially responsible sentiment, such as Fair Trade and the Forest Certification Council, there was no general certification for socially responsible businesses. "What we really need," they said to each other, "is a nonprofit that creates the standards for business."

Not long after that, they culled all that they had learned in their previous ventures, their meetings with leading investors and socially responsible entrepreneurs, their personal philosophies, and their attendance at numerous conferences and conventions, and began working to accomplish an ambitious and daunting challenge: creating the infrastructure for a new way of doing business. In addition to the lack of standards, another issue was that the mission and values of any company they created had to be integral and untouchable, virtually impossible for future leaders to change. "Our perspective was that the first phase of the responsible business movement had been a huge success, but then it was over. From Ben & Jerry's, Stonyfield, and The Body Shop to Tom's of Maine and Odwalla, there was now plenty of evidence of the market opportunity for values-led businesses to create significant shareholder value," recalls Coen Gilbert. "Values-led entrepreneurs and investors wanted liquidity, and they wanted to scale their businesses to create greater impact, but they didn't want to compromise on mission to do so. B Lab and B Holdings were envisioned as offering a solution to this problem."[17]

Building B Lab

In May 2006, Coen Gilbert and Kassoy attended a gathering at the Aspen Institute, a think tank dedicated to addressing societies' most difficult problems. They shared the B Lab concept with other social sector leaders, using the "B Corp" branding explicitly. At this gathering, they learned about a new corporate structure in the United Kingdom called the community interest company (CIC). CICs were introduced in 2005 so that companies could be set up as social enterprises that use their profits for good. This development told the trio and their partners that this type of company could exist and be credible—and with this encouragement, they were off!

Within the next month, they started to develop B Lab. Coen Gilbert converted the guest room in his house into an office. He jokingly recalls that he provided Houlahan with a small, sturdy folding card table as a sign of how grateful he was to have him as a partner on this journey. Coen Gilbert himself used a tiny wooden table that he had made years earlier. They each had a phone and a laptop, and that was it.[18]

Then they began to recruit leaders others would want to follow. They felt it was important to represent a diverse range of industries, geographies, and impact areas. In June 2006, they showcased a handful of potential B Corps at an IC members' retreat: Pura Vida Coffee, Give Something Back Business, Better World Telecom, and Working Today/Freelancers' Insurance.[19]

The next thing on their to-do list was getting Kassoy to commit to B Lab full-time. Kassoy was still working at MSD Capital, though he was spending one day a week with Coen Gilbert and Houlahan and calling in to the tiny "home office" every day. Coen Gilbert reflects on how important it was for Kassoy to join the team full-time: "In between visits, Bart and I would joke about what it would take to get our cautious investor friend to pull the trigger. We knew that Andrew would add a ton of capital markets credibility to our team, however, while we had known each other since college, and Bart and I had worked together for over a decade, we were just beginning to get a feel for how we would work together as a threesome. And the feeling was good. We complemented each other well, and in often fluid ways."[20]

Each founder's individual style complements the others'. Coen Gilbert is a leader—often jumping into a situation headfirst—whereas Houlahan and Kassoy are much more likely to read the room, listen, and get to know the players, including their blind spots. They are patient and they know how to make people feel comfortable and valued. Coen Gilbert's fearlessness often acts as a catalyst for the others' energy. As he puts it, "We knew that we shared a big audacious vision, that we'd be a pretty powerful team, and that we'd have a lot of fun together. That's why Bart and I fist-bumped and laughed when Andrew committed to join B Lab full time, but in his typical deliberate style, said he needed time to transition."[21]

On July 5, 2006, the trio held their first official day of full-time work at B Lab. This would become known as Interdependence Day and continues to be celebrated every year by B Lab and, in turn, by many B Corps. At first they considered writing a mission statement that would riff off the Ten Commandments—the Ten Commitments. Ultimately, they decided to mimic the U.S. Declaration of Independence instead, which tied in with the idea of interdependence in a more direct and powerful way. Mostly unchanged since 2006, in 2020 the B Lab's Declaration of Interdependence states:

> We envision a global economy that uses business as a force for good.
>
> This economy is comprised of a new type of corporation—the B Corporation—which is purpose-driven and creates benefit for all stakeholders, not just shareholders.

As B Corporations and leaders of this emerging economy, we believe:

- That we must be the change we seek in the world.
- That all business ought to be conducted as if people mattered.
- That, through their products, practices, and profits, businesses should aspire to do no harm and benefit all.
- To do so requires that we act with the understanding that we are each dependent upon another and thus responsible for each other and future generations.

Over the next thirty days, the trio created a case statement, an executive summary, and a full business plan for two entities: B Lab and B Holdings. They decided that the "B" would anchor the broader movement. "B Lab was the nonprofit whose mission was to build the 'for-benefit' sector; B Holdings was the for-profit B Corp which would begin that work on the ground by investing in values-led businesses through a values-led holding company," explains Coen Gilbert.[22]

Fitting Square Pegs into Round Holes

B Lab's timing was good. Conversations were happening in social venture spaces regarding the future of sustainable and responsible business. Ben & Jerry's was being purchased by Unilever, and Tom's of Maine was about to be bought by Colgate (Tom's became a B Corp in 2019). Many wondered whether those companies could still maintain their mission and purpose under their new owners. As Kassoy put it, "It got to two issues. One was the standards. . . . How would you really know whether Tom . . . actually is maintaining mission or Ben & Jerry's or any of those businesses? And the second one was, these folks got their businesses to a certain point and then got the pressure to sell and they didn't really have a choice. There was no alternative, and so that got to the fiduciary duty issue. . . . There were some pretty clear cases that said this is a problem. If you want these kinds of businesses to succeed, then we need a different way."

The Ben & Jerry's sale got off to a rocky start. Unilever began its acquisition of the beloved ice cream company by closing down production plants and firing a high percentage of employees. Many believed that corporate law—the fiduciary duty of directors to maximize profit—was the culprit and that this was a clear example of how traditional business was antithetical to social enterprises.

The solution was not immediately clear. Houlahan recalled that even back when they were still at AND 1, they were "feeling like a square peg in a round hole." They knew that their company did not fit into the traditional capitalist economy. From a fiduciary standpoint, companies had only one obligation: to maximize shareholders' value. Many leaders of socially conscious and responsible businesses started their business because they had at least two purposes, and for most of them, shareholder value wasn't at the top of the list. To upend shareholder primacy in business, the legal framework of the corporate structure had to change.

Although one of their original ideas—the holding company—was well received, readers will recall that the trio was often asked, "How will you decide who you will invest in?" Words like *green* and *sustainable* had been appropriated by marketers. "The more we were using them," Houlahan noted, "the less they meant, because there were no standards behind them."

The idea of creating a brand for good business—the B Corp—fully emerged at this moment. As more and more businesses adopted it, Kassoy stated, they became "advocates for and users of the policy solutions and the capital markets." Many entrepreneurs were running organizations that focused on people, the environment, or both. Similarly, there was a growing population of investors who were trying to drive capital in what would become known as impact investing—these were investors who sought a social and environmental return as well as a financial one. Finally, thought leaders such as professors at business schools were increasingly studying the space as well.

As Houlahan recalls, bringing these three powerful groups together—entrepreneurs, investors, and thought leaders—provided a foundation for profound change, just as deciding on the team's three-pronged move forward did: "A brand for good business was the umbrella for the different movements, all of which we viewed really as manifestations of the same intent: using the power of business to try to create social and environmental change." The brand would encompass a strong, scalable mission. It would work with companies to create a new legal framework or adapt an existing one that would allow them to embrace sustainability and social enterprise in an advantageous and competitive way. Finally, it would impose a set of standards that would have to be met for a company to be considered one that is *doing business for good*. As Houlahan says, "We kinda added up all the different business associations and put them into a bucket and [said], 'How big is the bucket?' We came in at a minimum of thirty thousand to forty thousand businesses that were self-declared triple bottom line companies. When you started to look at the size of that universe and then put it in the context of what type of awareness there is about that universe, there was a total disconnect and there seemed to be a need for a collective voice."

3

Putting the Spotlight on Interdependencies

In the fall of 2006, Coen Gilbert and Houlahan were in San Francisco meeting with prospective partners, investors, and B Corps. They were walking down Montgomery Street, as Coen Gilbert tells it, when they looked up and noticed a small sign hanging from a building with the Method logo on it. With its iconic transparent raindrop hand soap bottle design, Method had become one of the fastest-growing responsible businesses, widely recognized as a next-gen revolutionary company that was taking on the stagnant home products industry. Coen Gilbert and Houlahan decided to walk in and see if they could meet with the company's leaders. Not surprisingly, the receptionist turned them away, so they decided to have lunch instead. As they sat at a restaurant on the same block, munching tortilla chips and guacamole and sipping Negro Modelos, Coen Gilbert fired off a quick email to Method's cofounders, Adam Lowry and Eric Ryan, introducing himself and Bart as "two fellow Stanford-buddies-turned-business-partners (mentioning AND 1 at the top for credibility) who admired Method's environmental and design leadership." He mentioned a bit about B Corps, that they were at a nearby restaurant, and that they'd love to return to say a quick hello. "Within ten minutes," Coen Gilbert recalls, "Method's CEO Alastair Dorward emailed back saying he would be happy for us to pop in." They spent about twenty minutes chatting and Dorward promised he'd share their conversation with Method's cofounders.[1]

While Coen Gilbert and Houlahan were chatting with Dorward, Adam Lowry recalls, "I was doing a bunch of work trying to figure out how to overcome the issues [of] a traditional C-Corp structure, which is what we were." When Dorward called to tell him about B Lab, Lowry thought to himself, "This might be the solution I've been looking for." Within a month of that serendipitous meeting in San Francisco, Coen Gilbert met Lowry in Philadelphia to discuss Method's interest in becoming a B Corp. Lowry shared his thoughts on the standards that B Lab had set, and particularly how to govern them.

Their brainstorming was creative, collaborative, and very in sync. Lowry recalls, "You know when you have a conversation where you very quickly figure out that you are looking at the world in exactly the same way as someone else?" There was one thing in particular that, based on their past experiences, they were both clear on: Method and AND 1 had similar methods of product development and, more specifically, were both rooted in continual improvement, which would be a cornerstone of the B Corp movement.

The hardest task for B Lab wasn't creating the first generation of standards for their B Impact Assessment. There were books written by responsible business leaders and a number of other more narrow product- or practice-specific standards to look to for inspiration. The more difficult task was creating a dynamic process and a governance structure that would ensure that all voices and perspectives would be heard. The standards had to be able to evolve over time to incorporate new industries, new viewpoints, and new ideas.

Creating the B Impact Assessment

Third-party certification already existed for organic food and "green" products, and consumers recognized those logos and knew what they meant. But, as Houlahan recalls, the socially conscious business sector initially "seemed slightly stagnant." The B Lab founders wanted to create a set of standards that people could recognize and understand not only to increase consumer awareness but to drive impact. "Especially as people continue[d] to use the words *green, sustainable, responsible, charitable, local*... the more we were using them, the less they mean[t] because there were no standards behind it," Houlahan reflects.

The B Corps founders wanted to ensure that the certification process they created was standardized across companies of different sizes and comparable across industries, allowing companies to assess the true social and environmental impacts of their operations and work to improve them, and giving consumers and investors the means to hold them accountable. This level of transparency would help to alleviate consumers' natural skepticism and the fear that companies are engaging in greenwashing, just publicizing social and environmental good works to obscure the other problems they create.

As we have seen, it is easier and cheaper to just *look* good as opposed to *being* good. The German auto maker Volkswagen, for example, pushed sales of diesel cars in America by lauding their low emissions while at the same time installing devices in the cars to meet green requirements only when they were being tested.[2] Cosmetics and body care companies use the term *natural* in their marketing despite it having no agreed-upon meaning. Lush Cosmetics, as noted earlier, uses preservatives, parabens, and parfum in its "natural" products.[3] The average consumer doesn't have the inclination or time to dig through a company's product lines and history to ascertain whether the claims it's making are truthful or, to put it more generously, the whole truth.

When B Lab was founded, the socially responsible investing (SRI) community was fractured and marginalized. A large part of this had to do with the fact that SRI investors were not sharing their screening methods with the public—they were part of their proprietary investment models. Meanwhile, the Global Reporting Initiative (GRI), an NGO that focused on defining reporting metrics for larger, mostly publicly traded companies, had launched its first guidelines in 2000. It was a robust reporting framework but it was not designed to be used as a ratings system. For example, all companies using the GRI guidelines reported on carbon emissions, but no mechanism was in place to tell the public whether the amount reported was good or bad, and one company's measurements could not be compared with another's. As Coen Gilbert explains, "It offered no judgment. It also did not require companies to report on all GRI metrics, so selective reporting could still occur."[4] As for the Social Venture Network and other communities like it, they had no tangible membership requirements aside from a fee. This meant that anyone could join. While standards like those being developed for B Corps could be counterproductive to the community building and fellowship that was the core of their mission, a standards-based certification could help their members stand out in a cluttered marketplace. That's likely why so many SVN members were early adopters of the B Corp certification.

As they developed the BIA, the B Lab trio kept GRI's reporting standards in mind, as it was the closest comparison on the market. At first they hoped they could somehow use a threshold score on someone else's standards—or multiple standards—as the requirement for B Corp certification. But this plan did not pan out, as one of the GRI founders made it clear that the organization was not interested in pursuing a rating system. According to Coen Gilbert, they "recognized the value of a rating system that added credible third-party judgment to their credible third-party definitions, but they hoped that others, like us, would do that work." The trio quickly realized that even NGOs or nonprofits focused on this type of work covered only certain narrow aspects of social or environmental performance. There was just no publicly available, overarching, and detailed rating system that they could adapt—they would have to create their own.

The BIA went through several iterations before the team landed on a version that worked. Coen Gilbert remembers fondly that it began as "an Excel spreadsheet. More precisely, as is typical with me, it started with a series of long and winding conversations which Bart soon tired of, saying, 'Let me spend a day or two with this and see if I can pull something together that we can look at.' 'Sounds great,' I said. Two days later, Bart shared with me and Andrew the beta version of the first B Impact Assessment." Houlahan had really "put some meat on the bones," as Coen Gilbert puts it. The first BIA was a blunt instrument, "like humans' first tools," but it was also unique and useable—it got the job done. "The BIA, even in its Neanderthal Excel spreadsheet existence," Coen Gilbert says, "was the first comprehensive assessment tool for overall company social and environmental performance."[5]

The initial B Lab standards relied heavily on the practices espoused by Ben & Jerry's cofounder Ben Cohen and SVN chair Mal Warwick in their book *Values-Driven Business: How to Change the World, Make Money, and Have Fun.*[6] It also drew from the small business sustainability reporting standards of the GRI, practices aggregated by a systems-thinking entrepreneur named Betsy Power, and their own experiences at AND 1. Adopting the products, practices, and profits buckets from the original Declaration of Interdependence, Houlahan's beta spreadsheet then divided them into a dozen or so subcategories. Each subcategory and its individual metrics were weighted, so that the tool could properly and wholly assess a company's social and environmental performance.

Though they borrowed from sources they respected and agreed with, not everything they wanted had been covered by others before.

When the trio asked themselves, "What does a good standard need?" they answered that it must be independently governed, transparent, and dynamic. And there was one more factor they kept in mind that set them far apart from the rest: the BIA needed to be *comprehensive*. Houlahan explains, "Our point of view is that you have to look at the whole company—you can't look at just consumers or just the supply chain. What we're trying to benchmark is the positive impact created in society by these businesses." The B Corp standards they created examine a company in a holistic way; they include standards for workers, the company's products, the local community, and the supply chain as well as for the environment and the governance structure. Houlahan describes it this way: "This is a corporate certification. What that means is that if you're perfectly green, but you treat your employees like crap and you're not engaged in your community, then you're not going to pass. Or if you're an ESOP [employee stock ownership plan] with beautiful working conditions, but you're dumping your effluents out the back door, then you're not going to pass. At the end of the day, that would be a product certification or a practice certification. If you're trying to certify the whole corporation, you need to assess the whole corporation."[7]

Excel spreadsheet in hand, the trio was ready to beta-test the first iteration of the BIA on an actual, real-life company. They asked a few companies with diverse experiences and in different industries to complete the assessment with them over the phone, including Patagonia and Pura Vida Coffee—a socially conscious coffee company focused on paying coffee growers fairly and reinvesting profits into their communities. The feedback they received during this initial testing period was incredibly useful, particularly when it came to how they phrased their questions. Most important, they learned "that our standards will always be a work in progress," says Coen Gilbert, recalling his initial conversation with Method's Adam Lowry.

The B Impact Assessment

As the BIA has developed, it has come to focus on both a company's operations and its business model. The assessment itself is split into five key sections: governance, workers, customers, community, and environment. It has undergone six iterations, with the most recent version released in January 2019. With every version, B Lab refines, deepens, and extends the assessment. From the beginning, the questions that companies answer have been tailored to their size, sector, and geographical region. In order to achieve certification, a company must score at least 80 points out of a maximum of 200.

It is important to emphasize that the BIA provides a unique assessment of a company's entire operations. While the GRI provides a useful set of measures to help businesses, governments, and investors understand and explain the impacts they are making on the environment and the global community, it does not evaluate a company's performance. Similarly, SASB—the Sustainability Accounting Standards Board—offers reporting guidelines that factor in industry differences and materiality concerns, but this framework is geared toward publicly listed companies, whereas the BIA can be used by any company. Finally, the BIA is different than more specific assessment tools such as the CDP—Carbon Disclosure Project—which is exactly what the name suggests, an assessment that examines and rates corporations on their carbon, water, and forests impact.

After a company initially submits its assessment, it provides documentation to select responses in the assessment. A standards analyst at B Lab then reviews the answers and has a phone call with the company to address any consistency or accuracy concerns. Often a company's score drops below 80 after this review. In many cases this is an opportunity for the company, rather than a hindrance, as the BIA helps it identify new areas in which to create impact that it can implement to cross the 80-minimum-score threshold. Christina Forwood, director of the B Lab standards review team, explains there are many different types of improvements that companies can make. For example, some have created "Workforce Development programs with partner nonprofits to hire individuals from chronically underemployed backgrounds to provide quality jobs and training to support their integration in the workforce." And others have purchased renewable energy credits in order to meet the 80 points bar. The spirit behind the assessment is educational, aspirational, and focused on improvement. "It isn't just focused on whether or not the company is doing something, but how they can start doing it, if they aren't already." Dan Osusky, director of standards, explains, "so we're actually creating a roadmap for companies to improve themselves."[8]

For some certified B Corps, achieving the benchmark of 80 was the easy part—continuing to improve after that, as the certification standards evolve, has been the challenge. Because it's employee owned, King Arthur Flour hit 80 during its first attempt at certification; the workers and governance scores were high right out of the gate. But the company decided to keep improving and working on its score. "That is the beauty of the B Impact Assessment," King Arthur Flour's co-CEO Ralph Carlton told me when I visited him in the company cafeteria in modern-day Camelot, as King Arthur Flour's sprawling main campus in Norwich, Vermont, which encompasses a flagship store and a baking school, is called. "It may be difficult to complete successfully, but once completed, it not only offers incredible insights into the business, but also lets members of the executive staff know what is lacking and what needs to be addressed in order to evolve into a stronger business." During its first go-around, the company did not have a great environment score. As of 2019, the company has raised it to 116 points.

At Preserve, a pioneering company that turns recycled plastic into attractive consumer products, completing the BIA led leaders to discover that certain aspects of the business weren't well communicated to the rest of the team. "It's a really interesting process of getting different groups that might not talk to each other about these issues talking," explained CEO and founder Eric Hudson. Executives at Preserve realized several things about their company that they immediately set out to fix when they first completed the assessment. For example, they didn't have good maternity and paternity leave. "We noticed that we were putting people into situations where they had to make difficult decisions about work or family, and we didn't want to do that," explains Hudson. As Nora Livingstone of Animal Experience International puts it, "You don't know what you don't know. The B Corp certification process lets you think outside of the lens you have been looking through while planning and managing your company. Going through the process helps you understand benefits in ways you never thought of before and that can be hugely inspiring and help get your creativity flowing."[9]

At Ben & Jerry's headquarters—which is as quirky as the company's ice cream flavor names, featuring a two-story slide in the entrance and psychedelic art throughout—Rob Michalak, director of social impact, recalls that the company used the assessment as an opportunity to do some internal assessments and testing of its own. It took the company close to two years to get everything worked out so that it could properly complete the BIA. "As you go through it," he said, "it really helps your organization and management hold up a mirror to what your company actually is. It takes away some of the mythology." The improvement process goes both ways as well. For example, Ben & Jerry's was doing environmental work that the BIA didn't capture, as it assessed environmental impact in a different way. This led the management at Ben & Jerry's to consider whether B Lab's approach was better. If not, the company would give suggestions to B Lab that could be incorporated into the next iteration of the BIA.

The BIA is constantly evolving to become a stronger tool. Since B Lab collects certification fees from companies, a conflict of interest could develop; potentially, the enterprise could lower some standards to allow bigger, higher-paying companies to qualify. So, in September 2007, B Lab established an independent Standards Advisory Council to manage the BIA.

A new version is released every two years, with improvements and tweaks based on participant responses and research. For example, in 2010, New Resource Bank was the three hundredth B Corp to be certified, but its certification required an adaptation to the BIA. Vince Sicilano, its CEO, explains that the assessment had been "more suited for a CDFI bank—a community development financial institution." While New Resource Bank was pursuing certification, Sicilano and the B Lab team "spent a lot of time talking about a commercial bank versus a CDFI bank and eventually they came up with questions that were broader and fit a range of financial institutions. The BIA's continuous improvement is one of its greatest assets as it allows increasingly diverse types of companies to make their voices heard and eventually become a part of the movement."

Adam Lowry, an early Standards Advisory Council member, pressed the importance of pragmatism alongside continual improvement. "Perfect is the enemy of good" became a motto for the team—the standards had to be good, but they couldn't be perfect, because impact measurement was still in its infancy. Usability was also key, as standards that were so hard to meet that not even widely acknowledged leaders could achieve them would dissuade most companies from even attempting to certify. "A pragmatic approach to building rigorous and usable standards built B Lab's credibility with the leading entrepreneurs who would become the first users of these standards," notes Coen Gilbert, "which in turn would reinforce the credibility of the standards and make them more attractive for others to follow."[10] Lowry remembers that he "was counseling those guys early on" about the difficulty they would encounter in creating the social metrics. "The most important thing is the process that you use to improve and make the standards better over time, because whatever we pick today is going to be wrong by definition," he told them.

As of 2019, the Standards Advisory Council is split into two groups: one for emerging markets and one for developed markets, with about ten people in each. The council oversees all the decisions regarding what goes into the BIA. The assessment is set up to allow those completing it to leave feedback, and "we get around 3,000 pieces of feedback through that tool each year, and that's expanding," Osusky says. The council reviews and compiles this feedback, and its members also work with other standards organizations, calling on their valuable expertise and mechanisms. The council is also responsible for addressing any specific, material, and credible complaints made about any certified B Corp by, for example, a customer, an employee, or a supplier. When addressing these complaints, the council assesses whether a B Corp is staying true to the spirit of the community as expressed in the B Corp Declaration of Interdependence. Osusky points out that B Lab's mission is "to drive improvement," which makes remediation a much more important goal than banning a company from B Corp status.[11]

A crucial distinction that is underlined in the most recent version of the BIA is the difference between policies and outcomes. In an article for *B the Change,* the digital media platform for the B Corp community, Dan Osusky discussed this issue: "Many argue, justifiably, that the B Impact Assessment is not in fact an 'impact assessment' in that it focuses more on the practices of a company and not on the actual outcomes that the company creates." The newest version of the BIA aims to change that. Although many of the questions are about policies and practices, questions related to outcomes are much more heavily weighted. Can you gain extra points by formally writing out your recycling policy? Yes. Will it gain you as many extra points as having a zero-carbon footprint? No. "As much as possible," explains Osusky, "we design our questions, including those featuring policies and practices, based on objective research and examples that can inform what practices and policies are actually most likely to produce positive outcomes."[12]

Recruiting the First B Corp Cohort

In 2006, while the BIA was still a work in progress, Jeffrey Hollender, the CEO and cofounder of the sustainable consumer product brand Seventh Generation, agreed to meet Coen Gilbert and Houlahan to discuss B Lab and their B Corp idea. This was a big step for the team. Seventh Generation was considered an iconic responsible business, right alongside Ben & Jerry's and Patagonia. Hollender himself was a leader in socially responsible business and had just published a book called *What Matters Most: How a Small Group of Pioneers Is Teaching Social Responsibility to Big Business, and Why Big Business Is Listening.*[13]

They met at Seventh Generation's brand-new Leadership in Energy and Environmental Design (LEED)–certified offices overlooking Lake Champlain in Burlington, Vermont, a state that would eventually become a hub of B Corp activity. The meeting was very big picture and positive—both Hollender and Gregor Barnum, Seventh Generation's director of corporate consciousness, understood the potential power of the B Corps idea. For a company that *had* a director of corporate consciousness, this was no surprise. But Hollender also felt a bit cynical—could this team adequately evaluate whether a company was socially responsible? In this same vein, he knew that for the socially responsible business movement to move forward and grow, it needed to be more institutionalized. Hollender also recalls that at the time, corporate responsibility was overly focused on environmental issues; social issues were barely discussed. He let Coen Gilbert and Houlahan know that he was worried that they would over-index on environmental metrics, which are easier to measure, and ignore social metrics. He challenged them to build an assessment that was truly comprehensive.

Hollender asked how much it would cost to become certified. The B Lab team had already pegged certification fees to company sales: one-tenth of 1 percent. Following this logic, Seventh Generation, a roughly $100 million business, would pay an annual certification fee of $100,000. This was the first time that the B Lab team had presented such a high price tag to a potential B Corp. Barnum looked at Hollender. Hollender smiled and said, "That's a lot of money." It is, Coen Gilbert and Houlahan replied, because it's a big vision. "Okay," said Hollender, and Seventh Generation was on board. Hollender's act of leadership was game changing. From that point on, B Lab could tell other CEOs that Hollender and Seventh Generation were on board—even at the price of $100,000 a year.

In reflecting on how the B Lab team convinced established companies to sign on to an untested proposition, Houlahan says, "We had a simple, singular message, which was about leadership. We said, 'The reason why you started your business was to have impact and to provide a model for others to follow. We're going to give you a platform to disseminate that model. We're going to call it something. We're going to bring together a community of likeminded entrepreneurs who are going to stand at your side.' "[14]

In 2011, Hollender was fired from the company he founded when corporate profits became more important than social mission and he, the biggest advocate of the latter, became a hindrance. "As excited as I was about Seventh Generation," he said in his first public response to his dismissal, "it didn't go to the heart of the issues I really cared about. . . . I was interested in issues of justice and equity."[15] However, it is important to note that despite Hollender's termination and what, at the time, seemed like a rejection of B Corp's ideals, Seventh Generation has, in fact, continued to remain a certified B Corporation. It has continued to increase its BIA score and later navigated a successful mission-aligned sale to Unilever.

The first nineteen certified B Corporations were specifically targeted by the B Lab trio. The three wanted to attract companies that others would follow, so they approached recognized leaders in business networks like Investors' Circle and Social Venture Network, and companies that were diverse in industry and geography. New Leaf Paper was "trying to 'green' one of the most difficult, environmentally challenging industries," according to Houlahan, whereas Give Something Back's business model was to give "100 percent of their profits back to charity." Other targeted companies spanned the home products industry (such as Method and Seventh Generation), coffeehouses (Moka Joe Coffee and Pura Vida Coffee), fashion (Indigenous Designs), and home building (A-1 Builders). The West Coast is known for its progressive spirit and many of the initial B Corps hailed from California or Washington State. Another hotspot was the founders' hometown of Philadelphia.

Today, the main reason many companies join the B Corp community is that they want to influence the market beyond their own individual success. But those first B Corps were adding value to the B Corp brand, not vice versa. Their leaders believed in the mission so strongly that they jumped on board with virtually no guarantees or expectations. At this early stage there was no management or business case really, but they decided nonetheless that the risk was worth taking. Houlahan recalls, "One of the early presentations . . . had little quotes from each of them about why they joined the community. Different people focused on different things. Some focused on legal aspects, some focused on the standards, but above all, it was about leadership."

Community over Competition

In the early days, when companies were first beginning to go through the certification process, the existence of certified B Corps helped convince some companies and dissuade others. Andy Fyfe, who works on business development at B Lab, explains it this way: "We always thought that with Patagonia, EILEEN FISHER, New Belgium Brewing, Ben & Jerry's, it's going to set an industry precedent; once you get that, it's going to be a domino effect, and all the other companies in the industry are going to follow. [But] I think it sometimes has an adverse effect." Some smaller companies that were interested in the movement would look at a company like Patagonia and assume they had to be at its level to achieve certification. As Fyfe points out, often these smaller companies were more nimble and so "could actually be scoring higher than Patagonia," but they might not believe that until they saw it for themselves. This has led to an emphasis on community over negative or detrimental competition.

The B Corp movement allows companies, whether big or small, to stand toe to toe while encouraging positive competition. In other types of certifications, the competitors with the highest scores can say, "We know our product is better than theirs." As Fyfe puts it, "We have a broader aperture than just your soap versus their soap. It's also about a company having a workforce development program that hires ex-felons, or building a new facility that is net positive energy. . . . It's beyond score, it's beyond product, but it's a power of the community."

The B Lab team's focus is on getting B Corps to ask themselves, "What can we do together that we can't do alone? How can we go farther together?" A clear example of this is that B Lab decided early on that there would be no rankings. If a company is certified, it's met the bar.

Growing the Founding Class of B Corps

Coen Gilbert describes King Arthur Flour as very "middle America . . . they're sold in every grocery in the country." He realized that the company would be a good fit as a B Corp because "there's a different hook there than the hipster, venture-backed, disruptive soap company Method or the squeaky green save-the-earth folks at Seventh Generation." King Arthur Flour, he realized, would appeal to a broader base.

Coen Gilbert recalls sitting down in King Arthur Flour's then CEO Steve Voigt's office in 2006. Voigt "half-jokingly slammed a piece of paper down on the small round table" between them. It was the BIA. Voigt had taken it to assess how his company would fare and he wasn't too pleased with the results. Voigt found it unfair that his company lost points for not having many minority workers—this was Vermont, after all, where there wasn't a large minority population. Coen Gilbert shared a story about Greyston Bakery's open-hiring policy, which creates opportunities for people with criminal records and for people with little (if any) work experience or formal education. "In Yonkers, where they are located, that is mostly people of color. Do you think Greyston deserves to earn points for these practices? Yes, of course."[16] Coen Gilbert explained that that is the beauty of the BIA: no company will ever have a perfect score, especially because its standards must keep adapting to the changing world.

Coen Gilbert emphasized that to achieve 80 out of 200 points, a company must show excellence in at least one area—like labor practices or the environment—and proficiency in other sections. He also emphasized that King Arthur got credit for being employee owned, which others didn't get. It didn't take long for Voigt to say, "We'll be a B Corp."[17] Voigt retired from King Arthur Flour in 2014, but the spirit of the B Corp movement has clearly resonated deeply with him—he continues to work to expand employee ownership and benefit corporation legislation across the nation.

Most of the leaders whose companies were part of the founding class of B Corps were people whom one or more of the B Lab team had met through the communities at Investor's Circle, SVN, and BALLE (Business Alliance for Local Living Economies). For example, Judy Wicks, cofounder of BALLE, loved the B Corp idea and pledged that her café, White Dog, would become one of the founding B Corps. Don Shaffer, the executive director of BALLE, was a partner in Comet Skateboards and connected the team with Jason Salfi, the CEO, who also quickly came on board.[18]

The B Corps Public Debut

The founders were invited to introduce the B Corp concept at the national BALLE conference in June 2007. It was a memorable occasion for all of the participants. After Shaffer introduced them, Kassoy and Coen Gilbert made their way to the stage, surrounded by the leaders of the nineteen founding B Corps, while Houlahan was backstage making sure that their new website was going live. Coen Gilbert spoke briefly and then, as he describes it, "one by one, these leaders jokingly elbowed each other out of the way in their eagerness to step up to the podium to share why they had become a B Corp."[19]

Mike Hannigan, founder of Give Something Back, led the charge with a "power-to-the-people" type of speech. He was followed by Jeff Mendelsohn of New Leaf Paper, who spoke of disrupting industry and the next generation of entrepreneurs. Then came Wicks. Coen Gilbert recalls that she gave "unique credibility to the B Corp idea for this particular audience. . . . The reasons, frankly, were less important than who was sharing them. This reflected our most important insight for growing the B Corp movement: business leaders will be most influenced by their peers, not by B Lab."[20] Kassoy was particularly pleased that both Method and Seventh Generation were represented, as the icon of the original effort was Seventh Generation, and Method was the new, hipper version of it. "It was great to have two competitors standing up there, because it said, 'There's enough room in this space.' "[21]

Lowry of Method also remembers that moment well: "It really coalesced together into, I wouldn't say critical mass, but that nucleus of supporters, the standards, the companies that are going to live in the ecosystem. The collective commitment that said, 'Hey, this is something that needs to be done.' " Before the presentation, Coen Gilbert asked each of the participants to explain why he or she had chosen to have their company certified. "For me," he recalls, "there was a mismatch between what business needed to be to meet the demands of people in the world in the twenty-first century, and the government structures that we had available. We needed to change that, and it needed to be something that not just sort of covered the few; it needed to be something dynamic, not just some eco label or certain case." From one large ESOP company that was several centuries old to some small local businesses, it was clear to all in that room that the driving force behind this movement was its mission, its purpose, and the passion of the people propelling it forward.

The B Lab team used the momentum from the conference to drive the movement forward, waiving the certification fee for the first two-year term for all founding B Corps and inviting them to a group signing of the B Corp Declaration of Interdependence in December 2007 at the White Dog Café in Philadelphia. Eighty-one companies signed. Inspired by the energy that night, Harry and Kay Halloran and the president of Halloran Philanthropies, Tony Carr, committed

$500,000 in philanthropic support to B Lab, B Lab's first outside funding, a significant milestone. Until then, B Lab's start-up had been financed through a $1 million loan from the cofounders, who had also waived their salaries for the first year.

Looking back on that original group, Coen Gilbert notes that "there were too few women and no people of color." If the community of B Corps was meant to reflect the diversity of the country and eventually of the world, this would require a "sustained, significant, and intentional effort since the pool of business leaders already in the responsible business movement were overwhelmingly led by white males."[22] But at the time, the three founders were proud of the diversity of industries they'd attracted—from new, edgy brands like Comet Skateboard to established firms such as King Arthur Flour, founded in 1790—as well as their likenesses in terms of culture, mission, and goals. "It's kind of amazing, in retrospect, that anyone actually signed on to this," Houlahan reflects. "Our brand was meaningless, the only thing that mattered was being able to tell the story of who was a certified B Corporation."

4

Getting the Law on the Stakeholders' Side

After Elizabeth Warren called out benefit corporation legislation as a model worth emulating in her 2018 *Wall Street Journal* op-ed, Coen Gilbert published a piece in *Forbes* noting that many of the states that had passed it were led by conservative Republican governors. And twelve states passed the legislation unanimously. "While promoting 'Accountable Capitalism' may not be surprising coming from a liberal icon like Sen. Warren," Coen Gilbert wrote, "it may surprise some who haven't been following the rise of the benefit corporation to know that Republicans, the world's largest investors, and an increasing number of business leaders have been promoting a similar idea for years."[1] Creating a new economy centered on people, planet, and profits is not a Republican or Democrat issue. It is a human issue. And the only way to fix our broken economic system is by changing our laws.

B Corp certification has had a legal component from the beginning—companies must amend their governing documents to expand their fiduciary duties to include consideration of the interests of all stakeholders—workers, communities, and the environment. Small businesses, the vast majority of which are legally chartered as LLCs, had an easy time navigating this change, as they just had to amend their existing operating agreements to reflect this definition of fiduciary duty. For corporations, the objective was more challenging. In thirty-one states with so-called constituency statutes that allow

directors discretion to consider the interests of nonfinancial stakeholders, B Lab could give companies basically the same language they
gave to LLCs, and they could amend their articles of incorporation.
However, nineteen states, including some very important ones like
California and Delaware, did not have constituency statutes, so
any amendment would appear to conflict with underlying corporate
law. This conflict would create a legal risk if a corporation had
to choose between following the amendment and following the de-
fault law.

Changing those laws was especially critical when considering the
"exit problem." As mentioned earlier, values-led businesses such as
Ben & Jerry's and Stonyfield ran into challenges when they were sold.
Houlahan explains: "Each of these poster-child companies had been
acquired by large multinationals for large amounts of money. That
was great news to some. However, it was also sometimes to the significant dismay of their founders and often of their most evangelical
consumers, who feared selling meant selling out. The fear of a forced
sale or of a happy sale that turned into an unhappy marriage was having a chilling effect on the next generation of values-led entrepreneurs, who worried that raising traditional venture capital or pursuing
traditional strategic sale options would lead to an erosion of the vision
and values which had led them to start their business in the first
place." These businesses wanted to grow and create bigger impact, but
not at the expense of their mission.

To provide a legally sound platform for entrepreneurs and investors who wanted to start and invest in companies explicitly seeking to
create both shareholder and social value, B Lab championed new U.S.
state laws. The laws would provide clarity to business leaders, general
counsels, and investors that the fiduciary duty of these companies'
directors and officers includes creating public benefit, even when a
company is up for sale. States have jurisdiction over the incorporation

process in the United States, so the creation of a new legal form requires legislative action at the state level.

As we will explore in more detail below, the proposed legislation also mandated higher standards of transparency, annual reporting to shareholders and the public about the corporation's social and environmental performance, and mechanisms to help ensure that these corporations and the positive social and environmental impact they created were built to last, such as requiring a two-thirds-majority vote of shareholders to remove those higher standards.

As of early 2020, thirty-five states and Washington, DC, had passed benefit corporation legislation and six states were working on it; Italy, Colombia, Ecuador, and British Columbia have also passed benefit corporation laws, and a number of countries around the globe are working on it.

The Law and Shareholder Primacy

As we've seen, shareholder primacy is encoded in U.S. corporate law. While statutes rarely explicitly deny businesses the right to consider the social and environmental impacts of a potential seller's operations, when firms have multiple offers, the company enters *"Revlon* mode,"* named after a landmark case. In 1986, the Delaware Supreme Court issued an opinion in *Revlon v. MacAndrews & Forbes Holdings* stating that firms were obligated to sell to the highest bidder. This means that once the sale of a company is inevitable, the fiduciary obligation of its directors is solely to maximize immediate stockholder value, which most often means selling the company to the bidder offering to pay the highest share price. Penalties are exacted if the directors and the board don't do so, ranging from court-ordered conflict disclosure to an injunction against a proposed transaction that involves a buyer other than the highest bidder.

Although it remains a point of contention, the *Revlon* decision was not unprecedented. As far back as 1919, in *Dodge v. Ford*, it was stated that "a business corporation is organized and carried on primarily for the profit of the stockholders. The powers of the directors are to be employed for that end."[2] In *eBay v. Craigslist* in 2010, the Delaware Chancery Court held that a corporate mission that "seeks not to maximize the economic value of a for-profit Delaware corporation for the benefit of its stockholders" is invalid because it doesn't line up with the director's fiduciary duties. If additional missions are being pursued, the court found, they must also lead to an economic benefit.[3]

The B Lab team believed that *Revlon* mode and the more general focus of corporate law on shareholder primacy denies entrepreneurs, managers, investors, and consumers the freedom to build, invest in, or support businesses that seek to create long-term benefits for society. As Coen Gilbert says, "There are tons of individual companies that have managed to effectively balance social and business impact. Still, we need to institutionalize the values, standards, and accountability that allow companies to do that. We need systems in place. We need to change the rules of the game instead of continuing to clean up messes."[4]

Lessons from California and Aid from Bill Clark

California was the first state the B Lab founders targeted. It seemed the most logical place to start, though the enterprise did not go as planned. As Kassoy recalls, "Basically, we looked around and we said, 'Where are there concentrations of B Corporations, other sustainable businesses that are active, the right legislative environment, and lawyers that we know who would be receptive?' One place that was pretty obvious was California."

As noted earlier, a constituency statute is a provision that permits, but does not require, corporate boards to pay regard to the interests of all corporate stakeholders in their decision making. In 2008, working with attorneys from California law firms Hanson Bridgett, Montgomery & Hansen, and Wendel Rosen, "we got a constituency statute passed in the legislature despite a massive battle with the California bar association," recalls Kassoy. "It passed almost unanimously in both houses of the legislature." Unfortunately, Governor Schwarzenegger vetoed it due to vigorous opposition from the Corporations Committee of the California Bar. However, he encouraged its champions to keep trying. Kassoy explains, "He ended up, after talking to the bar association, vetoing the bill but writing a letter in which he said, 'California should be at the forefront of all states in considering alternative models of corporate governance for the new millennium. This is potentially another opportunity for California to once again lead to a new era of innovation. I urge the legislature to consider and study new styles of corporate governance that can offer alternatives to the current model, but that maintain the vital shareholder protections that have helped turn California into the economic powerhouse of the world.' "

Schwarzenegger "asked the sponsors to work on creating a distinct corporate entity, not simply an enabling constituency statute," Coen Gilbert notes. "This was our preferred solution as well; we just did not think anyone would be supportive of what we perceived as a more radical innovation."[5] Until Bill Clark entered the picture.

Bill Clark is a man of strong Christian faith who views his involvement with B Lab as "a divine appointment." Clark got married shortly after graduating from college. His wife had dropped out but they realized she should return to college right away, before life got in the way. Clark had intended to attend Westminster Theological

Seminary in hopes of building a career at the college or university level with a focus on ancient languages. When his wife went back to college, those plans were put on hold, and he searched for a job that would allow him to support her and their growing family. He ended up working as a paralegal in the government regulation department of Philadelphia's largest law firm, Morgan, Lewis & Bockius. After his wife graduated, he headed to the seminary to fulfill his own dreams. He did well there and eventually graduated with a degree in theology, but he spent every summer at Morgan, Lewis & Bockius. Clearly, he had found what he was really passionate about: law. It seemed a shift in priorities was in order.

Eventually, Clark went to law school and became an associate at Morgan, Lewis & Bockius. His mentor at the time had written the Pennsylvania Business Corporation Law, which was going through a rewrite. Clark's focus became statutory drafting and corporation law, which meant he wrote or was otherwise responsible for laws on partnerships, limited partnerships, limited liability, nonprofit corporations, business corporations, insurance companies, credit unions, and more. He got involved with committees that worked on national statutory writing as well.

Eventually, he moved to AND 1's law firm, Drinker Biddle & Reath. Clark heard about the sale of AND 1 and the founding of B Lab, but he had no connection with the trio or those organizations at the time. It was only after B Lab's plans in California fell through that they were brought together. Clark recalls that at first he was "a complete skeptic. I did not get it at all. I had spent my entire career working for 'the man,' the biggest publicly traded companies incorporated in Pennsylvania. Aetna, Comcast, folks like that, were clients, and I was kind of used to working the other side of the street. But I said I'll have some meetings with them and understand what their issue is and see what kind of a solution we can draft." Once he started to meet with the B Lab team, it didn't take long before he was fully committed to the cause. Looking back, Clark says that "my entire professional career was preparing me to work with B Lab. My move to Drinker Biddle & Reath was the final development that brought my entire career into focus because it put me in contact with B Lab."

Clark was the missing piece of the puzzle. Kassoy recalls that Clark "got really excited about this idea that there ought to be an alternative corporate form or an election that a regular company could make to do something broader in expanding fiduciary duty. He encouraged us to sit down with him and a blank slate to write a corporate code. He worked with us as we decided what a company should look like if it wants to create public benefit in addition to shareholder value."[6]

The founders spent over six months going back and forth with Clark to develop the initial model for benefit corporation legislation in California. Kassoy recalls that other groups in the United States were attempting things along similar lines: "Minnesota had had a citizens rights group that had tried to create a socially responsible corporation code at some point. Hawaii had tried something similar. You had thirty-one states [with] constituency statutes. And so we had lots of ideas floating around out there, and we spent a lot of time with Bill, basically writing a piece of model legislation, and then went and started talking to a few different states where we had some relationships."

As Clark put it, the model they were envisioning would be "set up so that all of the normal rules in the basic law apply except to the extent that the special charter provides for an enforceable expansion of fiduciary duty. An opt-in model would be consistent with what Schwarzenegger had suggested, and thus much less worrisome than a similar change to the base corporate code when you're asking politicians to vote for something."

Maryland Leads the Way

In the fall of 2009, Kassoy attended an Investors' Circle party in Washington, DC, at a community gathering space called Busboys and Poets. Jim Epstein, the founder of Blue Ridge Produce, a longtime member of the sustainable business movement and a B Corp champion, introduced Kassoy to Jamie Raskin, then a Maryland state senator. Kassoy recalls, "I started describing to him the work that we do. And he said, 'Oh, this is perfect! This is exactly what we need in Maryland. This would make us like the Delaware [a hub for traditional corporations] for sustainable business!' And literally, the end of the conversation was, 'Can I have your card? I'm going to get legislation written next week.' "

Kassoy was thrilled to have met a like-minded individual who could potentially help with B Lab's long-term goals, but he certainly didn't believe it would happen as quickly as Raskin had said. "I remember calling Bart and Jay the next day, and we kind of all laughed. We got a call two days later from [Raskin's] assistant saying, 'Can you get on the phone with him? Because we want to submit legislation next week.' It might have taken him two weeks instead of a week. But he literally submitted the legislation, found cosponsors, and just started driving it forward."

Three major events had spurred Raskin's urgency: "One," he recalls, "was the Upper Big Branch mine collapse disaster in West Virginia, another was the BP Oil Spill, and the third was the mortgage meltdown . . . it was a very tough time when you think about these corporate catastrophes."[7] The mine collapse, which cost thirteen people their lives, occurred largely because no one had followed up on safety citations made against the ICG Corporation. "It just seemed to me that we had gone back as a society to rapacious unregulated capitalism," Raskin told me. "If corporations are unchecked by law, then a corporate charter is a license to steal."

Raskin had been rereading Adam Smith and juxtaposing his ideas to the situation in the modern world. "I had come to the conclusion," he recalls, "that Adam Smith had been fundamentally distorted, mis-characterized, and exploited by contemporary right-wing politics." Raskin understood that Smith didn't believe that markets should dominate everything, nor that capitalism was just whatever happened. In fact, he would have feared what the reign of shareholder primacy had wrought: the "development of monopoly capital and predatory business activity where certain large businesses gain power over the political sphere and then use their influence to dictate to the rest of society the essential terms of public policy."

Shortly before the 2008 presidential election, Citizens United, a conservative nonprofit organization, had tried to air an anti–Hillary Clinton film but had been denied the opportunity based on a federal law—the McCain-Feingold Act—that prohibited corporations from producing "electioneering communications" prior to an election or making any expenditures for the success or defeat of an electoral candidate. In what some considered a shocking move, the Supreme Court ruled in favor of Citizens United in 2010, creating a precedent that would allow corporations to hold opinions and act on them as if they were people. "What the court did," Raskin says, "was basically say that CEOs could write checks from the corporate treasury in order to propel favored politicians to office or to beat politicians anti-thetical to their interests."

By creating a new legal entity, Raskin explained, these companies "could send a signal to potential investors, employees, and customers that they are a different kind of business because they have a social plank built into their charter. They have a specific public purpose that they're fulfilling in addition to the general Delaware incorporation model of trying to make as much money as possible."

When they began their work together, Raskin asked the team if they had an "actual plan." The three told him that they imagined their work on benefit corporations would take from five to ten years. Raskin replied that it should be a ten-week plan. When he presented the benefit corporation legislation to his colleagues, he kept his explanation brief and simple: "When corporations first began, they were on a very tight leash and had specific social purposes in mind. When this purpose was completed, they would go do something else." The Delaware corporation model, he continued, changed this drastically. It made it so that corporations could do whatever they want, could exist in perpetuity, and could have limited liability to shareholders, shifting all the risks from the corporation onto society, consumers, or employees. Because of corporations' vast wealth, it was now impossible to "put the genie back in the bottle," he said. Convincing businesses to voluntarily incorporate a social ethos into what they're doing was not a solution, but it was a huge step forward.

He reminded his colleagues at the Maryland General Assembly that benefit corporation legislation would be a financial boon to the state because companies would register in Maryland, would pay their fees to Maryland, and it would cost the state nothing. His Democratic colleagues, he recalls, liked the idea immediately. Although they were a bit more skeptical, most Republicans couldn't find anything wrong with the legislation. Those who opposed the plan, though few, spoke up. Some, Raskin recalls, thought it was a George Soros plot to rewrite all the rules of capitalism on the side of liberals. Others considered it just a feel-good exercise that wouldn't make a difference. When presented with these criticisms, Raskin invited the B Lab team to come to Maryland to testify and further elaborate on the proposed legislation. There was also a lot of debate centered on whether there should be incentives and inducements like tax relief for benefit corporations. Raskin shut these debates down, noting, "That's a conversation for a later day." In the end, Raskin relates, "we ended up having nearly unanimous support."

On April 13, 2010, Maryland's governor signed the legislation. On October 1, 2010, the legislation's effective date, eleven companies waited outside the offices of the Maryland State Department of Assessment and Taxation for the distinction of becoming the world's first registered benefit corporations. Big Bad Woof, an organic and environmentally friendly pet store, was the first, followed closely by Blessed Coffee, a Fair Trade coffee-importing business.

What It Means to Be a Benefit Corporation

Registered benefit corporations not only give entrepreneurs permission to take other interests besides those of shareholders into account but offer protection to founders concerned that taking in outside capital could lead their companies to "drift" away from their social mission. Under model benefit corporation legislation, companies are required to:

- Have a purpose to create a material positive impact on society and the environment from their business and operations, in addition to being financially profitable.
- Expand the fiduciary duty of their directors to consider the impact of their decisions on a broad spectrum of stakeholders, not just shareholders.
- Deliver information on their broader purpose by periodically preparing a public report using an independent, transparent, credible, and comprehensive standard for evaluating the positive impact of the company on the environment, their employees, their customers, their communities, and more.

In addition to its purpose to create a material positive impact on society and the environment generally, a benefit corporation may also elect to create a specific public benefit to a particular community or environmental issue. The demand for accountability ensures that a company's directors consider the interest of shareholders, employees, customers, and the local community. An annual "benefit report" that follows third-party standards (including the B Impact Assessment) for assessing and reporting on social and environmental metrics must be distributed to all shareholders and made available on the company's public website for complete transparency. B Lab is particularly focused on transparency around negative practices, such as disclosing if a company has had litigation in the last few years, because this is the only way that stakeholders can make informed decisions. In some states, benefit corporations can choose to elect a benefit director, an independent person who oversees the integrity of the assessment, or a benefit officer who might lead in preparing the report. Directors have no personal liability in general or for monetary damages for failure to create public benefit.[8]

Some benefit corporations end up pursuing B Corp certification as well. B Corps that are incorporated in states that have passed benefit corporation legislation are required to become benefit corporations after certification. Benefit corporations and B Corps have similar aspects: both are required to assess and disclose their overall social/ environmental performance against a third-party standard (for certified B Corps, this must be the B Impact Assessment), and both types of entities require that their directors consider all stakeholders when making decisions. But it is useful to highlight their differences. The fundamental distinction, of course, is that one is a legal form and the other a certification. Certified B Corps and benefit corporations differ most in the issue of performance. Certified B Corps must achieve a minimum score on the BIA and must recertify every three years. Benefit corporations, on the other hand, are not expected to maintain a minimum assessment score, nor is there any ongoing verification or oversight. Additionally, they differ in terms of cost. While certified B Corps pay an annual certification fee to B Lab based on revenue, benefit corporations are responsible only for state filing fees.

Is Benefit Corporation Legislation Necessary?

Some legal scholars believe that benefit corporation legislation is superfluous. In her 2012 book *The Shareholder Value Myth,* Lynn Stout argued that in corporate law, the "business judgment rule" gives managers and directors quite a lot of room to lead the business as they see fit, as long as they don't take advantage of their position or their power.[9] In an article in the *European Financial Review,* she wrote, "Certainly they can choose to maximize profits; but they can also choose to pursue any other objective that is not unlawful, including taking care of employees or suppliers, pleasing customers, benefiting the community and the broader society, and preserving and protecting the corporate entity itself. Shareholder primacy is a managerial choice—not a legal requirement."[10] She followed up on this when interviewed by the *Guardian* after Delaware passed benefit corporation legislation. Stout said, "It's a total misunderstanding—very common in the public mind—that you can sue directors and get them to pay damages for failing to maximise shareholder value."[11] In other words, according to Stout, the argument that B Lab makes regarding the dangers of *Revlon* mode, as well as shareholder primacy, isn't valid.

But former Delaware chief justice Leo E. Strine disagrees. In his essay "The Dangers of Denial," he exposes the flaws in the various lines of thinking that conclude that directors can easily promote the interests of other stakeholders in traditional businesses. One of his key points is that shareholders are the only ones who have any legal power—they vote for directors, enforce terms, hold directors accountable, approve transactions, and so on. No other stakeholder constituency is given any power. As he writes, "It is not only hollow but also injurious to social welfare to declare that directors can and should do the right thing by promoting interests other than stockholder interests. This argument does not pressure those with the ability to make sure that other constituencies are protected to do so, such as by giving them rights to protect other interests. Instead, it alleviates this pressure."[12]

Rick Alexander, the "recovering corporate lawyer" we met earlier in these pages, offers an even more direct rebuttal: "The way the law works in this country, it's what the judges say it is. . . . What the law is, to me, is not a complicated thing. Go read the *Revlon* case. It's the Supreme Court of Delaware, and it says shareholder primacy." In other words, lawyers and law professors can say that *Revlon* mode is avoidable or that it isn't the law in theory, but in fact the Delaware Supreme Court justices explicitly made it the law in practice through their decision.

State-by-State Progress

While Maryland's journey to benefit legislation was propelled forward by one man, the next state to pass legislation, Vermont, was influenced by a group of socially responsible businesses and individuals including Vermont Business for Social Responsibility (VBSR) and Vermont Employee Ownership Center (VEOC), which were instrumental in getting legislative interest and the support of the Vermont Bar Association. Benefit corporation legislation passed fairly easily in Vermont about a month after Maryland led the way. Kassoy finds it ideal that Vermont was the second, not the first, state to pass legislation:

> We're quite lucky that that happened, because if Vermont had been first, it could have easily been dismissed as, "Those are the crazy, socialist people up there. This isn't real business." Maryland is only behind Delaware [with] the second-largest number of publicly traded corporations. . . . It's got a serious business bar, a pretty well-known middle-of-the-road governor. And just the fact that it sits there next to Delaware and it's near DC, it created some credibility and gravitas that I

think Vermont wouldn't have created by being first, but it was phenomenal that we could have that one-two punch within a month of each other.

Coen Gilbert admits these quick successes were not part of B Lab's original plan: what happened in Maryland and Vermont surprised the team. "Yes, in our original business plan, law was an eventual goal. But we thought we'd be dealing with it in 5 or 10 years. But the chance came, we couldn't say 'Oh, the plan doesn't say to talk to you for 3 years.' We just said, 'Great, let's go!' "[13]

New York, Pennsylvania, Colorado, Oregon, and North Carolina all expressed interest in benefit legislation in 2010, and the B Lab trio set to work to introduce legislation in each of these states. The team's resources were limited; the three couldn't be everywhere at once. They focused on being present in certain states and providing a package of documents— a model based on Bill Clark's original legislation for California—to share with interested policy makers. While it was adaptable, "it also allowed us to capture exactly what we thought the best way of doing this should be," Clark says. The language in those early states' legislation isn't as consistent as it is among states that became interested later, but Clark notes that "they all share the three basic characteristics of changing the purpose of the corporation, changing the duties of directors, and requiring enhanced reporting on that broader purpose. Those are the three main characteristics of a benefit corporation."

The movement was often led by grassroots activists, and local business communities in each state had differing reactions. In South Carolina, the Chamber of Commerce immediately thought it was a good idea. Michigan's Chamber of Commerce, in contrast, was very concerned that companies would feel shamed if they didn't adopt the model—that somehow passing legislation to allow the option of being a benefit corporation would label all non–benefit corporations as "bad companies." Clark reflects, "That's a very interesting notion to fear, right? All of a sudden you're worried that it proves to be successful and you'll have to do it too." The takeaway from these various responses was that it was important for B Lab to identify the right people at the state level and go to them quickly to secure their support.

The B Lab founders worked hard to ensure that the efforts were bipartisan. "We have very conservative sponsors, very liberal sponsors, and 90 percent approval rating on all floor votes," says Holly Ensign-Barstow, director of stakeholder governance and policy at B Lab. From the start, B Lab has been reactive: the founders don't approach a state unless they already have interest from that state. It usually begins with local B Corporations, which often have existing relationships in the state legislature, and with local business networks and corporate lawyers. Once the interest is there, B Lab takes the next steps to move forward with legislation that has bipartisan buy-in, as Ensign-Barstow explains: "Depending on who it is, we generally have a call with them. Basically, we talk them through our recommendations in terms of how they think about moving and advancing the bill. In general, we want the sponsor to be a Republican. If the interest is from a Democrat, we recommend that they find a Republican who would be interested in cosponsoring at the very least. We recommend that they reach out to business organizations as well as the bar association. The bar association can sometimes be the most difficult actor to get on board, unfortunately."

Clark is quick to point out that passing this legislation requires a lot of convincing. One of his main jobs has been finding the right local lawyers to speak to and then persuading them to push forward. As these lawyers are responsible for corporation' and other business entity laws in their state, they often push back on the idea of an outsider telling them what to do. They also may have a hard time understanding why this is necessary and that the legislation won't ask companies to adopt specific missions.

Early in the process, other similar forms, such as the low profit limited liability corporation (L3C), the flexible-purpose corporation (California), and the social purpose corporation (Washington), were also being introduced and passed in some state legislatures. However, it was increasingly clear that B Lab's model was becoming the standard. A key factor in B Lab's success was its ability to promise regulators that passing the law would not create any additional costs. Plus, as Raskin points out, there's a hope among some that benefit corporations will "help us to reinstate the wall separating corporations from electoral politics." In other words, Raskin explains, "I would hope that benefit corporations could help us challenge Citizens United and the idea that corporate treasuries are political slush funds for the CEOs to advance either their personal interests or even the collective interests of the shareholders. As Justice Byron White observed, the corporation is the creature of the state and the state need not permit its own creature to consume and devour it. If people in corporations sincerely want to improve social well-being, they should do it directly in their communities, where we need them, not by intervening in elections and subsidizing political campaigns."

Taking the Fight to Delaware

Delaware is the de facto center of corporate law in the United States. More than 65 percent of Fortune 500 firms have chosen Delaware as their legal home, and about a third of the annual state budget comes from business filings. The B Lab founders knew they had to approach Delaware slightly differently than they might another state, and the work to get a B Corp statute on the books there proved especially challenging. The people championing benefit corporation legislation in Delaware did not use Clark's model, knowing its chances of success would be slim because of Delaware's general approach of creating its own version of corporation and other entity laws.

Rick Alexander spent twenty-five years dealing with traditional corporate law and was a leader in the movement to get legislation on the books in Delaware. Much of his past work focused on the Delaware statute itself, and he had always strongly believed in shareholder primacy. Alexander was part of a group of Delaware lawyers who were essentially the trustees of corporate law when the B Lab cofounders approached them. He recalls, "We thought they were kind of silly and naïve and not something we wanted to mess with." Through the years, he explained, the lawyers had encountered many forms of constituency statutes—the type of legislative change the B Lab team had originally tried to get passed in California—and had rejected them all. "Whatever your political stripes might be, a corporation produces profits and is backed by people who put money in it. . . . If you think there are too many externalities, then you go to Congress and lobby for some legislation to make corporations internalize those costs."[14]

The trio approached the Delaware bar cautiously, equipped with some important local support, including Chief Justice Leo Strine and then-governor Jack Markell, who asked the Section of Corporation Law at the Delaware State Bar Association to meet with them. Alexander took the lead on the project, becoming very interested as he delved deeper into it. Everything changed for him when he read Lynn Stout's book—a turning point we discussed earlier.[15]

To make its case, in September 2012, B Lab brought in the founders and CEOs of a diverse set of B Corps, including Chad Dickerson from Etsy, Neil Blumenthal from Warby Parker, Fred Keller from Cascade Engineering, and Mandy Cabot from Dansko. Importantly, B Lab also made sure there were credible investors in the room, namely, Albert Wenger from Union Square Ventures and Ommeed Sathe from Prudential. Kassoy recalls that they held the meeting at a large law firm: "We went down there, and there were literally eighteen middle-aged white men . . . from each of the big Delaware law firms" sitting around a huge table. "We had this giant conversation to try to help them understand why it mattered to these entrepreneurs and investors to have a different corporate form. It was a seminal moment. After that, every time we had a meeting with any of these lawyers, they would talk about one of the specific examples from that meeting, saying, 'This is why we need a statute in Delaware.' It was a totally fascinating experience."

Negotiations were very tense when working on the text of the legislation. At one point, Clark thought that Delaware should change the name of its statute because it didn't match the B Corp brand enough and would reduce the impact of the movement. The threat of "greenwashing" came up again and again. At another juncture, the B Lab team reached out to the national B Corp community for advice and help. If Delaware decided to move forward with a watered-down version of the benefit corporation that would confuse the market, B Lab decided, the trio would launch a widespread publicity campaign to influence the state. When Strine and Markell heard about that plan, Houlahan recalls, "oh my goodness, that was a bad moment. That was a very bad moment because we had people who had been working with us in good faith to try to find an answer, and they felt we were planning a response that was going to be potentially very damaging to the State."[16] In February 2013, Strine called a meeting with Alexander, other key leaders of the bar, and the B Lab cofounders. When they were all in the same room, Strine invited the bar to share its draft statute and then announced that no one could leave until they'd all agreed on a statute together. Before the participants left the room that day, a member of the Delaware Bar Association said that when passed, Delaware's benefit corporation statute would represent a "seismic shift" in U.S. corporate law. On August 1, 2013, the legislation was signed.[17]

In certain areas, Delaware's legislation differs from that of other states. For example, it doesn't define a company's stakeholders, instead saying that the directors have to balance the interests of shareholders with those of others materially affected by the company. Under the benefit corporation legislation that B Lab developed in other states, a third-party standard has to be used and the results of that assessment must be transparent to the general public. In Delaware, there is no obligation to use a third-party standard to assess the benefit corporation's overall social and environmental impacts, which arguably leaves it open to a greenwashing risk. In addition, companies registered as "public benefit corporations" under Delaware law are required to make a report transparent only to their shareholders (as opposed to the general public) every two years (as opposed to the annual reporting requirement of the model benefit corporation legislation).

Unlike the model statute, there is no provision for what is known as a "benefit enforcement proceeding" that a shareholder can use, as Alexander explains, "to show that a company is not meeting its benefit obligations. In that proceeding, there's no business judgment rule protection." In traditional corporate law, the shareholders give the directors discretion with respect to business decisions as long as they're acting in good faith. Under the model statute, that protection extends to directors and officers but not to the company itself. "A shareholder could sue and say, 'I think there's a better way to achieve material public benefit,' " Alexander explains, contrasting the model statute with the Delaware provisions, under which there is no exception to the business judgment rule.

Challenges with Benefit Corporation Adoption and Implementation

While more than ten thousand benefit corporations have been established as of early 2020, entrepreneurs can still face significant pushback from the legal and financial community. Romain Aubanel is no stranger to start-ups or the benefit corporation—he cofounded

Court 16, an inclusive tennis club, and was part of the founding leadership team of Olea Medical, a medical imaging software company that was sold to Toshiba. Aubanel has registered two different companies as benefit corporations. The first was LNRJ United, which is essentially a family investment office. Since this company was backed by him financially, he didn't need to convince anyone about registering it as a benefit corporation.

Jack and Ferdi, his latest venture, is an app geared to "bleisure travelers"—people on business trips who also want to add some leisure experiences. When it came time to pursue benefit corporation status, Aubanel says he was "a bit shocked to hear the type of advice we were receiving." Everyone, he says, from investors to lawyers to banks, was either against the idea or had never heard of it. For example, the IT systems at Aubanel's bank did not recognize the benefit corporation in its account setup form. His lawyers believed that he would have an uphill battle with investors because he would have to spend so much time explaining and justifying the idea of a benefit corporation. There was a concern that he would push the company to be overly focused on its social mission to the exclusion of profits. "We're either too much on the profit side or too much on the unknown or uncharted side with the social dimensions," he said. "So this is a little difficult. This is not firmed up yet." Aubanel went on to explain that a related concern of potential investors regarded exit: "Are your shareholders who invested because of your social component going to create problems if your buyer isn't good enough on the social end of things?"

Moreover, Aubanel's lawyers thought that the transparency aspect of being a benefit corporation would be difficult, though Aubanel explains that was one of the main things that attracted him to the form. "We want to communicate to all of our consumers and users how what we are doing is different. We want to show that."

The transparency standard of benefit corporations has created some other challenges. For instance, it's recently come to light that many benefit corporations are not meeting the mandatory transparency requirements. Belmont University's J. Haskell Murray, investigating this issue in 2014, found that less than 10 percent of the benefit corporations he looked at were fulfilling the annual reporting requirement. Murray also found that the reporting requirements weren't particularly strong—the clause stating that third-party standards have to be followed to complete the annual report is written in a vague and uninformative way, leaving it too open to interpretation.[18] More recently, in response to Elizabeth Warren's Accountable Capitalism Act, Murray stated on his blog: "I have noted in my scholarly work how the state benefit corporation laws fail to align the purported 'general public benefit' corporate purpose with effective accountability mechanisms. This bill, however, takes one step toward aligning company purpose and accountability by requiring that employees elect at least 40 percent of the board. Of course, that still leaves out many other stakeholders that directors are supposed to consider, and shareholders are still the only stakeholders with the ability to sue derivatively."[19]

For benefit corporation legislation to achieve its goal, clearly its requirements must be enforced and maintained. Without oversight and consistency, it is possible that some companies could use the benefit corporation form as a sophisticated kind of greenwashing.[20]

Beyond the United States

Following its legislative successes in the United States, the benefit corporation idea sparked interest in other countries. One early initiative was the G8 Social Impact Investment Task Force led by Sir Ronald Cohen in 2013. Bill Clark and Andrew Kassoy were members of the task force's Mission Alignment working group, which recommended adoption of benefit corporation laws to G8 countries in its final report.[21] B Lab didn't devote a large part of its time to policy changes in other countries at the beginning, largely because the co-founders thought that most jurisdictions were fairly permissive with respect to fiduciary duty and therefore didn't need them to take on policy changes. In France, for example, shareholder primacy is not mandated—if a French company wants to be a benefit corporation, it just has to modify its articles of incorporation. (In Australia, in contrast, shareholder primacy is an absolute.) But the benefit corporation legislation movement took off on its own, and B Lab had to step in to protect and bolster the label.

In Italy, entrepreneurs Eric Ezechieli and Paolo Di Cesare were running a sustainability consultancy named Nativa. It was important to them that the company have a sense of purpose—in fact, they wrote it into their articles of incorporation. The commerce bureau rejected their application. "The happiness of all those who are a part of it," they stated, was not an acceptable reason for a company to exist. "We realized that legally, if you're a manager," explains Di Cesare, "you can't focus on improving the lives of your employees or the environment. You *must* maximize profits for shareholders. That's it. We thought: There must be another way." In 2013, Nativa became a certified B Corp, and its founders heard about the benefit corporation legal structure for the first time. It seemed they had finally found the answers they were looking for. They approached an open-minded politician, Senator Mauro Del Barba, and asked for his help. Within the next few years, the founders tested the waters by approaching different politicians and citizens, and they received supportive feedback. In 2014, they reached out to PD, the democratic political party in Italy, which responded enthusiastically. Legislation was drafted and quickly moved through the government in 2015 until it was approved by the Italian Senate and Parliament. By 2016, "Italy became the first country outside of the U.S., with a law for a new type of business that looks not just at profit but also at society and the environment." Of course, Nativa was the first *societa benefit* company to register.[22]

Interest in the movement later sparked in Colombia. As the B Lab team began working with lawyers in Colombia, the political situation in the country shifted and, as Clark put it, "pretty much sucked the air out of the politics of the country." The plan was put on pause until the man who had been pushing for it, then senator Ivan Duque, became president of Colombia in June 2018. After his election, benefit corporation legislation passed very quickly, though with a few provisions reflecting its Colombian context. Many other countries in South America have now proposed legislation, and in February 2020 benefit corporation law passed in Ecuador. Discussions are under way in Argentina, Australia, Brazil, Canada, Chile, Peru, Portugal, Taiwan, and Uruguay. In addition, in May 2019, the Canadian Province British Columbia unanimously passed benefit company legislation into law.

To overthrow shareholder primacy, there needs to be a fundamental change in the legal foundation of corporations. Benefit corporation legislation is an important step in this direction. Under benefit corporation law, directors' duties shift in a fundamental way such that they now need to consider all stakeholders, not just shareholders. But moving forward, it's crucial that benefit corporations are required to comply with the transparency requirements in the law. Without vigorous enforcement, there is a risk that the ideas behind the law will lose legitimacy and detract from the larger movement.

5

Investing for Impact

In 2006, before the official launch of the B Corp movement, the B Lab founders met Leslie Christian, who would become very influential in what they would create. They connected with Christian through Marjorie Kelly, whose book *The Divine Right of Capital: Dethroning the Corporate Aristocracy*, in which she directly identified shareholder primacy as an impediment to economic, social, and environmental success, had greatly inspired Coen Gilbert. Her latest book, *Owning Our Future: The Emerging Ownership Revolution*, explores cooperatives and community-owned businesses.[1]

With her platinum blond coif and black, thick-rimmed cat-eye glasses, Christian is a natural force. Starting in 1999, when she created one of the first SRI funds in her hometown of Seattle, she has been a leader in the socially responsible investment space. Portfolio 21 is an open-end, no-load mutual fund focused on companies' environmental and social impacts.

The roots of the SRI movement go back to the 1960s, when the civil rights movement and protests against the Vietnam War sparked a widespread passion for change. In the 1970s, concerns about the environment and the threat of pollution began to rise. This spirit affected some in the business world as well. At the height of the apartheid crisis, for example, many firms divested from South Africa. By the 1980s, several mutual funds had been established to address the concerns of socially responsible investors. These funds screened out companies that profited from weapons, alcohol, tobacco, and gambling as well as those that mistreated their workers, or whose practices were harmful to the environment. In 1990, the Domini Social Index was established, which identified U.S. corporations that had met its social and environmental standards.[2]

As encouraging as these developments were, Christian had a key insight: by the time socially responsible companies got into the public markets that SRI funds invested in, most had already been sucked into a capital structure and a set of market dynamics that pushed them toward short-term decisions that minimized their focus on people and the planet. Founders often felt driven to sell their companies rather than transition them to new ownership or to their employees because of their fiduciary obligation to their shareholders. To address these concerns, in 2004 Christian founded a holding company called Upstream 21—a "Berkshire Hathaway for values-driven companies," as she describes it. Upstream 21's first acquisition was a distressed timber company that was important to the local economy. "Their idea was, 'We're not going to flip it but hold it as stewards,' " Coen Gilbert explains. "That was a really powerful vision." Upstream 21 did not last long—it took a hit that it was unable to recover from in the 2008 financial crisis. But while she and her partner lost money, Christian remains positive about the experience. "We contributed to this movement of benefit corporations," she says. "We ended up knowing we'd learned a lot, and that we had made a contribution to something we cared about."

When they met, Coen Gilbert and Christian talked about how she had structured her company. Planting the seed that grew into the benefit corporation, she recalls telling him, "You have to make [the focus on stakeholders' interests] tighter legally, and here's what you can do. You can charter a company, you can put it into the articles of incorporation and make it unchangeable." Christian had done that herself with Upstream 21, which was the first company to have amended its articles of incorporation to explicitly require consideration of stakeholders' interests. As Christian explains it, "We developed a set of articles that defined the company's best interests to include its employees, the community, the environment, suppliers, customers, as well as shareholders. We put everybody on a level playing field, and specifically put it into the charter."

With all that in mind, the B Lab team began to move toward the investment world. As we will see, the B Corp movement has evolved the impact investing field in a number of ways. At a fundamental level, the development of the BIA provided a foundation for impact assessment. Investors helped accelerate the movement by encouraging the companies in their portfolios to use B Lab's tools not just to better understand social and environmental impact but to manage their firms. Large multinationals have contributed to the movement as well by buying certified B Corps as subsidiaries. By 2019, there were scores of financial services companies that had been certified as B Corps themselves, including venture capital firms, commercial banks, wealth managers, and insurance companies.

The Emergence of Impact Investing

The Rockefeller Foundation coined the term *impact investing* in 2007 to describe investments that focused on social and environmental goals as well as investment returns. Whereas SRI was focused mostly on screening out perceived "sin stocks" and on shareholder resolutions in public companies, impact investing was focused on the intentional creation of positive impact in primarily nonpublic markets.[3] But as Kassoy recalls, at the time, the critical issue "impeding impact investing was a lack of standards and ratings infrastructure to help [investors] know what [it] meant to measure impact."

The Rockefeller Foundation identified the BIA as the leading impact investing metric, and offered the team funding to turn the original BIA into a more robust rating system. In doing so, it also looped B Lab into discussions about how to drive institutional capital to mission-driven businesses. "Since 2007," explains former president Dr. Judith Rodin, "the Rockefeller Foundation has been committed to growth and development of the impact investing sector as a way to address social and environmental challenges and accelerate benefits to poor and vulnerable people. B Lab has been a critical partner in this work and . . . laid some of the foundational infrastructure needed to expand the sector and address the world's social challenges."[4] As Kassoy elaborates, the Rockefeller Foundation said, "[The BIA's] got the right platform to use for an investor-facing rating system. It needs X, Y, and Z changes, but it's fundamentally the right methodology." Today, the BIA is used to certify companies as B Corps, but it also acts as the foundation for many other B Lab tools and measurements.

Developing Assessment Tools

The Rockefeller Foundation created the Global Impact Investing Network (GIIN) in 2007 with a mission "to accelerate the industry's development through focused leadership and collective action."[5] The GIIN promoted B Lab's initial investor-facing tool, GIIRS (global impact investing rating system), which pulled information from the BIA to create a rating for a fund. The fund itself completed a fund manager assessment—a custom version of the BIA—and reviewed its responses with help from B Lab staff. Once the fund's portfolio companies had all completed their BIA assessments, B Lab aggregated the data to derive an overall impact business model and overall operations rating from an average of their scores that was weighted to reflect the amount invested. This was then translated into a medal rating (bronze, silver, gold, or platinum) and a star rating (one to five stars).

The fund also received ratings in specific impact areas, such as community, customers, environment, workers, and governance.[6]

B Lab believed GIIRS could allow institutional and high–net worth investors to conduct better due diligence, make more informed investment decisions, more effectively track and improve social and environmental performance throughout the investment life cycle, and better report absolute and relative impact. GIIRS was also intended to give consultants, investment bankers, and other intermediaries the data and analytical tools they needed to improve their own proprietary products and value-added services, as well as help companies and fund managers raise capital from mission-aligned investors based on the social and environmental impact of their underlying businesses or portfolio companies. This suite of measurement tools gave investors the tools to understand social and environmental impact in increasingly nuanced ways and has evolved into the B Analytics platform.

Starting with the Pioneers

The B Lab team knew they had to start with the people who already had an interest in sustainable investment and get them on board. That is, first they had to "get buy-in from the people who actually get it"—the investment community that was already focused on social investing. They thought, "If this worked, then we would go beyond just the impact investments, and ask Apollo and Blackstone and KKR to get rated too." As investment companies and banks experienced the certification process directly, it would lead to network effects that would help scale the movement.

New Resource Bank (NRB), a community bank focused on environmental sustainability, is an example of how this strategy can play out. As noted earlier, New Resource was the three hundredth certified B Corp. It spread the idea of being a B Corp to RSF Social Finance, a pioneering impact investor and another early B Corp that was one of its first investors, and the Netherlands-based Triodos Bank, which became a certified B Corp as of 2015. NRB merged with fellow B Corp Amalgamated Bank in 2017, creating the largest sustainability-focused bank in the United States and spreading the idea still further. When impact investors such as RSF and Triodos became active participants and proponents of its work, B Lab encouraged them to spread awareness to the companies in their portfolios and to other companies they interacted with.

As Kassoy explains, "We're trying to get investors essentially to be an accelerant to businesses using our impact management tools, like the BIA." The B Lab team encourages all investors to use the B Analytics platform as a way to analyze their portfolios. Thus the companies that are part of the investors' portfolios have to use the platform as well, at least to upload their information. This then often leads to companies looking into B Corp certification for themselves or at least using some of the BIA metrics or other tools on the platform.

In 2015, London-based Bridges Fund Management certified as a B Corp and became yet another example of investors expanding the influence of the B Corp movement to their industry as a whole. Even before the movement crossed the pond, Antony Ross, a partner at Bridges who leads its sustainable growth and social sector funds, told me that Bridges had been lobbying the government to "create some form of specialists, some brand that businesses could engage with" that would not only verify a business's dedication to its mission but also prove its dedication to its customers. Now Bridges assesses the businesses in its portfolios via their BIA scores to see where their impact is lacking and where Bridges can help—environmental initiatives and human resource management are two areas that it is especially concerned about. To date, companies that have gone through this process with Bridges include an ethical hotel chain, a company that provides maintenance services to housing associations, and a business focused on book recycling. Bridges looks first at what issues a business is addressing and what goals it might be able to achieve before considering things that traditional investors might consider. Ross explains that Bridges has funds that back private sector profit-generating businesses and funds that back mission-based enterprises. But "the holy grail for us . . . is mission-driven, profit-making enterprises."

Bridges's CEO and founder is Egyptian-born businessman Sir Ronald Mourad Cohen. A well-known figure in UK politics, impact investing, and venture capital, Cohen has earned too many accolades to mention. His family fled Egypt in the wake of Nasser's anti-Jewish measures in 1957, and the eleven-year-old Cohen arrived in the United Kingdom with minimal knowledge of English. Cohen's father enrolled him in a local school in London and promised the headmaster that Cohen would be at the top of his class in no time—a promise that Cohen was eager to fulfill. He adapted quickly, going on to excel at Oxford and Harvard Business School. After graduation, he founded one of the UK's first venture capital firms, Apax Partners, which he ran until his "retirement" in 2005. The second half of his incredible career began when he pioneered the first social impact bond in the United Kingdom.[7] Knighted in 2001, he has been called a "compassionate capitalist" and "the Father of UK Venture Capital."[8] Watching him onstage or in person, one gets the sense that he has the soul of a true English nobleman; his speech and demeanor reflect both his intellect and zeal. "I think it's a question now of inspiring the millennial generation to do again what it did in the tech revolution," he says. "But this time, *to do it for impact—doing good and doing well at the same time*" (emphasis added).[9]

Making the Case for Investing in B Corps

While the field of impact investing has enjoyed substantial growth, New Resource Bank's former CEO Vince Siciliano is acutely aware of the challenges it faces. "Financial returns are still paramount in most businesses and in most investment portfolios," he says. While many impact investors act as if you can have your cake and eat it too, "in reality, you're either increasing your risk in order to get the right return, or you're investing in companies that aren't really green. The real goal is to understand impact investments to such a depth that the apparent risk is reduced to an acceptable risk/return trade-off."

As B Lab worked to expand the social investment circle and reach out to traditional investors, the main questions the team had to answer was whether B Corp certification is good or bad for investors long term. How can a company take all of its stakeholders' interests into account, from the shareholder and the employee to the consumer and the local community, and still make money? If B Lab could not convince traditional investors that being socially responsible was also good for business, then the movement would be dead in its tracks.

The fact is that B Corps offer benefits that traditional corporations often don't, such as long-term sustainability, risk mitigation, and management quality. The B Lab team has worked hard to educate investors about these factors. For instance, when the cofounders first approached Silicon Valley investors, they were met with quite a lot of skepticism. But, B Lab's Holly Ensign-Barstow recalls, "by the end of the meeting[s], they were thinking about portfolio companies that it did make sense for." If investors could be convinced of the risk-mitigating benefits of the B Corp movement, they would be on board.

Bridges Fund Management outlined many of the pros and cons of investing in B Corps in its publication "To B or Not to B: An Investor's Guide to B Corps." The pros include:

- Changing the investor profile, changing the mindset, and attracting young talent. Investing in B Corps shifts the investor profile as millennials become asset owners as well as employees. Changing the investor profile matters if investors want to keep their finger on the pulse of what's important to the younger generation. Research has clearly indicated that companies with strong values or mission-focused companies yield more positive results over the long term. Additionally, B Corps are attractive employment options for workers who have a passion for using business for good. These employees bring their A game because the company they work for represents them in a fundamental way.

- Benchmarking. Investing in B Corps creates more opportunities for benchmarking. B Analytics tools can help investors keep track of their portfolio companies in ways they couldn't before. The "improve your score" report gives companies a pathway toward future improvement, something that other benchmarks haven't been as good at doing. The incentive of recertification also creates a big advantage here. It keeps companies on their toes as they think about how they can continue to improve their score.
- Generating new business opportunities. B Corp certification creates opportunities for branding as well as, through the B Corps community, for partnerships and collaborations.
- Building trust. B Corp companies build high levels of trust with their stakeholders because of their commitment to using business as a force for good. This gives them more strength, resiliency, and long-term stability, leading to a higher valuation for the company.
- Becoming mission-locked. "Mission drift" is often a problem for value-driven companies. Since B Corps' missions are baked into their DNA, they are much less likely to compromise them.[10]

Of course, the Bridges document does investigate several questions that remain about the B Corp movement. These are broken down into five overarching categories.

- Can the B Corp brand gain enough traction to become main-stream? This is a concern that the B Corp movement is currently struggling with—a significant effort must be made to increase branding and consumer awareness. The recent partnerships with large multinationals are helping to allay this concern.
- Will the BIA assessment continue to create a strong benchmark? To overcome any doubts on this score, the B Lab team must keep doing what the organization has done from the beginning—improving and enforcing the rigorous standards of B Corp certification.
- Can B Corps really create value through their communities? The B Corp movement can offer real advantages to its members in terms of new customers or business partnerships.
- Does B Corp status create governance issues? The legal framework does change the way a company is governed and could, as we've seen, seem like an obstacle to some investors. However, as B Lab and certified B Corps continue to work closely with their investors, this is becoming less of a concern.
- Will the "mission-lock" be too restrictive to potential investors? Certainly being a B Corp means that its leaders have less leeway in some respects. As with the previous concerns, the goal is to show-case the many advantages and opportunities of being a B Corps that offset this potential obstacle.[11]

Of all the pros, my interviews suggest that perhaps the most important is B Corps' connections to the changing investor landscape. Susan Baker, a vice president of the social investing pioneer (and certified B Corp) Trillium Asset Management emphasized the forces behind this shift, saying that "surveys show that women and millennials have been at the forefront of turning interest in sustainable, responsible, and impact investing into action. It's this action that is helping to drive companies to develop or deepen commitments to sustainability in their mission and business strategy." Every day, industries are becoming more diversified and less bound to the interests of wealthy, white, traditional, mostly male investors. For example, in 2016, Trillium urged J. B. Hunt Transport Services to adopt a policy prohibiting discrimination based on sexual orientation, gender identity, and gender expression. The shareholder proposal passed, and Hunt expanded its protections for employees.[12] Shortly after that, putting his money where his mouth is, BlackRock's Larry Fink joined a coalition led by Trillium that opposed a Texas bill regulating transgender access to public bathrooms.[13] Only a year later, the investment firm began prioritizing diversity as well as other matters focused on human capital.

Companies are becoming much more aware of such issues and are making the changes needed to attract new individuals as investors and to portray themselves as the right type of investment company for this new era of investing. And companies want not only to attract long-term investors but also to attract the best talent. Baker notes that "Target comes to mind as one large retailer telling us, ahead of its peers, that in order to attract the best talent it had to prioritize and demonstrate a commitment to environmental, social, and governance issues in the way it did business."

Better Business

One of the most important hurdles that companies embarking on the B Corp journey must overcome is concern about their investors' reactions. Seth Levine, a founding partner at the Boulder, Colorado–based venture capital firm the Foundry Group, notes that this often stops companies from pursuing certification. "I think the reason that most companies haven't [discussed it with investors] is because they haven't thought about it, or they think it's too hard, or there's a generally wrong notion that being B certified means you can't be profit oriented. That's true for some companies, but that wasn't our conclusion.

We felt like it was completely aligned with our broader mission . . . which is to make our investors money."

The Foundry Group is an interesting example to look at when considering investors and B Corporations as it is both a certified B Corp *and* a traditional venture capital firm, not an impact investor. But as Levine looked at the BIA, he realized that Foundry was already doing or had plans to do many of the things that it measured, and many of its items represented better business practices in general. "There was nothing . . . in the paperwork requirements that was in any way in opposition to our returning as much money to our investors as we possibly could, which is ultimately what we exist to do," he says. While the B Corp movement is revolutionizing traditional capitalism, it is not dismantling the system—it seeks to use business as a force for good while creating gradual change and positive impact. "Measuring something you care about helps you change your view on the things you're doing," Levine explains. Foundry had some good practices in place, such as domestic partner benefits, but the BIA helped the company identify other things it hadn't yet considered, such as recycling and evaluating its suppliers. Levine recalls, "There were some things that we looked at and said, 'Hey, these get us points and these are things that we want to do, so let's marry those two things together.' "

When Foundry Group made the decision to certify, its leadership team didn't really discuss it much with their limited partner (LP) investors. But after becoming a B Corp, a question the Foundry Group team occasionally had to answer was whether the company would invest only in B Corporations. The answer, according to Levine, is "No, that's not core to our mission. We are B certified, we have examples of B Corporations that we've invested in, but that's not a driver of our investment criteria." Still, the Foundry Group hopes that being a venture capital (VC) firm *and* a certified B Corporation will encourage other companies to make the move while attracting entrepreneurs who are aligned with its values.[14]

B Corp advocates like Foundry are attracting other investors to the movement. Over $2 billion has been invested in certified B Corporations and benefit corporations within the last few years. Over the next ten years, B Lab hopes it can turn its full attention to its primary battleground: the public capital markets and the large institutional investors that dominate them.

B Corps as Agents of Change

Another important change lever in the effort to shift investment ideology away from shareholder primacy has been the efforts of B Corp companies to convince their investors to join the movement themselves. "What we're good at is interacting with the agent of change," says Kassoy, "and that is the enterprise or entrepreneur."

The massive Brazilian cosmetics company Natura provides a good example of this. It was a public company when its leaders decided to become a B Corp, so it had to change the language in its corporate articles. This required a shareholder vote, potentially a big challenge, given how many large institutional investors it has. The Natura team made the argument as to why this change was consistent with the company's identity. The investors said yes without much, if any, hesitation. Coen Gilbert hopes this is evidence that "large institutional investors are becoming more comfortable with this [movement]."[15]

While Natura was public first and B Corp second, Laureate Education did things in reverse. The world's largest for-profit higher-education operator, it became the first benefit corporation to go public in January 2017. In 2015, when Laureate certified as a B Corp, the company was struggling. This was due to the negative press that for-profit education providers were receiving, particularly in the North American market. Instead of focusing on education, many of those schools concentrated on sales, pressuring students to take on significant debt based on false promises of employment opportunities. A well-known example is Trump University, founded in 2005 by Donald Trump with the ostensible mission of providing training in real estate. The university was not accredited and did not, in fact, provide any type of college credit, degree, or grades. Instead, it offered three- to five-day seminars in real estate, asset management, and wealth creation. By 2010, Trump University had largely ceased operations, but not before being pummeled by lawsuits and allegations of fraud. In testimony recently released, Ronald Schnackenberg, a former salesman for Trump University, stated that Trump University was "only interested in selling every person the most expensive seminars they possibly could" and that, based on his experience, it was a "fraudulent scheme" that "preyed upon the elderly and uneducated to separate them from their money."[16] When Laureate Education began to consider going public, its leaders knew that potential consumers and investors would hold the negative reputation of schools like Trump University against them. Todd Wegner, former senior manager of global public affairs and B Corp program manager at Laureate, explained to me that Laureate saw B Corp certification as a means to benchmark and more formally understand the company's impact, while also gaining credibility via a rigorous third-party assessment. Laureate also reincorporated as a benefit corporation before registering for its IPO in 2016.[17]

Laureate's founder and former CEO Doug Becker led the charge, taking the time to immerse himself in the B Corp movement. He further explained his company's reasoning to me: "As we thought about entering the public markets, we thought to ourselves, 'How can we tell a different story? How can we tell a story about a company that is a for-profit enterprise that really believes in the power of education to transform lives? What can we do to articulate that and say that Laureate is something different and make investors pay attention?' "

An important step was explaining the movement to Laureate's board members, many of whom represented the company's large private equity investors. One who was already familiar with the B Corp movement, Becker points out, "was very supportive, but also very appropriately thoughtful, saying that it sounds like a great idea but we have to really, really understand that there's a lot of untested law and unprecedented aspects to this." On the flip side, other board members were "a little bit questioning about why one would need to defend the idea that business could be good. Why is that even necessary?" In the end, however, Becker says that the overall feedback was more along the lines of "Do what you think you need to do, but when it's time for us to make a serious decision, make sure we really understand the risks and downsides associated with this."

The first and most important question was whether Laureate would receive a lower IPO valuation because it was a B Corp, since it would not be maximizing shareholder value. Laureate's leaders spent a lot of time on due diligence around the legal and profit-based ramifications of the change. Becker recalls that "when we talked to the different bankers and did some studies of IRR [internal rate of return] under different scenarios, nobody could answer the question of whether this would be good for the stock or bad for the stock, but it stood up that it should be fine, that it was probably going to be neutral." Though some concern that removing the focus on profit maximization remained, it was clear to the company's leaders that they had to do their best to show the world "that we weren't like the rotten apples," Becker says, and that without this legal framework and certification, "it would've looked like window dressing." Becker notes, "We actually had the CEO of Ben & Jerry's come and speak to our board because we wanted them to get educated. We wanted to hear from someone who went through the process and is still implementing their core mission."

Laureate leaders reflected that investors such as KKR (Kohlberg Kravis Roberts)—a classic "old-school corporate raider" and pioneer of the leveraged buyout—"largely understood our inherent social mission." This helped convince other institutional investors that benefit corporations are good, solid investments.

The sustainable footwear start-up Allbirds, founded in 2015 and B Corp certified in 2016, had a slightly bumpier road to securing buy-in from investors but eventually succeeded. Allbirds was recently valued at $1.4 billion; the company's investors include mainstream firms such as T. Rowe Price, Fidelity Management and Research, and Tiger Global Management. When it was first looking for backing, though, the company heard a lot of nos because it had a direct-to-consumer model and Allbirds' founders, Tim Brown and Joey Zwillinger, had no experience in the industry they were entering. What investors called "naïveté," however, Brown and Zwillinger saw as a hidden advantage: they never took "Because it's always been done that way" as an appropriate answer, and this led them to innovate, using avenues that many traditional footwear companies wouldn't have approached. They eventually raised $77 million over five funding rounds.

Big, traditional capitalist investors are starting to make a seismic shift. Zwillinger told me that he recently heard Henry Ellenbogen, vice president of T. Rowe Price and manager of its New Horizons growth fund, say "that this is the way things are headed, and not only is it the right thing to do, it's going to also help business. And it's something that he as an allocator of a very large amount of capital in the world feels a responsibility to continue to focus on. There is no tension between us and our investors; it feels like it's kind of a wind in our sails instead." As Zwillinger further reflected in an interview with Coen Gilbert, "Investors have never questioned for a moment why we're doing what we're doing, nor have they questioned our benefit corporation legal structure. Some companies have faced challenges as publicly traded B Corps, but frankly I think this is the way the world is headed."[18]

A Growing Focus on Multinationals

Every time a B Corps is acquired by a large multinational or a subsidiary of a multinational becomes certified, bigger and more traditional investors take notice. Happy Family offers an example of this. Founded in 2003, this passion-driven company, headquartered in New York City, became one of the fastest-growing organic food brands geared toward babies and toddlers. Its stated mission was to make organic and healthy baby food available to parents at all income levels. That mission caught the eye of RSF Social Finance and led to a working capital loan in 2009. RSF put Happy Family in touch with the Kellogg Foundation, which committed $4.6 million in debt and equity in 2012. All in all, the company raised $23 million from early investors, but Shazi Visram, its founder and CEO, believed that Happy Family needed additional resources to truly scale. At the same time, Visram worried about taking venture capital funding, as she believed it could jeopardize the company's values and mission. Happy Family had become a certified B Corp in 2011, and she didn't see how traditional VCs and a mission-driven B Corp like hers could work hand in hand. So in 2013, she sold the company to Group Danone, which has always had health and nutrition at its core. The deal benefited both companies, giving Danone a way into the U.S. market in the segment and Happy Family the support it needed for further R&D and growth.[19]

As Visram, who was Happy Family's CEO until December 2017, said, "These guys are the real deal. When they talk about social responsibility, they really mean it. Nowadays, there's a lot of bigger food brands who acquire little guys to build credibility, especially with Millennials, as we're all changing and demanding to know what's in our food."[20]

Danone has since become a major player in the B Corp movement. As noted earlier, as of early 2020 it had seventeen certified B Corps in its portfolio, including its North American subsidiary, and was aiming to be the first multinational food company to obtain global B Corp certification. "At Danone, we believe that each time we eat and drink, we can vote for the world we want to live in," Emmanuel Faber, Danone's CEO, has said.[21] Since Danone North America certified, several other multinationals have reached out to it to ask about the process. Faber told *Baking Business* that he hopes it starts a movement. "To get certified," he said, "you have to sign a Declaration of Interdependence. You become a part of a movement that is interdependent, and it talks to the fact you cannot succeed alone. I really hope many more brands and companies, big and small, will join the party."[22]

A similar story unfolded after Unilever acquired Ben & Jerry's, the progressive ice cream company whose deep social mission encompasses the use of Fair Trade–certified suppliers and environmentally friendly packaging; paying premium prices to dairy farmers; donating 7.5 percent of its pretax revenues to charity; and creating business opportunities for local communities and disadvantaged populations. Located in Waterbury, Vermont, Ben & Jerry's main ice cream store and factory reflect its fun-loving, activist nature. At their headquarters in nearby South Burlington, Vermont, freezers with free samples are scattered throughout the building and employees get to take some ice cream home every week. At Ben & Jerry's, employee and consumer satisfaction is always sky-high.

At first, there was widespread concern that Ben & Jerry's would stop being the pioneering, justice-focused company its customers loved. But while the transition was marred by plant closures and layoffs, Unilever ultimately allowed Ben & Jerry's to function with more autonomy than any of its other subsidiaries and even created an external board whose responsibility is to preserve the company's social mission. This was written into the binding acquisition agreement. This board reports to no one but itself and even has the authority to sue Unilever. At the same time, it tripled Ben & Jerry's revenues, creating more jobs and impact, and has also contributed significant funds to community projects and corporate philanthropy led by its employees.[23]

Unilever's own history helps to explain this arrangement. It was formed in 1929 when a soap maker and a margarine maker merged. By the 1980s it was the twenty-sixth-largest company in the world, with interests in plastics and shipping as well as food and personal care products. Then, in a move that shocked many, Unilever decided to restructure. Moving away from the industries that, some argued, had made the company a success, Unilever began to focus on environmental sustainability. In 2009, when Paul Polman took over as CEO, he redoubled its commitment.

Ben & Jerry's had been a subsidiary for close to a decade when Polman arrived, and the B Corp movement was just beginning to take off. Ben & Jerry's became a certified B Corp in 2012, and since then it has had a greater effect on its parent company than the other way around. Unilever now holds several subsidiaries that are certified B Corps, including Pukka Herbs; Sundial Brands, a hair and skincare products company best known for its Shea Moisture brand; and Sir Kensington's, a condiment maker. Seventh Generation, a founding B Corp, was acquired by Unilever in 2016, in the largest acquisition of a socially focused business to date, at somewhere between $600 and $700 million. Taking a page from Ben & Jerry's story, Seventh Generation will remain semi-independent and has established a social mission board.[24] "We're proud to join Unilever and its shared vision for purpose-led business on a global scale," John Replogle, Seventh Generation's CEO at the time, declared. "Working together we are confident we can have a positive impact on the health of billions of people around the world, truly fulfilling our mission of nurturing the next seven generations while transforming global commerce."[25]

Most recently, Unilever acquired Olly, a B Corp vitamin and supplement company founded by one of Method's original partners. Polman often spoke publicly about the benefits of becoming a B Corp, intimating that Unilever itself planned to become globally certified. Although Polman retired at the end of 2018, his successor, Alan Jope, the former director of Unilever's beauty and personal care division, has been with Unilever since 1985 and plans to uphold Polman's vision. Unilever's commitment to the B Corp movement has influenced the investment community—and, indeed, the global economy. As more multinational companies join Unilever and Danone in the movement, traditional capitalism and its main players will have no choice but to adapt and change, or risk being seen as out of step with the times.[26]

Another founding B Corp and household name that took a similar route is Method, which sells cleaning products made from plant-based ingredients. In 2012, Method merged with the Belgium-based Ecover, a mission-aligned home products company, becoming the largest green cleaning products company in the world.[27] Meanwhile, SC Johnson, a massive maker of household goods, also became focused on choosing better product ingredients and improving its impacts on health and the environment. In 2017, it acquired Method and Ecover.[28] And in November 2019 it was announced that B Corp stalwart New Belgium would be acquired by Japan's Kirin Holdings. This quick succession of acquisitions and mergers signals quite clearly that even large, traditional corporations are beginning to see the benefits of sustainability and, more specifically, the B Corporation movement.

Other important trends also suggest that investment in B Corps is reaching maturity. The crowdfunding pioneer Kickstarter was an early B Corp and is also a benefit corporation. Recently, Beta Bionics, a company focused on commercializing the "bionic pancreas," which would help children and adults with type 1 diabetes, raised $126 million in its second round of funding (Series B/B2). A small portion of its original funding came through WeFunder, a fellow B Corp that enables equity crowdfunding, which became legal in 2016. Most of the investors in the Beta Bionics equity crowdfunding "were families and people with Type 1, folks with skin in the game that may not be focused on having their shares return money to them," explained Edward Raskin, vice president of business development and corporate strategy at Beta Bionics. Other certified B Corporations have used equity crowdfunding as well. Meow Wolf, an arts and entertainment group, launched its WeFunder campaign in July 2017 and quickly raised $1.07 million.[29]

While crowdfunding underlines the growing grassroots acceptance of benefit capitalism that has grown over the last decade, it is getting top-down support too. For instance, in 2018 the Department of Labor (DOL) released a bulletin stating that funds governed by the Employee Retirement Income Security Act (ERISA) can take measures of expanded fiduciary duty such as ESG (environmental, social, and governance) metrics into account. In the past, the DOL had held that ESG factors may be associated with higher risk and lower returns, and so should be "rarely" considered.[30] This change could have a very strong influence on the way that investments in benefit corporations, and impact investing overall, shape the country's economy.

This short decade has seen massive change for B Lab. As more and more multinationals and institutional investors come on board, the B Corp movement will move closer to its tipping point, when the dominant ideology of shareholder primacy is replaced with a more humane and sustainable form of capitalism.

6

Employees as the Heart of the Company

Founded in 1981, Rhino Foods began as Chessy's Frozen Custard—
an ice cream shop run by Ted and Anne Castle in Burlington, Vermont.
Ted Castle grew up in Rochester, New York, and fondly remembers his
childhood visits to Abbott's Frozen Custard stores. After college and
marriage, he and his wife decided to bring frozen custard to Vermont.
Chessy's eventually became a manufacturer of cookie dough and baked
pieces for use in ice cream as well as a co-packer of ice cream sand-
wiches for several national and international brands. From its first day,
the Castles wanted their business to have a positive impact on the world
in multiple ways, starting with their employees.[1] Ted Castle's workers
call him "the Big Cheese." A fun-loving CEO, he strives to do what's
best for his employees, even if that means literally giving them his car
when theirs has broken down.[2] Rhino Foods prides itself on Castle's
desire to run a company that "develops its employees, has a positive
impact on the community, and shares innovative workplace practices."[3]

For instance, during Rhino's early days, Burlington experienced a
boom in refugees. Ted, with input from his staff, made the company-
altering decision to open its hiring pool to them. He admits that
when the first wave of Bosnian refugees arrived in Burlington back in
1990, he was reluctant to hire them because they weren't proficient in
English. Rhino Foods has an open book management policy that
links decision making to the performance of the business, essentially
allowing employees to act like owners. Financials are shared, as are

long-term plans and goals. If the refugees couldn't speak English, thought Castle, how could they participate in this core component of the company's operations?[4]

Fortunately, his team pushed him past his reservations, and he quickly discovered that many refugee workers have an incredible work ethic and are loyal, stable employees. Rhino doesn't just offer refugees temporary jobs; it makes them permanent employees and has developed a set of programs to help them settle into life in America. At first, the company brought translators in to aid communication among employees. This slowly shifted to at-home language software courses, which eventually led to the development of on-site ESL classes as well as diversity and inclusion training for the whole company. As of 2020, Rhino Foods had about 180 employees, 30 percent of them refugees from Vietnam, Bosnia, Nepal, Bangladesh, Somalia, Congo, Ghana, or Kenya.

This is clearly at the opposite end of the spectrum from other "innovative" ideas about employees more typical in today's world, such as the gig economy, whereby companies externalize their human resources. B Corp employees are excited to come to work because they believe their jobs have real value.[5] Not only do certified B Corporation's attract passionate, socially driven employees, they hold on to them for much longer—there is a strong positive correlation between the strength of a company's social mission and its employee retention rates. In addition to specific examples, numerous studies have shown that treating employees as interdependencies as opposed to externalities creates significant value.

Benefits of an Employee-Centric Culture

B Corporations offer employee benefits that go above and beyond the typical health insurance packages and HR policies offered by traditional corporations. They are integrated into the everyday culture of the company with a main goal of increasing performance. Not only do employees feel valued when their workplace is focused on their well-being and happiness, they are also eager to be at work. Many B Corps also offer benefits that have an impact on employees' life-styles. For example, Nature's Path, a producer of organic foods, offers employees on-site meditation rooms, a $500 subsidy for gym memberships under their "Get Fit" program, and the use of the company's organic food garden.[6] Other companies focus on improving policies such as maternity/paternity leave or days off for community service.

The relationship runs both ways. Casper, an online mattress retailer, has an internal competition in which employees pitch new initiatives. As Andy Fyfe from B Lab's business development team told me, "One of the suggestions they received was certifying as a B Corp. It didn't win in the voting (it came in second), but the staff, the leadership, everyone kind of rallied around it and said, 'Actually, that's still worthwhile. Let's see if we can go after that.' And the founders were into it. A lot of the younger employees show up already knowing about the importance of being a B Corp." Casper was certified in 2017.

Rhino Foods' Caitlin Goss says the company's workplace culture and commitment to being a B Corp has influenced every aspect of its decision making. Thanks to B Lab's Inclusive Economy Challenge— an annual call to action encouraging certified B Corporations to improve their impact on issues of equity, diversity, and inclusion by committing to a minimum of three different and measurable improvements—Rhino Foods began to think about its hiring process above and beyond what it had already been doing. "We kind of stepped back and said, 'Let's challenge that bias. Do we have people here that have barriers to employment? And could we create more of a runway to create opportunity for people?' " Internal hiring happens more often than not at Rhino Foods now, and employees are encouraged to move up the ladder, which leads to economic benefit through better employee retention.

The Alchemist, a family-run brewery, has professionalized every position. Whether you're a cleaner, an administrator, or you work the cash register at the brew pub, you have a salary and full benefits—and the opportunity to enjoy Alchemist's award-winning beers, such as Heady Topper. Also, there are yoga classes every week, the kitchens are fully stocked with whole foods, and a chef is on staff to prepare lunches for employees. Green Mountain Power, a clean energy company, and Method pay significantly more than a living wage to their lowliest employees (25 percent more for the former, 40 percent for the latter). When I talked to these companies' leaders, all of them emphasized that these practices give them a significant competitive advantage in the labor market, and their employee turnover is quite low.

Social Mission and Employee Retention

Setting aside their obvious social benefits, evidence shows that employee-driven strategies have several economic benefits. For instance, a 2015 article in *Organization Science* emphasized the strength of the relationship between a corporation's social initiatives and its employee retention.[7]

This has clearly been seen at Rhino. Another of its innovations is an income-advance program that provides grants for emergency situations, so employees don't have to resort to payday or other high-interest loans. In its first ten years, the program provided $380,040 to 379 employees, helping them salvage their credit histories and establish banking relationships. Rhino benefited financially from the program via "reduced absenteeism, higher morale and more focused employees"— in fact, it has seen a 36 percent increase in employee retention since the program began.[8]

The Ian Martin Group, a Canadian technical recruiting firm, has worked to ingrain B Corp values into its DNA. Tim Masson, its CEO, has seen the effects in the company's office in India. There are many recruiting firms with offices in India and a lot of competition for limited talent, which means that employees change jobs frequently. The average turnover rate is 70 to 80 percent, but Ian Martin's turnover is less than 10 percent, thanks to its employee engagement. In response to a question on its annual employee survey ("What's good about working at Ian Martin?"), an employee answered, "We're a certified B Corp and it feels like I have solar panels on the roof of my house. I get that same feeling. I just feel good about myself for working here."

Boloco, the burrito chain discussed earlier, expects high turnover in its stores, as that is the nature of the industry. Even so, it spends less time worrying about retention than most of its peers and so can devote more attention to employees' futures. John Pepper, Boloco's CEO, believes in helping people reach their goals as much as he can. If the dream is to stay at Boloco, that's great. If the dream is to do something else, he will help employees do that—for instance, by helping them develop new skills outside the restaurant business.

Since it opened in 1999, Boloco has offered English classes on site. These classes began informally, conducted by a Boloco employee, but have now grown to the point that outside education companies come in to teach. Pepper often has to remind the ESL teachers that the lessons need to be tailored to the English-speaking world as a whole, not just to the restaurant industry. Boloco pays its employees to take these English classes because, as Pepper points out, if they had to take a second job to afford them, they wouldn't be in the right frame of mind to learn. Additionally, if the classes were free but took up time when they could be working, they would likely not pursue them, as many of his employees aren't in a position to sacrifice hours of their day without pay. This initiative may seem small, but it has had ripple effects throughout the company. Many of Boloco's general managers today did not speak English when they started at the company a decade or more ago. Not only are they now on the management team, many are also enrolled in leadership training and continue to pursue greater opportunities for themselves. Boloco has also encouraged many employees to pursue higher education or job opportunities outside of the restaurant industry.

Such positive effects on employees and employee culture don't occur just at the entry level; they extend to the highest levels of B Corps. At BAMA Companies, a bakery and snack products company, the retention rate is especially high in management positions, which BAMA attributes to its decision to hire internally. CEO Paula Marshall explains, "We're growing our team members inside . . . unless we absolutely have to go external, it's going to be an internal promotion." Other benefits BAMA offers include access to health clinics that are 100 percent covered, chiropractors and doctors in-house on a weekly basis, and a wellness coach. With such benefits, the company's mission, "People helping people be successful," creates a really attractive workplace.

When a new employee enters a B Corp and is immediately encouraged to participate in the company's mission and uphold the company's values, that person becomes invested in the company's continued success. When it also offers a positive workplace environment and cultivates a strong employee culture, retention is even higher.

A Focus on Family at Badger

In the mid-1990s, carpenter Bill Whyte was suffering from dry, cracked skin. No product on the market would heal his hands, so Whyte set out to create his own, working in his family's kitchen. After much trial and error, Badger Balm was born. His fellow carpenters soon started asking for their own batches of Badger Balm, and by 1995

W. S. Badger Company was officially founded. The secret to the original Badger Balm's success was that it used simple, natural ingredients, a tradition that the company upholds today by adhering to strict standards for its ingredients and its supply chain.[9]

Also key to the company's success is its emphasis on its employees and their families—something that is familiar within the B Corp world, but rare in traditional business. Bill's wife Katie Schwerin, Badger's cofounder and COO, states on the company website: "We are committed to supporting children and family life, and also to spreading the word, so that other companies can join us in these efforts. We hope to inspire a new movement of businesses taking a lead in this kind of specific and significant support for families."[10]

Nestled in the landscape of southern New Hampshire, Badger's corporate headquarters looks like a big log cabin. It feels welcoming and homey, like a place you'd go to for a weekend to enjoy some rest and relaxation. The company's focus on family care begins from a child's birth. Its lactation room, which they call the Lavender Room, won Badger an award for being a breastfeeding-friendly company. When Badger won, it was asked to provide a hard copy of the company's breastfeeding at work policy and realized it didn't have one—the community just naturally accommodated breastfeeding mothers. After participating in the BIA, Badger put a number of written policies into place. Badger's Babies at Work program allows employees to bring their babies to work until they are six months old or crawling. This is in addition to the five weeks leave that the company offers (on top of the federally required twelve weeks) for the primary care parent. They also offer leave for the nonprimary caregiver.[11]

When they are six months old, employees' children can be enrolled in the Calendula Garden Children's Center, Badger's daycare facility down the street from headquarters. Employees with older children can apply for childcare reimbursements through a company program that offers them up to $800 a year per child to cover the extra costs of childcare during school vacations.[12]

Because Badger believes in the importance of parental influence, its employees don't ever have to miss their child's dance recital or Little League game: Badger allows for flexible scheduling, and employees can also work "school hours" when their children start going to school. Such initiatives have had a strong effect on employee retention—the average employee tenure is more than five years. In 2018, true to form for the family-focused company, Badger's Bill and Katie handed the company to their two daughters, Rebecca and Emily, and made them co-CEOs, or collaborative executive officers.

Attracting the Best Employees

B Corp certification provides a signal to potential job seekers that a company will be committed to its employees, and candidates' familiarity with a company's brand and social mission has a direct impact on their decision to apply. Even if a job applicant knows little else about the company, studies have shown that a strong social mission and a positive employee culture can attract potential employees, especially those who understand CSR and social mission. This means that employers should promote their social missions when recruiting. B Corp certification is one way to do so.[13] B Lab's Andrew Kassoy can attest to this; he says he receives emails and letters all the time from people who are looking for B Corps jobs or would like to leave their current company for a B Corp.

Studies show that when an employer's brand performs well on the market and in the public consciousness, interest from potential job applicants increases. It's particularly important for a brand to perform well in local communities. The positive effects of this don't end when applicants begin work, however. A favorable reputation also increases an employee's engagement within the workplace.[14] It's important to think about the employer's reputation as an aspect of the relationship between the employer and the employee—a positive, impact-driven one encourages communication and relationship building, allowing employees to truly feel like stakeholders. In some ways, they can feel like "corporate partners" rather than "just employees." Their connection to the business runs much deeper than in traditional corporations and this, in the long run, makes all the difference in terms of its success.[15]

A few years ago, the Ian Martin Group considered how to make it easier for people seeking purpose in their work to connect with the available jobs. This line of questioning led to the creation of B Work—a B Corp job board—in partnership with B Lab. At Bwork.com, people can search through current job postings at certified B Corporations across the globe and find an employment opportunity that matches their own personal values and purpose. Job searches can be refined by region, job type, employment type, and industry. The searches can also be refined by company type: certified B Corp, registered benefit corporation, pending B Corp, and companies with a verified BIA score. "As companies, we assess candidates based on their résumé and skills profile," says Tim Masson. "Why shouldn't candidates also have detailed information about companies so they can filter and select a place to work that aligns with their goals and values?" Masson believes this process will work to both employees' and employers' advantage.

At Cabot Creamery, a century-old dairy cooperative, Jed Davis, director of sustainability, remembers the first time his human resources manager called to tell him that the company had received an application that answered the question "Why are you interested in working at Cabot Creamery?" with "Because you're a B Corp." Davis says this is now a regular occurrence in interviews. As a result of this trend, Cabot has altered how it markets its available positions, using its B Corp status as a way to communicate to a younger pool of candidates that it's an employer of choice. The company utilizes the B Work job board and encourages fellow B Corps to do the same.

Similarly, Samantha Pause, senior vice president and chief marketing officer at Mascoma Bank, has had several new employees tell her, "Mascoma's B Corp status is the reason I signed on." New Belgium Brewing's Katie Wallace says that when she began noticing an uptick in people who said they were interested in the company because it's a B Corp, she asked her HR team to give her a number, and it shocked her. Only a few years ago, zero candidates mentioned B Corps. Today, fully 25 percent of candidates mention wanting to work for a B Corp as one of their top reasons for applying. Ranya Hahn, director of human resources at Participate Learning, which partners with organizations and school districts to engage learners in online communities, notes that at job fairs she meets many students who ask about the companies' B Corp status. Additionally, Participate Learning attends an annual networking night hosted by North Carolina State University at which the company is showcased alongside other B Corps. This typically leads to an influx of interns who are eventually hired into entry-level positions and often stay with the company long term.

The Importance of Employee Ownership

The recent focus on employee ownership is the opposite of what "gig" economy firms like Uber and TaskRabbit promote. According to a report by McKinsey Global Institute, 20 to 30 percent of the working population in the United States and Europe belong to the "gig" economy.[16] From the employer's perspective, using part-time or temporary contractors instead of full-time employees is a strategic move to avoid having to provide benefits. Thanks to employers like Walmart and Amazon, where layoff chances are high and the pay is poor, many American workers struggle to obtain financial security from a single employer. *USA Today* profiled a man named Michael Alfaro from Michigan who works full-time as a customer service representative and then works the late shift at an electronics store most weeknights or weekends. Recently, he also took on a third gig position to help pay off his student loan and credit card debt.[17] Stories like his are not unusual. More Americans than ever before are working multiple jobs, though few of them are finding happiness or fulfillment in the workplace.

Instead of thinking of employees as externalities, increasingly businesses are incorporating employees into the ownership of the company. King Arthur Flour has always had family values at its core. For five generations, it was family owned. In the 1990s, owners Frank and Brinna Sands wanted to retire but also wanted to ensure that the company would remain in good hands. Since they had no family members interested in taking over, they decided to hand down the company to their other family—King Arthur Flour's employees. In 1996, they started selling the company to employees, and by 2004, it had become 100 percent employee owned.[18]

The transition to employee ownership was simple and direct. Frank and Brinna Sands began with a 30 percent transfer, followed a few years later by a 40 percent transfer. At that point, they realized that 100 percent employee ownership had huge tax advantages—no federal or state income tax—so they took the final step and went the whole way. Today, all workers who have been with the company for more than a year and log more than eight hundred hours annually, whether they are seasonal, part-time, or salaried, are eligible for King Arthur's employee stock ownership plan. Since the company became employee owned, it has seen a substantial growth in its sales and profit. King Arthur Flour is one of the top three flour brands in the United States, and the company often wins awards as a "Best Place to Work."[19] Research has long shown that formal ownership of a company leads to "psychological ownership," as employees bond with the company more intensely.[20]

It is not surprising that many certified B Corps and benefit corporations lean toward employee ownership—it enhances workplace culture and aligns with values of transparency and employee engagement. Fifty by Fifty, an initiative focused on increasing employee ownership, published a report arguing that more employee-owned companies are needed to build a more sustainable economy. Fifty by Fifty compared the BIA scores of thirty-five employee-owned B Corps to non-employee-owned B Corps and found that the former scored significantly higher. The study also found that investor-owned firms rarely enjoy the same levels of employee commitment that employee-owned companies do.[21]

Employee ownership is also key to a balanced organizational culture. The women's clothing brand EILEEN FISHER has an ESOP for 40 percent of the company. Founder Eileen Fisher decided to pursue this route over a decade ago. She did not want to sell to a larger company and she did not want to go public, as that would leave the company at the mercy of shareholders. Instead, she realized that the people who would make the best decisions for the company are those who put their "blood, sweat, and tears into it." EILEEN FISHER also has a very generous profit-sharing program.[22]

The environmental consulting firm EA Engineering traded on NASDAQ for a while, during which time the company was in constant turmoil. After it transitioned to 100 percent employee ownership, there was a huge increase in morale and employee retention. "Now we focus on who we are and what we're doing," says Loren Jensen, founder of the company. "We returned immediately to the task of understanding environmental problems and knowing what to do about them. Nobody buys stock except in the hope of a good return on investment. The problem this poses for a company like

EA is you confuse the goals. It was very difficult to manage in that environment."[23]

Proponents of employee ownership argue there is no better way to pursue sustainability and responsible business. Jeffrey Hollender says, "I don't think you can be a responsible business without being committed to employee ownership because otherwise your business acts as a way to concentrate wealth." He notes that America has developed a problem of wealth concentration. "Responsible businesses have to take that head on, get over their fears about giving employees access to their financial statements, and understand they're being agents of wealth concentration if they're not committed to employee ownership." An article written by Amy Cortese for *B the Change* points out the increasing need for such a shift in perspective. "More than a third of U.S. workers are categorized as independent contract workers for hire in the 'gig economy.' Meanwhile, unions, which once were workers' strongest advocates, have seen their ranks and power erode. Growing disparity of wealth and income has spawned renewed interest in ownership models that can help develop a more inclusive form of capitalism that shares wealth more broadly."[24]

Diversity and Inclusion Drive Value Creation

Perhaps the most distressing problems in today's workplace culture are gender discrimination and sexual harassment, which continue to run rampant in the twenty-first century. Uber—the ride-sharing giant—has come under intense scrutiny because of the dangers that female drivers—and female customers—face in Uber vehicles, and because of the company's toxic workplace environment. Several of Uber's female engineers have filed lawsuits against the company, claiming that they are being promoted less often and paid less money than their male colleagues. Engineers of color have also sued, claiming that they are paid less than their white and Asian American colleagues.[25] Susan

Fowler, a former software engineer at Uber, published an exposé in 2017 that alleges instances of blatant sexism and sexual assault, including on her first day of work, when her manager propositioned her. Some female Uber drivers have dealt with harassment and assault on a daily basis, leading them to work less and, in consequence, earn less. And in 2014, reports started to emerge of male drivers, many with criminal records that Uber's background check failed to identify, sexually assaulting female passengers.[26]

For many companies, diversity and inclusion are policies they proudly display but do not follow. B Corps are focused on inclusion in the broadest sense of the word, redirecting companies to understand that issues of diversity and economic inequality need to be addressed not only within society but within firms. In 2016, B Lab launched the B Lab Inclusive Economy Challenge, inviting certified B Corps to set and meet three specific measurable goals to use their business to build an inclusive and equitable economy that works for everyone and for the long term. Inclusion and diversity are related but different concepts. Diversity means counting people; inclusion means making people count, treating all people as we'd like to be treated. Going one step further, equity is making sure that all people have the resources they need to succeed. The goal of B Lab's Inclusive Economy Challenge is to create an equitable, diverse, and inclusive economy with those values as the core of business, from hiring to sourcing to ownership.

Equity, diversity, and inclusion are at the heart of many B Corps. Bernie Glassman, Greyston Bakery's founder, didn't start his business with the goal of making great brownies; he started it with the goal of providing jobs and job training to people who face barriers to employment. At Greyston, anyone who wants a job can apply, regardless of background. This includes previously incarcerated persons, the homeless, and people who have struggled with addiction. The bakery's commitment goes beyond just offering someone a job. The company does its best to remove obstacles for its employees, both on the job and in their lives outside work, helping them with everything from finding safe housing and childcare to developing a plan for long-term success. By giving its employees these opportunities, Greyston combats the effects of wage disparity and long-term poverty.

Yonkers is New York's fourth-largest city, and 34 percent of its population lives below the poverty line.[27] Greyston plays an active role in the community, offering workforce development courses, a transitional employment program, housing for the formerly homeless living with HIV/AIDS, and an early-learning center that are available to all. In an effort to expand its practices to other companies, Greyston opened the Center for Open Hiring in 2018, offering education, training, and advisory services to companies that would like to implement open hiring policies themselves. The center also has a research facet that aims to improve and advance open hiring practices. One of the company's long-term goals is to open a bakery in Amsterdam by 2020, thereby taking the open hiring model global.[28]

Research has shown that workplace diversity and inclusion can promote employees' performance, attachment, and engagement while improving their perceptions of their own careers and of the organization.[29] Effective workplace diversity management is also positively associated with civility in the workplace, increased employee retention rates, innovation, organizational voice, and enhanced sales performance.[30] "More than 250 companies have embarked on the journey of taking B Lab's Inclusive Economy Challenge—one they knew would be challenging, sensitive, slow-going and last multiple years," according to Coen Gilbert. "These companies set a collective goal to improve the practices at their individual companies so that they could begin to shift cultural expectations about the purpose of business and how our economy can operate to increase security and prosperity for all."[31]

The businesses that embraced the challenge have made measurable progress on issues such as equitable pay across race and gender, equitable benefits for part-time and contract workers, shared ownership, workforce and board diversity, and renewable energy (because climate change has an outsized impact on the most vulnerable populations and future generations). Although diversity plays a big role in this challenge, inclusion is equally important and includes goals regarding parental leave as well as the creation of income- and wealth-building opportunities for low-income or underrepresented populations. For example, companies will be asked what percentage of their management team is made up of women or people of color, but they might also be asked about their parental leave policies, what percentage of their suppliers are located in low-income communities, and what percentage of ownership is held by nonexecutive team members.

B Lab gives participants support and structure. It developed an inclusive economy metric set comprised of roughly twenty of the highest-impact practices to help companies chart a path and lay out their annual goals. B Lab sends out monthly emails with resources, inspiration, and advice, and companies have access to virtual forums so they can help each other achieve their goals. Quarterly progress reports are required to ensure that participants are accountable, and peer circles are set up for more direct support and encouragement. Best practice guides created by B Lab are now available for a number of topics such as board diversity, governance and inclusion, and transparency in inclusion issues in general.[32]

The Inclusive Economy Challenge has afforded some companies the opportunity to improve on existing policies; others realize that they didn't have equitable policies or a culture that supports diversity in place. The Redwoods Group, a North Carolina–based commercial insurance company, realized it wasn't paying everyone equally. "Decisions that are made five or ten years ago get forgotten and then you don't re- alize that there's a gap," explains in-house counsel John Feasle. To fix the problem, the company increased the salaries of several individuals and minimized the gap. Sometimes the fixes are easy. Other times they're a bit trickier to figure out. For example, Redwoods believes in supplier diversity but, as Feasle points out, diversity exists in many di- mensions, and sometimes it is not clear what to prioritize. "Is your first consideration whether the supplier is minority owned, woman owned, local, a B Corp, in your community, etc.?"

Many B Corps have demonstrated their commitment to diversity and inclusion without taking on the challenge; for them, this type of work is just a part of being a values-led, triple bottom line business. Trillium, for example, has a workforce that is over 50 percent female. EILEEN FISHER's workforce is 84 percent female. At TriCiclos, the first B Corp in South America, street waste pickers and members of the local homeless community are given the opportunity to operate recycling stations, allowing them to increase their income, contribute to the local community, and gain dignity.[33] Natura has more than 1.8 million consultants, among them many previously unemployed and underemployed women, who receive training and can participate in the company's profit-sharing program; as a result, they often be- come agents of change in their local communities.[34]

One area in traditional businesses where there is significant room for growth in inclusion is senior management. In recent years, share- holders and institutional investors have been paying more attention to the appointments of board members and top management team members, as studies have shown that diversity improves organiza- tional performance by providing new insights and perceptions. Much more work remains to be done to ensure that women, people of color, and members of various cultural and socioeconomic backgrounds are welcome in C-suites and boardrooms.

At a recent B Corps Annual Champions Retreat, I attended a session in which a participant likened the recognition of diversity and inclusion today to the recognition of technology departments in the 1980s and 1990s. This was quite evocative for me. During the 1990s, I worked at a large U.S. bank. At the time, technology was "siloed": the IT staff was often housed separately (frequently in the basement of the building) and was not seen as integral to companies' abilities to deliver products and services. Given today's technology-fueled economy, such practices certainly seem antiquated. In recent years, staff members focusing on diversity and inclusion have often been siloed in HR departments. But as companies increasingly work to meet the needs of diverse consumers, and as challenger brands show how diverse and inclusive workplaces can lead to more innovative and higher-impact solutions, companies are starting to recognize the greater importance of diversity and inclusion for their long-term success. Effectively building an inclusive workplace is challenging and requires the efforts of more than a few key leaders and the human resources department—the ethos needs to be diffused throughout the entire company.

Helping Employees in Times of Crisis

One of Rhino Foods' most innovative program for employees is its income advance loan program. After a year of employment at Rhino, any employee can request a same-day loan of up to $1,000 that is repaid through weekly payroll reductions. This ensures that if an emergency occurs, employees have support. The program is run by the North Country Federal Credit Union. According to Caitlin Goss, Rhino's director of people and culture, it's "really unlocked a lot for people. Now they have a relationship with a bank, their credit score is improved, they . . . have more of a framework of how to save."

At the inception of the program, longtime Rhino Foods employee Paul Philips, affectionately known as the "Freezer Geezer," took out a $1,000 loan. Due to a mistake he made when filing taxes, Philips's credit score had plummeted, and he was unable to take out a loan elsewhere. His story is far from unique. A 2017 survey conducted by Harris Poll found that 78 percent of working Americans live paycheck to paycheck and cannot handle an emergency expense.[35] Philips used the income advance program five times, leading to a huge increase in his credit score. That allowed him to purchase a new car for the first time in his life and, shortly after, a new house.[36]

What does this mean for Rhino? It means that the company has hardworking and loyal employees who always know that Rhino gave them a chance when others would have closed their doors. Before the program was implemented, employees would ask the company for a direct loan when an emergency struck. Rhino would usually provide it, but Ted Castle realized doing so didn't help employees in the long run. The income advance program has proven so successful that Rhino, in partnership with B Lab, has created a guide that other companies can use to see how such an initiative would impact them and how to implement it. Rhino also coaches companies directly.[37]

The creation of the income advance program at Rhino Foods has had a ripple effect across the B Corp community. At its core, a program like this one puts employees at the center of the business, acknowledging and appreciating the value of the individual employee. As of 2018, more than thirty businesses and five credit unions in Vermont are using the program, and other companies across the country are showing interest in it. Heather Paulsen of B Corp Heather Paulsen Consulting heard about it and started working with a local financial institution to set up Helping Employees Access Loans (HEAL) in the hope of making emergency loans available to all B Corps employees in Mendocino County.[38]

Castle told me that with the arrival of the coronavirus, the necessity for businesses to "scale opportunities for financial security for employees that make good business sense" has been fast-tracked. For example, large and well-known B Corps like Patagonia and AllBirds committed to closing their stores while still paying employees.

At Rhino, the approach was to consider "our employees' physical health, their emotional health, and their economic health. When you put all those strings together it's pretty hard to figure out what you're supposed to do. We're trying our hardest to balance all of that, so we set up a task force that meets every morning. We also meet with the whole leadership team at noon to work through the complex issues and make decisions."

One crucial concern is the potential conflict between public health and individual welfare, because when people live paycheck to paycheck, they need to come to work, even if they are feeling sick. So Rhino created an incentive for people to stay home if they were not feeling well. "One thing we did is a program where if somebody doesn't want to come in due to health care or they're feeling sick, we decided to give them $40 to stay home and recover. Is that the perfect number? We don't know, but it's a start and it's better than nothing."

These trends suggest that the days of employees being given the bare minimum they need to survive while executives fill their already-overflowing pockets may be coming to an end. The world's workforce is shifting and demanding more. At the same time, the B Corp movement is ushering in a new way of building strong workplace cultures that focus on the value of individual employees and their importance as stakeholders. Whether a B Corp is privately held or employee owned, they've all got one thing straight: there are tremendous strategic and financial benefits to be gained by placing employees at the heart of a company.

7

Finding Kindred Spirits: The B Community

It was a devastating scene across much of Colorado in September 2013. Record-breaking rainfall caused flooding that destroyed more than three hundred homes; whole counties had to be evacuated. The storm came as a shock to virtually everyone—no weather forecasters had predicted it.

Namaste Solar, an employee-owned cooperative that designs, installs, and maintains solar electric systems, has been a B Corp since 2011 and is headquartered in Boulder. The flood deposited up to three feet of mud throughout its building. Disheartened as they were, Namaste's employee owners set about the work of recovery.

On September 17, buses full of fellow B Corp employees descended on them, ready to help. As it turned out, the B Corp Champions Retreat was held in Boulder that year. The B Lab team had considered canceling the conference, but decided to utilize its local presence to help the people of Colorado instead, turning the retreat into a three-day volunteering experience. Alongside FEMA, the Red Cross, and other local organizations, members of the B Corp community rolled up their sleeves and dug in.[1] "We received a rejuvenating shot in the arm that day," recalls Blake Jones, Namaste Solar's founder. "The B Corp community helped us to accomplish in a few hours what would have taken many days on our own, bolstering our spirits in a way that words cannot describe. We felt so supported—and so loved—by our fellow Bs. We will forever be grateful to the B Corp community for helping us during our time of need."[2] I heard many similar stories of B Corps rallying together in the face of the economic disruption caused by the coronavirus.

As B Lab has developed, its community has developed alongside it, according to cofounder Coen Gilbert: "It's easy to talk about tools and resources and individual stories, but in our experience, community has been one of the most powerful offerings that we have created that drives performance within individual companies while creating the conditions for collective action and systemic change."

The B Lab community goes way beyond acts of support and generosity. John Elkington, a cofounder of the sustainability consulting firm Volans, reflects that being a CEO or a business leader pushing for an agenda of social change can sometimes feel isolating. Elkington would know, as he has been a pioneer of socially responsible business for decades—in fact, he is credited with coining the phrase "triple bottom line." For much of his career, he has worked on change, innovation, and impact, often battling boardrooms of naysayers and doubters to do so. Elkington's manner is direct and focused—he states his opinions straightforwardly, though always with tact, and when pressed on a subject that excites him, his passion comes through in his tone.

Elkington says that the B Corp movement has given people like him the comfort and the power of having a community. He describes meeting Louise Kjellerup Roper for the first time when Volans was looking for a new executive director. When he learned she had previously worked at two other B Corps (Method and gDiapers), he knew he had found a kindred spirit: they held the same values and beliefs, and they were dedicated to fighting for them. Identifying as a member of this community eases business relationships. Vince Sicilano of New Resource Bank explains, "When the potential client hears that you're a B Corp, it cuts about three hours of discovery."

New Resource began with a group of individuals and organizations who recognized the need for a bank that would finance sustainable companies. Sicilano told me about his first meeting with Keith R. Mestrich, Amalgamated Bank's CEO, after they were brought together through the Global Alliance for Banking on Values (the two banks ultimately merged). "He was a new CEO, embracing the social mission aspect, and I encouraged him to pursue B Corps certification for his company. For a bank, it makes a real difference if you use it right."

The web connecting New Resource Bank to the B Corps community also includes one of the bank's founding investors, RSF Social Finance. RSF was founded in 1936 as the Rudolf Steiner Foundation—Steiner (1861–1925) was an Austrian scholar, critic, philosopher, social reformer, philanthropist, and mystic. During its first fifty years of existence, RSF offered grants to businesses in line with its mission, which was to cultivate transparent relationships focused on social, economic, and environmental benefits.[3] In 1984, it began offering loans, and later began to make direct investments. RSF's investment in New Resource Bank made perfect sense. Then president and CEO Mark Finser stated in a 2006 press release that "for RSF, this is a natural extension of our mission. We connect investors and philanthropists with socially beneficial projects that promote a healthy and sustainable world."[4] RSF Capital Management, RSF's for-profit arm, became a certified B Corporation in 2009 and has been a strong proponent of the B Corp movement ever since—much like New Resource Bank itself.[5] Although RSF doesn't require its portfolio companies to be certified B Corps, it requires all its borrowers to take the BIA survey and supports the certification process. Bart Houlahan reflected that "RSF has been a pioneer in B Lab's work from day one" by providing funding and board advisory support to B Lab.[6]

Also in that web of interconnections is NRB investor Triodos, a Netherlands-based bank that became a certified B Corp in 2015.

Founded in 1980, Triodos touts a values-based banking model and early on launched the first "green fund" on the Amsterdam Stock Exchange. Triodos, which compensates for 100 percent of its own CO_2 emissions, invests in companies involved in solar energy and organic farming as well as in cultural organizations. With branches in Spain, Belgium, the United Kingdom, and Germany, its international work has grown to include investments in the developing world through microfinance institutions.[7]

The power of the interdependent network developing within the B Corp movement means that people are jumping on board every day. Harnessing so many actors in diverse ways is a challenge that the B Lab team, and B Corps themselves, consciously work on. Beginning at a grassroots level, B Lab has teamed up with local B Corps to create groups of leaders focused on their city's or state's B Corp community. They come together on formally constituted B Local boards or informally through social networking to host events, market the B concept, and encourage new businesses to participate in the movement. They may also create networks within their industries and geographic regions focused on broader change. Within and across these communities, certified B Corps and registered benefit corporations can enter into partnerships for mutual support. For example, many B Corps encourage their suppliers to take the BIA. In addition, many B Corps prioritize other B Corps as suppliers, particularly when expanding their businesses to new locations.

Although B Lab has played a big role in encouraging such bottom-up initiatives, it has also encouraged the growth of the B Corps community through a top-down approach. B Lab has created a myriad of resources to be shared and utilized by B Corps, registered benefit corporations, and others interested in the movement. For example, it launched the B Hive, a social networking platform. And its annual Champions Retreat in the United States has spawned similar gatherings of B Corps and allies in South America, Europe, the United Kingdom, Australia, and East Africa.

Fostering Strong Local Roots

Early on, the B Lab team saw that certain areas were attracting more certified B Corps than others and viewed the development of these geographic clusters as a way to extend the movement. As these communities grew naturally, the B Lab team worked to help support and encourage their growth. One of the first such communities was in Colorado, around Denver and Boulder. In 2014, B Lab secured a grant to create an office in the state. As Colorado native Andrew Kassoy explained at the time, "The idea in Colorado was to build a team of people whose whole job is to build and serve the local certified B Corp community, and then use that as an example to build a larger community of businesses around it who are committed to using business as a force for good. It's sort of like a laboratory where you can learn how to get a bunch of businesses working together in a concrete way to effect change. We wanted those businesses to actually be working together collectively." Ideally, even companies that didn't become B Corps would be influenced to measure their impact, promote policy change, and work with B Corps on specific initiatives.

When the grant funding for B Lab in Colorado expired as planned in 2017, Colorado had more than one hundred B Corps; hundreds of other local companies were using the BIA, many of them registered as Colorado benefit corporations (five hundred as of 2019). Local B Corp leaders established B Local Colorado, a board of passionate, driven individuals who host events weekly and continue to focus on growing the B Corp presence. Kim Coupounas, the first director of B Lab Colorado, says, "They are supporting each other's businesses, working to bring others into the community, and working to advance responsible business and shared prosperity in the state of

Colorado and across the mountain West." Over the last few years, a number of great partnerships and collaborations have emerged. For example, the Center for Ethics and Social Responsibility at the University of Colorado–Boulder partnered with the local B Corp community to create a manual that would allow users of the B Impact Assessment to help other companies achieve certification.[8] At one point, the university's MBA course Topics in Sustainable Business required students to help a company complete a "sustainability-based pursuit." For many, this came down to helping a local business complete the BIA.[9]

The GrowHaus is an indoor farm in Denver that organizes events with B Local Colorado to encourage individuals to "B of Service." GrowHaus and B Local Colorado host volunteering opportunities for companies and individuals who are interested in giving back (and who are often interested in the B Corp movement as well). Wordbank, a marketing firm and aspiring B Corp, attended one in 2018. The Wordbank team explained, "The drive to 'use business as a force for good' is what inspires us to step up and volunteer at local organizations like the GrowHaus. Teamed with these organizations, we can alleviate the social and environmental issues that impact our community."[10]

Colorado's government has also launched initiatives to foster the growth of the B Corp movement. The "Best for Colorado" campaign has been particularly successful in encouraging Colorado businesses to take the BIA. An interesting spin on the "Best for" campaign is that companies don't have to be certified B Corps or benefit corporations to participate. Instead, they complete a modified version of the BIA and compete to be recognized as a company doing good.

B Lab has taken opportunities to build similar capacity in other strategic locations, such as Vermont and North Carolina, while some local communities, such as Montreal and Portland, Oregon, have grown on their own. In Los Angeles, for example, certified B Corps created their own B Local community in 2016 with a mission to "improve the vitality, happiness and growth of the Los Angeles B Corporation community by sharing knowledge and collaborating on best practices that inspire change."[11] In Latin America and Australia, concentrated groupings of B Corporations attest to the movement's global impact. "The theory of change," as Kassoy puts it, "is that as these companies become more engaged, they create ripples that wash across the regional economy."

One important local ripple has been the local BLD (pronounced *build*—it stands for B Corp Leadership Development) events that have sprung up to connect local organizations and develop B Corp employees. These events are organized and led by and for members of local B Corporations. As Ted Castle of Rhino Foods notes, "That's the way anything grows. We have to become ambassadors; we can't depend on B Lab to do it all." The first BLD event took place on May 22, 2014, in San Francisco. Cohosted by B Lab, B Corp Beneficial State Bank, and Golden Gate University, it attracted more than 150 employees of local B Corps. Honeyman Sustainability Consulting, founded by Ryan Honeyman, was also a cohost.[12] Honeyman coauthored *The B Corp Handbook: How to Use Business as a Force for Good*, which is now in its second edition, and has himself helped a few dozen companies undergo B Corp certification.[13]

BLD events feature breakout sessions hosted by local B Corps and give attendees the opportunity to meet like-minded individuals and trade best practices and advice. BLD events continue to thrive in the Bay Area thanks to the efforts of B Corps like Allbirds, Method, Athleta, New Leaf Paper, Change.org, RSF Social Finance, and many more—close to two hundred certified B Corps at last count. Berett-Koehler Publishers, an independent publisher and benefit corporation focused on changing the publishing industry to benefit all stakeholders, has made waves recently with its call to "to create a world that works for all."[14] Numi Organic Tea, another Bay Area B Corp, was created in response to the lack of diversity in quality and innovation among tea companies. Today, it is a leading brand in the organic tea industry and a model for fair labor practices.[15] A B Local board has been established to continue to grow the presence of B Corps along the California coast, as well as in many cities and states in North America, including Asheville, Boston, Colorado, Illinois, Los Angeles, Montreal, New York, North Carolina, Philadelphia, Portland (Oregon), Southwestern Ontario, Vancouver, Virginia, Wisconsin, West Michigan, and the Mid-Atlantic.

B Corps Community in Vermont

Vermont has long been a hub for sustainable and responsible businesses, so it's no surprise that the B Corp movement has flourished there. In fact, some of the largest and most influential certified B Corps can be found in Vermont. Many would even argue that the movement for business with a social mission truly originated when Ben Cohen and Jerry Greenfield of Ben & Jerry's fame opened their first ice cream shop in Burlington, with social responsibility at the core of their business model. Ben & Jerry's officially became a certified B Corp in 2012, one of the first subsidiaries of a large multinational to do so. Other prominent certified B Corps in Vermont, many of which readers will now be very familiar with, include Rhino Foods, Cabot Creamery, King Arthur Flour, Seventh Generation, Green Mountain Power, and the Alchemist Brewery. Green Mountain Power was the first utility company in the world to become a certified B Corporation. Cohen and Greenfield congratulated the company and expressed their hope that "their commitment and their business success will inspire others."[16]

Most of the B Corp leaders in Vermont are involved in Vermont Business for Social Responsibility, so they spend a lot of time with one another, encouraging and cultivating better business for their communities. "It's like a family," Jennifer Kimmich, cofounder of the Alchemist Brewery, says. Cabot Creamery has set up mutual events and joint advertising with the local B Corp network—something that has also happened nationally with Patagonia, Ben & Jerry's, Seventh Generation, and others.

Caitlin Goss at Rhino says that collaboration among B Corps "creates an ecosystem where we would have competition otherwise. . . . The B Corp community helps us understand businesses that aren't in our industry, but that might be helpful and supportive, and that we can share ideas and best practices with." Rhino Foods is constantly in communication with fellow Vermont B Corps to discuss workforce planning, strategy, and future partnerships. Carey Underwood of King Arthur Flour adds that "there is a strong network in Vermont. These are the companies I go to first if I have a question."

Boloco's John Pepper realized that his local area in New Hampshire, right across the Connecticut River from Vermont, was not very familiar with the B Corp movement. When he was invited to host a Chamber of Commerce event, he decided to reach out to his fellow B Corp leaders in Vermont. As he tells it, they held a "joint reception. The Alchemist [Brewery] came and they served free beer. We did it at [a Boloco] restaurant. . . . It was such an awesome event. It really showed the power of being a B Corp." Afterward, Pepper made it his goal to partner with as many B Corps as possible so that his community could grow to be as connected and interdependent as the one in Vermont.

Partnerships Built on Shared Understanding

The understanding between B Corps begins well before a company is certified and officially in the movement and continues well after. When B Corps are looking to purchase products and services, they look to others in the community first because they know how B Corps run their businesses. The B Lab team expands this effect by encouraging member companies to spread the word about potential suppliers and partners.

Prior to its acquisition by fellow B Corp Amalgamated Bank, New Resource Bank created a banking package with deposit benefits tailored specifically to certified B Corporations and committed a part of its assets to financing socially responsible businesses. Amalgamated Bank committed to double that amount by 2020, and, as the country's largest socially responsible bank, continues to work toward creating a positive economic impact in the world. Much of this is possible because of the partnerships built over time between New Resource Bank, Amalgamated Bank, and the broader B Corp community.

For many B Corps, the opportunity to partner with other B Corps is a big selling point for certification. In fact, many companies had already been selective with their supply chain and other partnerships; joining the movement gave them the opportunity to strengthen those positions. Luke's Lobster, which achieved B Corp certification in 2018, is a prime example of this. In 2009, Luke Holden, a twenty-five-year-old ex–Wall Streeter, took a sharp left turn on his path through life and decided to open a lobster shack in the heart of New York City with his father, Jeff, and freelance food writer Ben Conniff, also in his early twenties, whom Luke had met through Craigslist. They decided to give themselves a couple of months to get up and running. The 2008 financial crisis was still very much affecting the economy, so opening a lobster shack in the middle of Manhattan was rather risky, if not flat-out crazy. Holden, however, had been craving a down-home, no-frills lobster roll and couldn't find one anywhere in New York.[17]

Luke's Lobster's mission is simple: it provides traceable and sustainable seafood to its customers. The company now has more than two dozen locations across the United States, and in 2017 it did $50 million in sales. From the beginning, Luke's Lobster believed in encouraging like-minded businesses within its supply chain. The company buys directly from cooperatives up and down the East Coast, where it can verify quality, safety, and price. Holden says that stakeholder primacy was the driving force behind Luke's Lobster since its inception, but "we didn't know to call it that in the beginning." When the founders were getting ready to open their first West Coast location, they reached out to the B Lab office in San Francisco and inquired about potential partners. This led to a partnership with Sufferfest Beer Company: "As fellow B Corps focused on sustainability, supply chain optimization, employee wellness and living a healthy lifestyle, there was an immediate attraction between the two brands," says Caitlin Landesberg, Sufferfest's founder and CEO.[18]

Interestingly, Luke's Lobster had partnered with B Corps in some of its other locations, even before it achieved certification itself, because B Corp certification "acts as a filter," Holden says. "It is more efficient than trying to weed through potential relationships to learn whether they will do what they say they'll do. You're much more likely to get quality and follow-through in a long-lasting way from a B Corp." His partner Conniff agrees, emphasizing that sharing the same principles not only ensures better service and relationships but also offers opportunities for learning. "The sharing of ideas and seeing the wonderful things partners are doing gives us examples and lists of goals to continue to improve our business," he says.[19]

Luke's partnerships with B Corps are far-reaching. The company tries to use a clean energy model developed by fellow B Corp Inspire in as many of its locations as possible. Its trash is taken out by Recycle Track Systems, also a B Corp, and its office workers enjoy coffee provided by B Corp Wicked Joe Coffee. Aside from offering beer in collaboration with Patagonia Provisions and Sufferfest, Luke's Lobster works with United By Blue, a B Corp that sells organic apparel, to run a seasonal lobster bowl campaign, which raises awareness and promotes coastal cleanups by removing a pound of trash from coastal waterways for each bowl sold. Although it is a fairly new B Corp, Luke's Lobster has long used the B as a "bat signal" to create valuable connections and partnerships.

Partnerships the Ben & Jerry's Way

Ben & Jerry's has long partnered with other B Corps. Rhino Foods has supplied cookie dough for its ice cream since 1991, well before the B Corp movement even existed.[20] Ben Cohen met Greyston Bakery founder Bernie Glassman at a social innovation conference over three decades ago, and the two hit it off immediately. Since then, Greyston has been baking the brownies used in many of Ben & Jerry's ice creams. In fact, the company bakes thirty-four thousand pounds of brownies every day for this purpose.[21]

Thanks to their mutual connection to Ben & Jerry's, Ted Castle, CEO of Rhino Foods, and Mike Brady, CEO of Greyston Bakery, have also become frequent collaborators. For instance, Greyston is interested in implementing Rhino Foods' successful income advance loan program. They've also discussed doing an employee swap, which would allow employees to learn new skills while fostering a deeper sense of community between the two companies.

In support of Protect Our Winters, a local NGO focused on climate change, Ben & Jerry's and New Belgium Brewing teamed up to create Salted Caramel Brownie Brown Ale and a matching ice cream. A few years later they teamed up to create Chocolate Chip Cookie Dough Ale and a matching ice cream in support of the same cause. Rob Michalak, director of social impact at Ben & Jerry's, noted that the companies' shared B Corp connection was the impetus: "For us it was like, 'Oh, man, New Belgium, you're so cool.' And they're going,

'Yeah, Ben & Jerry's, you're pretty hip, too.' It's like hey, wait a minute, we could do something here and have a lot of fun and create all the benefits."

B Corp Networks for Change

B Corps also create partnerships and networks focused on promoting larger change in the world. Rubicon Global, a leader in cloud-based sustainable waste and recycling solutions that has received significant funding from actor Leonardo DiCaprio, Goldman Sachs, Tudor Investment Corporation, and others, and World Centric, a supplier of certified compostable food service products, are both focused on reducing waste. In 2016, the two companies announced a partnership that would see Rubicon encouraging the use of World Centric products among its customers in an effort to reduce the waste found in landfills. World Centric CEO Aseem Das stated, "We believe our compostable products and Rubicon's organics diversion and recycling model both represent major steps toward that goal, and we look forward to working together to create a more sustainable world."[22]

Likewise, in 2016, Patagonia led a group of five B Corps—the first-ever partnership of its kind—to create a $35 million tax equity fund that made solar power available to thousands of households. Tax equity funds work as a win-win between property owners and financial institutions—the owners get solar power and the financial institutions receive tax credits, deductions, and the like. The fund helped purchase over fifteen hundred solar energy systems and made them available to homes across eight states. The five B Corps and their respective roles were as follows: Patagonia was the tax equity investor; Kina'ole was the fund manager; New Resource Bank and Beneficial State Bank were lenders; and Sungevity provided the solar power. Patagonia CEO Rose Marcario noted, "B Corps know how to make money while creating broader benefits—but any company would be smart to leverage their tax dollars this way." Sungevity's then CEO Andrew Birch added, "This B Corp partnership clearly demonstrates that corporations can work together in creative ways to simultaneously benefit their respective bottom lines, the personal finances of homeowners and the environment."[23] A similar fund created by Patagonia and Kina'ole in 2014 purchased one thousand rooftop solar systems in Hawaii.[24]

In 2015, Cabot Creamery partnered with Little Pickle Press, a B Corp publisher of media for children, on an awareness campaign, creating a picture book entitled *The Cow in Patrick O'Shanahan's Kitchen,* which showed readers where their food comes from. Fifteen percent of the book's net sales were donated to the ONE Campaign— a nonprofit that fights preventable disease and extreme poverty around the world, particularly in Africa. Both companies are invested in creating and expanding awareness of food origins, so this partnership was a natural fit.[25] In 2016, the two companies launched an iOS app titled Farm2Table, an interactive version of the picture book that includes animations and games.[26] Cabot Creamery also partners with various B Corps on its Reward Volunteers program. Participants log how many hours they volunteered through an app or an online widget, which makes them eligible to win prizes from other B Corps such as King Arthur Flour, Gardener's Supply, and Divine Chocolates. Root Collective, an ethical clothing company, partnered with Elegantees, their direct competitor, to create a T-shirt made by survivors of sex trafficking in Nepal. Profits benefited anti-trafficking efforts.[27]

Like most business leaders, B Corps members are "inherently competitive people," according to Coen Gilbert. When they hear about what other companies are doing for their workers, for the environment, or even for their investors, they are pushed to do more with their own companies. But at the same time, they are a community. Whether

B Corps are competing with each other in the marketplace or partnering together to promote charities, actively enact change in their communities, or raise awareness about important issues, it's clear that their deep connections to one another are a true strength of the movement.

Fostering "Connective Tissue"

As B Corps have banded together to support one another and create social good, B Lab has created large-scale initiatives to encourage the growth of the interdependent web of connections. These initiatives include an annual retreat for B Corps, an exclusive social media portal for B Corp employees, and a variety of incentives and partnerships.

Champions Retreats

For the past decade, mission-driven leaders of the B Corp community have gathered at annual Champions Retreats to network, attend workshops, and expand the B Corp movement. It began as an invitation-only gathering in the high desert of Southern California, to say thank you to the thirty or so early "champions" who were doing the most to grow the nascent movement. The retreat has since turned into a three-day event hosted in a different city each fall. "Champions Retreats are about engagement, helping people to see that B Corp is more than a certification for individual businesses—it is community coming together to build a movement," explains Kassoy. The Champions Retreat allows people to experience and to create "the connective tissue," as Coen Gilbert calls it, that B Corps share.

The B Hive Network

In 2015, B Lab launched the B Hive, a private online platform for employees and executives of B Corps that allows its users to create profile pages with relevant information about their company and areas of expertise. Groups can be formed within the network—for example, a "Women in B Corps" group—to engage with people more intimately and directly.[28] The B Hive allows for instant collaborations, including selling goods and services, partnering on new initiatives, and troubleshooting. Many of the B Corps I talked to said that when they are looking for a product or service, they try the B Hive first to see if that can find a B Corp partner.

The B Hive also allows for informal interactions among B Corp employees. For example, when Kristin Carlson of Green Mountain Power needed some help with customer relations, she was able to get on the phone with Rose Marcario, Patagonia's CEO. This option was available to her, she says, not just because of the B Hive, but because the two are bound by the same network of people and companies— they know and recognize the handshake. The B Corp community not only encourages a sense of a strong identity among its members, it also creates loyalty and respect. For example, Jacob Malthouse of B Corp Big Room describes the importance of communities and support within the B Corp movement this way: "I think those peer groups are actually pretty interesting in terms of potentially preventing mission drift. Once you become part of those groups, there is a business advantage to being a part of them. . . . [You] want to be a part of that group and that means you have to stay true to what you believe in."[29]

In-Network Incentives

B Corp certification makes a company eligible to participate in B Lab's service partnerships. For example, Salesforce offers B Corps discounts for its Client Relationship Manager (CRM), and Intuit offers free Quickbooks licenses. Netsuite and Inspire Commerce also offer discounts on their software.[30] Early in the movement, Ogden Publications, publisher of *Mother Earth News,* the *Utne Reader,* and other sustainability-focused periodicals, ran approximately $500,000 of free advertisements as part of B Corp's first collective brand campaign.

Being in the B Corp movement provides other interesting benefits. Graduates of the Yale School of Management who find employment at a nonprofit organization after graduation are offered loan forgiveness. In 2009, the program was expanded to graduates who find employment at certified B Corps within ten years. The announcement of the program came as a surprise to the B Lab founders. "[We] think," says Kassoy, that "it was very much driven by students saying, 'Hey, there's a perfectly valid form of creating social benefit beyond just going to work at a not-for-profit. It's this!' " Now Columbia and NYU have similar programs.

It's not just schools. Cook County, Illinois, established an ordinance that gives impact ventures (including B Corps) preference in its procurements of goods and services. LA County and the City of San Francisco also have procurement policies specific to benefit corporations and certified B Corporations. Tax incentives that benefit the B Corp movement have also begun to emerge. In Spokane, Washington, for example, certified B Corporations enjoy reduced registration fees and no head tax. In Philadelphia, they receive a business tax credit. This type of practice will almost certainly become more commonplace.

All of these developments encourage the interdependence that is at the heart of the B Corp movement. What happens at one business can influence other businesses in the community, and the movement grows. B Corps, says Kassoy, "are using their relationships to help us create partnerships with other kinds of business organizations or Chambers of Commerce or accelerators and incubators or business schools. Other kinds of business organizations that take us from retail to wholesale. . . . You get those companies measuring what matters, now you're impacting their employees and their consumers." From busloads of B Corp employees arriving to help a fellow B Corp in the wake of a natural disaster to the close-knit local communities in small towns and states, the B Corp movement could not have experienced the growth and success of the last decade without these passionate individuals and companies.

8

Going Global

In the fall of 2007, Colombian businesswoman Maria Emilia Correa was helping her daughter settle in at Reed College in Portland, Oregon. While in the supermarket looking for dish soap, she picked up a bottle of Method. Its transparent packaging had stood out amid the sea of opaque, familiar-looking bottles, and the tagline on its label really seized her attention: "You don't need gloves to use this product." "That line reaches everyone. You don't need to be an expert to understand that using this product does not harm your health or the environment. It is a fantastic way to allow everyone to act," Correa recalls. She had spent fifteen years working in sustainability for major corporations, and one of her most frustrating experiences had been "listening to people in marketing departments saying, 'It can't be done.' " When Correa took a closer look at Method, she learned that it was a certified B Corp. The stars certainly aligned that day—Correa would end up becoming a leader of the B Corp movement herself, revolutionizing Latin America's business community.

The B Corp movement has expanded into South America, Europe, the United Kingdom, Australia, and more recently East Africa and Asia. As in the United States, B Lab has followed a grassroots strategy in which local entrepreneurs introduce the idea of B Corps to their countries. This has resulted in a set of uniquely tailored theories of change in different locales. While the expansion has been significant—as of 2019, more than half of B Corps are headquartered overseas—there have also been challenges, particularly in translating the U.S.-based standards underlying the BIA into a tool that can be used around the world.

A couple years after her original exposure to Method and B Corps, Correa partnered with Gonzalo Munoz in Chile on a new recycling concept, founding a company called TriCiclos whose goal is to teach citizens how to be more sustainable through recycling. TriCiclos developed and installed recycling stations that clearly explain how sorting and recycling should occur. It also hired "street waste pickers" from local communities to help them keep their neighborhoods clean and to provide them with increased income.

From its beginning, TriCiclos focused on a triple bottom line. "TriCiclos means three cycles, right? We founded the idea based on balancing social, environmental, and financial benefit," explains Munoz. They ran TriCiclos the way they'd always wanted to, which was the opposite of how the companies they had previously worked for functioned. Correa stated that she had become an entrepreneur because she had grown very frustrated with the idea of CSR. "It is a wonderful promise that has not been able to deliver." Although the resources and capabilities were there for business to have an impact, Correa felt something crucial was missing: the alignment between shareholders and management. Extended fiduciary duty—in other words, extending the legal obligations of the firm beyond shareholders to include nature and society—allows companies to act intentionally to create positive impact with a long-term view. "That, for me," she explains, "changes the history of business."

In 2011, Munoz was helping to plan the Aconcagua Summit, an offshoot of the Zermatt Summit that is focused on "humanizing globalization." He and Correa wanted to get Coen Gilbert to speak at the conference, but they couldn't find anyone who could connect them. They reached out to friends, but they kept coming up empty. They didn't give up, however, because they knew that what B Lab was doing and what they wanted to do lined up perfectly. "There's no point whatsoever in trying to invent it again," Correa thought. "It's been invented. Let's join forces with these guys." Correa eventually reached out to an Argentinean friend, Pedro Tarak, who, as legal advisor to the vice president of Argentina during the country's first period of democracy, had promoted environmental change and citizen participation. Tarak, Correa says, "has an amazing global network," but he didn't know the B Lab team—yet. The next day, Tarak called her back. He said, "You won't believe it. Last night, I met an American who knows these guys."

With Tarak and a Chilean friend and social entrepreneur, Juan Pablo Larenas, the director of the Chilean Entrepreneur Association (ASECH), Correa and Munoz got on the phone. Munoz remembers the conversation well. The four had planned it all out and knew exactly what they were going to say, but when it was his turn to speak, Munoz feared that Coen Gilbert and Kassoy seemed bored. He said, "You know what? I feel extremely uncomfortable to have this conversation about saving the world and trying to solve the problems in the economy without seeing your faces. . . . I need to watch other people's eyes to connect. We need to do this in a way where we are connected. We need to feel like we trust each other." Munoz started describing his life, his family, the room he was in, his dreams for the future—and "in that moment," he says, "Jay said, 'Okay, now we're in.'"

Correa, Munoz, Larenas, and Tarak flew to New York City for two days in the fall of 2011. "It was love at first sight," Correa recalls. Munoz remembers that it was right around the anniversary of 9/11—a particularly difficult time for Coen Gilbert, Kassoy, and Houlahan—and Munoz himself had just lost his partner in a horrific plane crash.

"It generated an extra connection between us, and now we're brothers," says Munoz. The Latin Americans pressed the need to make B Corp into a global movement: "We need to have a systemic change," they said. "We need the markets to change. We need consumers, investors, media, and academia to act for a better world, and the change has to be systemic."

Before Coen Gilbert could tell them about B Lab's plans, Tarak jumped in: "Okay, thank you so much, Jay, but let me tell you why I am here." The four friends from South America began to talk honestly and openly about their vision—"I would say after two hours, we were the best of friends," recalls Correa. Munoz remembers it much the same way: "It was mostly about bonding and connecting at different levels, of course on an intellectual level, an ethical and value level. We also connected more emotionally, and then we found out what we were willing to do on a practical level."

The four Latin Americans brought two important things to the table. The first was that they wanted B Corp to be a global phenomenon and intended to translate the B Impact Assessment and B Lab's other resources into Spanish and Portuguese. The second thing they addressed was that in South America, change was not going to happen cleanly or systemically, as the B Lab team expected it to happen in North America—they needed to be prepared for its messiness. During that meeting, the group agreed to "date for a while before they got married." But within the year, there were licensing agreements and partnerships between B Lab and a new entity called Sistema B that would receive the vast majority of the certification fees of South American B Corps—a partnership model that would be the basis for other global partnerships as the movement expanded around the world.

After the meeting in New York, the four went back to Santiago, looked at one another, and asked, "Where do we begin?" They were still just friends sitting around a table, wanting to enact change. Their first order of business was to raise funds to get the organization off the ground. At first, the Sistema B team members relied on volunteer efforts and their own professional networks to fund and support the introduction of Empresas B (B Corps). The Chilean Economic Development Agency (CORFO), a government organization, provided support for the movement in that country. The Multilateral Investment Fund (FOMIN) provided the funds for Sistema B's staff salaries, and CAF, the Development Bank of Latin America, helped support the creation of public policies and education. Kassoy also introduced the Sistema B founders to the Rockefeller Foundation, which wanted to support a meeting in Santiago focused on kicking off the B Corp conversation in Latin America.

The Santiago event was set for January 2012, and it turned out to be bigger and better than anyone could have imagined. A few days before it was scheduled to happen, the office of the minister of economy in Chile contacted them to say that the minister was planning to attend the meeting. Correa assumed he'd deliver some opening remarks or give a speech and then leave. "No," his office told her, "the minister doesn't want to open the meeting. He wants to be there with you during the day." They could not believe their luck. They had expected twenty-five to thirty-five people to attend. When the day arrived, the room quickly filled up with eighty people representing more than ten Latin American countries, the United States, and Spain.

By February 2012, TriCiclos had been certified as the first Empresa B. That same year, B Lab formally announced the partnership at the Clinton Global Initiative meeting, with Kassoy stating, "By extending the B Corp movement into emerging markets in South America . . . the B Corp movement will have dramatic impact on the development of more inclusive and sustainable economies."[1]

A Different Theory of Change

The B Lab team's theory of change was based on a tipping-point model. As Correa puts it, "They say, 'Systemic change will happen when we reach a significant number of certified B Corporations. That's going to change the system.' " This view is complemented by the Latin American perspective: "You need to have all actors on board," she says. "Sistema B brings a complementary theory of change—change happens not just because of critical mass, but because of the critical connections between pioneers, who are the new entrants to the market, and the evolving ecosystem. A new system requires other actors to come in: consumers who buy new products and services, investors and public policy that supports a new economy, academia that teaches a new way to do business, and opinion leaders who bring new futures into the everyday conversation."

Because of this, the Sistema B quartet focused its strategy not just on companies but on bringing more stakeholders to the table, particularly "communities of practice": academia, large market players, opinion leaders, investors, and public policy makers. This might not have been how B Lab originally set out to change the world, but it has definitely been incorporated into the team's own practices. As Correa argues, "Systemic change happens because of multiple variables acting towards change. Social change is unpredictable. It emerges. You can put all the ingredients there, but you cannot predict what's going to happen or when it's going to happen."

The Growth of Sistema B

Sistema B was born simultaneously in Chile, Argentina, and Colombia in 2012, and it quickly expanded into Uruguay and Brazil. The first thing the team had to establish was a definition for the term *empresa social* (social business) that would be the same across all twelve

South American countries. From there, the founders had to build out and create an ecosystem—there was no existing social enterprise structure. Even the continent's geography was challenging, playing into everything from how to set up legal frameworks to how to support employees.

The team pinpointed five initiatives that were put into play in 2014. One of them is B Multipliers, low-cost workshops that train twenty people at a time in the same way that Sistema B employees are trained. The participants are then encouraged to work on their own to grow the movement. To date the program has trained more than two thousand people whose backgrounds range from teachers and students to consultants and executives. Correa says, "I get, maybe once a week, an email or a phone call from someone I don't know . . . saying, 'Hi, I'm a B Multiplier and wanted to ask you such and such.' " Thanks in large part to B Multipliers, Sistema B now has offices in ten countries and a strong presence in five more. As each national team grew, it received initial funding from Sistema B headquarters in Chile until it was able to access local funding and take on its own fund-raising.

During its first few years, Sistema B's focus was largely on certifying B Corps—the movement couldn't exist without them. But, Correa recalls, "it was very time consuming and expensive in terms of resources." They did the math at one point and realized it was taking on average five full-time days to get one company to start the certification process. If their goal was one thousand B Corporations, Correa remembers thinking, it would be almost impossible with existing staff. "There's no way to scale that. We started looking for ways to scale the impact without enlarging the organization," she recalls, which eventually led to a number of new outreach strategies such as a partnership with Bancolombia. From the B Lab side, the most pressing challenges at the time were organization oversight and the globalization of B Lab's standards.

Bancolombia and the BIA

In May 2016, Bancolombia partnered with B Lab and Sistema B to spread the use of the BIA to its suppliers. Headquartered in Medellín, Bancolombia is the third-largest bank in South America and the largest in Colombia, with assets of over $55 billion. It has always had a strong mission of providing "more human banking" to customers and had been looking for a platform to crystallize that mission.[2] Its leaders were introduced to the B Corp movement by Correa, who encouraged them to use the BIA. Although they realized that becoming a certified B Corp would be quite a challenge, they embraced the movement. Their objectives included strengthening the bank's relationship with its suppliers, improving the sustainability of its supply chain, and understanding which of its suppliers were mission oriented and in what ways.[3]

In the first year of the initiative, Bancolombia asked close to 150 of its suppliers to use the full-length BIA and report their results. It also asked them to identify two or three areas of improvement to work on. More than 100 of them completed the BIA, which helped Bancolombia better understand the scale and makeup of its supply chain. Its leaders also realized that compared to other businesses, those suppliers outperformed on governance, labor, environment, and community practices. In fact, over 30 of the businesses that took the BIA qualified for certification. The results were impressive and spoke to a larger shift in the makeup of the global economy: of these 100-plus companies, women held 36 percent of executive positions in Bancolombia's supply chain; 68 percent of them have an environmental policy; and they created over 17,500 jobs that year.[4]

Bancolombia plans to run a similar pilot project with borrowers and scale it from there, using the BIA as a road map. The bank's leaders made this process a suggestion rather than a requirement, but its early success likely stems from the fact that Bancolombia took the

BIA itself and can attest to how useful it is. The benefits of this plan can be seen across the board: it reinforces the bank's mission and brand, creates longer and better relationships with suppliers and lendees, and helps mitigate risk for lendees, who have access to more data about Bancolombia than they had before.[5]

B Lab UK

B Lab UK was founded in 2013 by James Perry, director and cofounder of COOK, which sells prepared organic meals, and Charmian Love, cofounder and at the time CEO of the London-based consulting agency Volans. Love, a Canadian with a background in art history and an MBA from Harvard, founded Volans with Pamela Hartigan and sustainability pioneer John Elkington. Volans was one of the first certified B Corps in the United Kingdom in March 2013, quickly followed by SustainAbility in April—which also had Elkington as a founder. COOK was certified in November 2013.[6]

The author of seventeen books and over forty reports on corporate responsibility, Elkington was inducted into the Sustainability Hall of Fame by the International Society of Sustainability Professionals in 2013. His life in social entrepreneurship started at age eleven, when he raised money for the newly created World Wildlife Fund.[7] When he first met the B Lab trio, he realized they moved in the same worlds: "We were all part of a broader movement, and [B Lab] was an attempt to frame some of the stuff and label it in a particular way," he reflected.

In the early 2000s, Elkington was working with Pamela Hartigan at the World Economic Forum and the Schwab Foundation for Social Entrepreneurship to get social entrepreneurs onto the main discussion panels at nationwide conferences. "Social entrepreneurs were very different from traditional NGOs because they were pro-enterprise," he explains. In 2002, the World Economic Forum (WEF) held its annual meeting in New York City. WEF reserved a ballroom at the Waldorf Astoria Hotel for a session on social entrepreneurship. Key people like WEF founder Klaus Schawb and social entrepreneur Mohammed Yunus were there, but otherwise "pretty much nobody turned up," Elkington recalls. "People couldn't see the relevance." Until more recent times, Elkington's experience was that NGOs didn't want to deal with business, and businesses didn't want NGOs in their boardroom. Elkington noted that in the 1980s nonprofits like Greenpeace would say, "The only way forward with business is to tie them down in regulations. We can never trust them." He disagreed; he believed that businesses had to be set up to have agendas that included social and environmental change, which is why he had developed the "triple bottom line" idea in 1994.

By the time Volans connected with the B Lab team, many UK companies were identifying as values based or mission led, but few had seen the need to certify. Charmian Love and James Perry helped bring energy to the movement. Richard Johnson of Volans recalls, "Char would always say, 'This is it. The triple bottom line is coming. The army's here.' " Love recalls that "there were many hands to the pump—the founding of B Lab UK was truly a community effort. The success today is because of the actions taken by an entrepreneurial and energetic community who deeply believed in harnessing the power of business as a force for good."

In many ways, the United Kingdom had been primed for B Corp's ideas. In 2005, the UK government introduced a new type of corporate form for for-profit social mission organizations called the community interest company (CIC). Like benefit corporations, CICs are required to issue an annual report summarizing their benefit to the community. However, a key difference is that CICs are subject to an "asset lock" that ensures that their assets are used only for community benefit, and as a result the return to investors is capped. As COOK's

James Perry explained it to me, benefit corporations don't have "the sacred-secular divide, and so capital markets can participate in the social business field." CICs have "found themselves excluded from the capital markets," he continued. "So they have had to create their own capital market which relies on a degree of subsidy." As of March 2019, the number of CICs in the United Kingdom exceeded fifteen thousand, and they were projected to continue growing at an annual rate of over twenty-five hundred.[8]

James Perry met Coen Gilbert in 2010. "He was pitching B Corps," he says, "and I was like. 'That guy—eureka!' He kind of had me at hello, really." At the time, Perry was part of the Mission Alignment Working Group for the G8 Social Impact Investment task force headed by Sir Ronald Cohen—readers will remember the passionate, seventy-two-year-old who is better known as the "Father of UK Venture Capital." Perry explains that when B Lab issued a license to set up B Lab UK, he and Love "set it up as a not-for-profit. . . . We got £200,000-odd of seed funding, and that was just about enough." From there, they "sort of corralled and cajoled" their friends who were also working in the social innovation space. As Perry recalls fondly, "It was real bootstrap stuff. No money. We didn't get paid or anything. We just did it from conviction." They hoped to have fifty founding companies at their launch event—a goal they exceeded.

Part of what's behind the growth of the UK B Corp community is the rise of challenger brands in consumer goods, many of them focused on sustainability. Competitors attend the same events, spend time together, and help each other out—much like Method and Seventh Generation did in the earliest days of the B Corp movement. As these and bigger companies push social business and impact investing forward, the B Corp movement has picked up incredible speed in the United Kingdom and continues to do so, setting an example for other parts of the globe.

B Lab Europe

Also a nonprofit entity, B Lab Europe began at about the same time as B Lab UK. At the beginning, a handful of European companies began to bring the concept to their marketplaces, including the Put Your Money Where Your Meaning Is Community (known by its acronym PYMWYMIC), an investment company in the Netherlands, and the French and Italian sustainability consultancies Utopies and Nativa. Since then it has grown steadily. As of 2019, B Lab Europe has formal chapters in Benelux, Switzerland, and Spain, and a strong presence in Italy and France.[9]

Marcello Palazzi, cofounder of B Lab Europe, had been involved in the CSR movement for many years, focusing much of his work on Sweden and Denmark, the countries he credits with starting the CSR movement. Back in 1989, Palazzi founded the Progressio Foundation, which has undertaken several hundred ventures, and start-ups in more than thirty different countries. I met him in a café in Rotterdam, just a short train ride from B Lab Europe's headquarters in Amsterdam. Palazzi is a driven, ambitious man whose presence is larger than life, thanks in part to his emphatic hand gestures and his way of pulling in his listeners.

When Palazzi discovered B Lab, he immediately believed that it was going much further in the direction of better business than anyone else he had encountered. A partnership agreement between B Lab and B Lab Europe was signed in February 2013, and in January 2014, Palazzi and his partner, Leen Zevenbergen, started working on B Lab Europe full-time. In April 2015, B Lab Europe officially launched with a founding class of sixty-five B Corps.[10] As of 2019, there were over five hundred B Corps in Europe.[11]

From the beginning, B Lab Europe's strategy has been to look for local partners that can spread awareness and help companies with certification in their own language and with an understanding of their culture. B Lab Europe also set up a team of standards analysts to assess companies' BIAs not only in Europe but also in countries in Africa, Asia, and South America. Palazzi describes B Lab Europe as "evangelists. We talk about it, we promote it, and we share the information. We organize events, we talk at conferences. Most importantly, we go out and meet the CEOs and potential people."

The French food company Danone has been a major player in the growth of B Lab Europe. "Our B Corp certification journey started several decades ago," its CEO Emmanuel Faber says, before B Lab even existed. As far back as 1972, Danone declared that it is "committed to pursuing a 'dual economic and social agenda.' This continued with the implementation of 'Danone Way' nearly 20 years ago: our audited, scorecard-led integrated reporting and monitoring process for all of our business entities around the world."[12]

The biggest challenge B Lab Europe has faced has been dealing with so many different legal frameworks. In many countries, such as Denmark and Sweden, progressive laws mean that the work B Corps do is already the basic level of good work expected. Thus, they have to do even more and score even higher on their BIAs to prove to their consumers and potential employees that they aren't just regular progressive companies such as the country is already used to; they are something new.

The progressive nature of social business in Europe also helped with work on benefit corporation legislation. In 2015, Italy became the second country in the world to offer the benefit corporation legal structure, thanks in large part to Nativa and B Lab Europe. In some European countries, just as in some states in the United States, companies can focus on the welfare of their employees, community, and environment without having to change the law. The true difference in European countries and also in some constituency statute states in the United States is that they can, technically, consider stakeholder interests as long as doing so continues to serve shareholder interests.

B Corp certification and the B movement in general have helped some European companies protect themselves from takeovers. Palazzi notes the example of AkzoNobel, a multinational headquartered in Holland, which survived a takeover attempt from U.S.-based PPG Industries: "The Dutch court actually gave a verdict in favor of rejecting the bid that came from PPG because the overall interest[s] of the company go beyond the financial interest." Unilever offers another example. Heinz and 3G attempted a takeover, and the question for Unilever's home country of the Netherlands became "What about employees who are working in the Netherlands? What about the national interest? Europe is becoming smart about this," Palazzi says—and the B Corp movement has played a role.

Further Expansion around the World

B Lab Australia and New Zealand
B Lab Australia and New Zealand was founded in 2013 and officially launched in August 2014. Danny Almagor, the CEO of the impact investing company Small Giants, met Andrew Kassoy at the Skoll World Forum and decided then and there to become the first B Corp in Australia.[13] After that, it didn't take long for Australia's B Corps community to explode. Once companies began to certify, a group of B Corp leaders lobbied B Lab in 2012 for permission to start B Lab Australia and New Zealand. Founding members and key players in this process included Small Giants, Net Balance, the Projection Room, Wholekids, and Australian Ethical. James Meldrum, who founded Wholekids, a producer of healthy snacks for kids, with his wife Monica, recalls, "Going back 10 years, when we first spoke to people about how we wanted to run the business, we got two responses—'this is too touchy-feely' or 'what are you trying to be?' "[14]

In 2013, the B Lab team was supporting the launches of both Sistema B and B Lab UK, so the trio was wary about taking on another market. Instead, B Lab encouraged the group from Australia to take the first steps, knowing that they would form a more formal partnership as soon as possible. The first year was thus a volunteer-led experiment. It launched with a founding class of forty-seven B Corps, a strong community, and an agreement with B Lab modeled after the Sistema B agreement. Initial funding came out of the pooled resources of many in the founding class, and their goal was to rely on the fees from certification within three years.[15] They also received support from a large Australian insurance company, Sun Corp.[16]

All of the businesses in Almagor's Small Giants portfolio certified as B Corps. He thinks big change is coming. "We talk about conscious capitalism, like the Occupy Movement. I think there are a lot of people with capital in positions of power who agree we can align profit with purpose. And I think that movement is growing."[17]

B Lab Australia and New Zealand faced a key challenge when it came to introducing benefit corporation legislation, as Australian corporate law is set at the federal level. The legislation was introduced in December 2016, but as of 2019, it was still being considered. Consistent funding was also a big issue at first. But the passion of the Australian and New Zealand B Corp community is evident; 120 members from sixty-one B Corps held their first Champions Retreat in 2017.[18]

B Lab in Asia

B Lab Asia is actually a coalition of organizations that includes a B Lab affiliate in Taiwan, a B Lab ambassador organization in Korea, B Lab Japan, B Corp China and, as of 2019, eighty-seven certified B Corps across seventeen countries.

B Lab Taiwan was launched in 2014. Its chair, David Chang, notes that because Asia is the world's most populous continent, it shoulders a disproportionate amount of its poverty, conflict, and environmental degradation. The movement has attracted the attention of the Taiwanese government—former president Yingjiu Ma described B Corps as a "new opportunity for agriculture, education, the service industry and the IT industry in Taiwan."[19]

B Corps are also beginning to gain traction in Hong Kong, where they are promoted by a prominent social entrepreneur, KK Tse, the founding chair of the Hong Kong Social Enterprise Forum and the CEO of B Corp Education for Good, which focuses on providing educational and training programs in sustainability and social innovation and is officially connected to B Lab. Education for Good has committed to "create a critical mass of B Corps to collectively drive the transformation of business as a force for good" within the next five years. The company is working to expand the B Corp movement across Asia.[20]

In the meantime, other organizations were working to determine whether B Corps could work in Mainland China. The Beijing Leping Foundation, an NGO, pressed for the establishment of a regional B Lab office in Hong Kong. Its initial estimate was that it would take five to six years for B Corps to become a legal form of institutional change throughout China. Leping was founded by Dongshu (Jaff) Shen, a well-known social entrepreneur whose work addresses China's social justice and development issues by promoting innovation and entrepreneurship. Shen likes to be provocative; you can see the twinkle in his eye when he asks a challenging question or makes an incisive point. His organization offers training to social entrepreneurs, micro-credit loans to low-income companies and groups, and management training for socially conscious businesses.[21]

Meanwhile, many companies in Mainland China were making independent efforts to be certified as B Corps. These included family businesses whose younger generations were eager to make a difference in the world (many had been educated in the West), companies that wanted to compete in the international market, and traditional social enterprises.

The first B Corp in Mainland China was certified in June 2016. First Respond's experience highlighted issues that other Chinese companies would face. Min Ko, the international affairs director of First Respond at the time, who led the organization through the process, was excited that it scored as well as it did on its first self-assessment. "I was almost certain that we would not have any problems getting certified," she says. But she and B Lab discovered that many of the requirements listed in the BIA were not applicable in the Chinese context. For example, B Lab assesses whether applicants are located in buildings with credible green building standards, such as LEED (Leadership in Energy and Environmental Design). Although such standards are widely accepted in the United States, it is hard to find green buildings in China, where the certification infrastructure is much less developed. While the B Lab standards are consistent, countries are not. Just as Scandinavian companies enjoy a head start, Chinese companies must start from behind.

Additionally, some of the terms used in the questions were hard to translate into a Chinese context. For example, Min Ko said she was confused by the requirement that "independent contractors are paid a living wage (calculated as hourly wage when living wage data is available)." Unlike the United States and Europe, China does not have official living wage data; the government only issues minimum working wage guidelines. B Lab responded that Chinese applicants could get credit as long as the wage was higher than minimum working wage, but how much higher should it be? Was $1 higher the same as $100 higher? Furthermore, basic needs in Shanghai, where First Respond was located, are completely different than in less developed cities in China. The minimum working wage of Shanghai is 1.7 times that of many cities in the interior. Without existing market infrastructure to reference and integrate into the BIA, as B Lab is able to do for U.S. companies through MIT's U.S. Living Wage Calculator, it is difficult for Chinese companies to answer this question, making it that much harder to earn the minimum 80 points. Moreover, there are roughly two hundred questions in the BIA, many of them requiring supporting documents. For companies whose main language is not English, that demands significant translation work.

Although First Respond's road to B Corp certification was challenging, it benefited from the designation almost immediately. As is the experience of many other B Corps, certification helped the company clarify its mission when talking to potential customers. Also, "it was an enlightening process for all our internal employees because now they understand the direction we are going after and what kind of real social impacts we are trying to create," Min Ko says. Min Ko in many ways embodies the grassroots spirit of the B Corp movement. After leading First Respond through certification, she moved to Leping, where she now heads up B Corp outreach for Mainland China.

Addressing the Challenges of Globalization

Back in 2014, Kassoy expressed concern about the scale, scope, and timing of B Lab's global partnerships. "We said yes too much internationally," he confessed, "and we have a bunch of partners in places who are awesome, and they're not scaling because [their market] is just not ready and they can't survive financially as a result, and we don't have the ability to support them."

Overseeing a global movement is no easy feat, of course. Richard Johnson, Volans's breakthrough agent, quips that "there are a lot of B Corps in the UK; they're just not certified." Johnson explains that when he originally introduced the B Corps concept to UK companies, there was a bit of backlash from those that already self-identified as social enterprises or mission-based companies. They felt as though this American organization was coming in and saying they could "do it better." Yet the international partnerships B Lab has set up are all different. B Lab understood from the beginning that it could not just show up and tell a country how to run its businesses: "That's not how the world works," Kassoy says. "Particularly with Americans showing up. Particularly when people in lots of places in the world think that while America may have a very innovative and creative economy, it is behind the curve in terms of being a responsible economy."

To address the potentially unhealthy power dynamics of being a U.S.-founded global movement, the B Lab board formally delegated certain responsibilities to a newly created Global Governance Council in March 2014, in which B Lab and each global partner had a role equal to every other global partner. Gonzalo Munoz from Sistema B remembers the B Lab team saying, "We're going to be just one more partner" on this council, which oversees three elements of the global movement—the approval of new global partnerships and the renewal of existing ones, earned income programs outside of certification, and any policy work outside of the promotion of benefit corporation legislation in various countries. One member of the Global Governance Council also sits on the B Lab board of directors.

Munoz recalls that in the first few council meetings, "everything was about the United States. You read the reports and everything was so complex and so disconnected [from] the rest of the world that part of my work was to show how this could be understood from the global perspective, generating bridges and bonds between B Lab and the global partners." It soon became very apparent that this was a problem. Houlahan explains, "The single greatest criticism of B Lab globally and the movement globally is that it's an American export, full stop."[22] To help mitigate this, every B Lab global partner gets to nominate someone to sit on B Lab's Standards Advisory Council. And each region has its own council that is managed by the larger one.

This ensures that B Lab's standards can be adapted for different geographies. Currently, there are three different versions of the standards: U.S., global, and emerging market.

In addition, the questions on the BIA have been adjusted to better fit each region. "The balance that we're trying to strike," explains Christina Forwood, B Lab's director of standards review, "is to make sure that it is relevant and insightful for all businesses while at the same time maintaining this broader comparability, as well as a trajectory towards what we're looking for as a global standard for what it means to be a good business. There are a variety of universal things that apply." B Lab has developed regional subadvisory groups to provide feedback and suggestions to the Standards Advisory Council for this purpose.

As we have seen regarding Scandinavia, governments in some countries mandate or provide benefits that would be seen as creating positive impact if they were adopted by companies in the United States, but companies elsewhere might not receive credit for them. "We want to make sure they are recognized as still providing a better or a good work environment," explains Forwood. "They pay taxes in that jurisdiction and therefore we're able to say, you know what, the companies in Germany . . . quite frankly just provide better jobs than companies in the U.S. . . . We don't want to just remove that from the equation." This is in some ways the opposite of the problem First Respond faced in China.

Marcello Palazzi says that Italy's benefit corporation legislation has been a watershed. "There have been over two hundred conferences and meetings about what is the purpose of the corporation and to whom are their owners accountable," he says. "Externalities—how do we make sure that all this negative cost actually gets paid by companies? It has created a real debate about issues of governance, of constitutionality, of accountability for the private sector companies vis-à-vis society. NGOs have gotten involved, academics have gotten involved. If you look at South America, there are now over 200 academics working on actually teaching some of this stuff. . . . It creates a different paradigm of business."

Every day, more and more entrepreneurs, sustainable business leaders, and political figures learn about the B Corp movement and work toward establishing it in their own countries. B Lab's first foray into Africa, B Lab East Africa, was established in 2016.[23] If the movement could grow its presence to over thirty countries in just a decade, it is likely to become completely global before long.

9

Widening the Funnel

In 2005, a craftsman and two programmers came together to create a unique online platform that the world now knows as Etsy. The craftsman, Rob Kalin, wanted to give craft makers the chance to sell their wares online. When the programmers, Chris Maguire and Haim Schoppick, left Etsy in 2008, Kalin hired a new chief technical officer (CTO), Chad Dickerson, who would later replace him as CEO.[1]

During Etsy's early years, its widely admired culture was often credited as a big reason for the company's success. When Etsy became a certified B Corporation in 2012, its office building was certified by the Living Building Challenge (an initiative focused on creating regenerative built environments) and its workplace perks included yoga and meditation classes, organic lunches, academic courses, and gender-neutral bathrooms (which were quite progressive at the time). Employee benefits included extended parental leave and impressive wages.

In March 2015, Etsy announced its intention to make an initial public offering. Much of the press coverage centered around its B Corp status and whether Etsy would be able to balance its social and environmental commitments with the financial pressures of the public markets. At the time, there were no publicly traded B Corps. Further, B Lab rules state that if a certified B Corp is incorporated in a state that has passed benefit corporation legislation, the company must become a benefit corporation within four years. Etsy was incorporated in

Delaware, and as that state's benefit corporation law went into effect in 2013, Etsy had until 2017 to become a benefit corporation or risk losing its B Corp status. Coen Gilbert explains, "The four-year on-ramp was designed to create a focused yet reasonable amount of time for companies like Etsy to socialize the legal issues with their board, investors, and other public market stakeholders."[2]

When Etsy went public, Dickerson posted a message to the Etsy community on the company blog stating that Etsy understood that the key to its success was being "a values-led community-based business that focuses on the long term." Dickerson imagined that Etsy would pave the way for other sustainable businesses to go public.[3] Unfortunately, that's not what happened.

On Etsy's first day on the market, its value doubled, surpassing $3 billion. It was a brilliant beginning. But after that, its fortunes quickly turned. For two years, its stock steadily decreased, and in the first quarter of 2017, the company faced a loss for the first time.[4] Investor activists took charge of the situation and demanded change. Seth Wunder and his hedge fund black-and-white Capital entered the picture, acquiring about 2 percent of Etsy's shares—not a large amount, but enough to cause a stir.[5] Wunder argued that Etsy's overhead was about double what it should be because of its headcount and generous workplace perks and benefits. The company's general and administrative expenses totaled about 24 percent of its total revenue—competitors' similar expenses were only about 10 percent—and the company had spent three years hiring a lot of people, increasing its staff by more than half.[6]

Wunder spelled out his concerns in two letters to Etsy's board in which he requested meetings about "what appears to be a lack of cost discipline at the company." Then, hours before Etsy's latest earning report went out, Wunder released the letters publicly, accompanied by a press release in which he outlined what he said were three key issues: slowing gross merchandise sales, the need for improvements in operations and corporate governance, and the "necessity" to maximize value for shareholders.[7] Not long afterward, Dickerson was let go, as was 8 percent of the staff—most of them members of teams focused on values alignment and workplace improvements. A few months later, Etsy announced another round of layoffs, totaling about 15 percent of its employees.[8] Dickerson was replaced by Josh Silverman, a board member who had also been asking pointed questions about the company's finances.

In 2017, Silverman announced that Etsy would not reincorporate as a benefit corporation and would let its B Corp certification expire. B Lab offered the company a year's extension because of the change in leadership, but Silverman turned them down.[9]

Coen Gilbert responded to Etsy's decision by pointing to Natura and Laureate, certified B Corps that are publicly traded; Laureate, also a benefit corporation, was traded on Nasdaq, the same exchange Etsy was on. Large public companies like Danone and Unilever have many subsidiaries that are B Corps. "While public companies have unique challenges in pursuing adoption of the benefit corporation legal structure," he acknowledged, "global institutional investors have already accepted the benefit corporation structure for public companies."[10] But Etsy's loss was a real blow, and it was not the only one the movement suffered.

Losing the B

Other high-profile B Corps have struggled with the governance dimension of certification in the face of real or perceived investor resistance. One such example is the Honest Company, founded with a mission of fostering a nontoxic world, particularly in the baby- and family-oriented product industries. Its products are made with clean ingredients and no synthetic chemicals and fragrances.[11] The idea for the company emerged when its founder, actress Jessica Alba, had an allergic reaction to traditional products while pregnant with her first child.[12]

The Honest Company would seem like a natural fit with the B Lab's mission, so it's not surprising that it was certified as a B Corporation in 2012. It remained a B Corp until 2017 but, according to a staff member who responded to a query on the company's website about why it dropped the certification: the Honest Company was "unable to make the legal transition to a public benefit corporation" because this corporate change "would raise a number of legal and compliance issues for our company that could lead to risk and uncertainty."

The company faced some challenges that may have also played into its lapsed certification. Unilever was interested in buying the Honest Company, but in early 2017 that deal fell through when it decided to acquire fellow B Corp Seventh Generation instead. Not long after, the Honest Company overhauled its corporate structure, replacing its cofounder and CEO Brian Lee, who had been a vocal B Corp advocate.[13] Around that same time, the Honest Company faced several lawsuits over its ingredients, as many consumers believed they had been lied to. Reports found that not all of its products were created with 100 percent clean ingredients, as its marketing seemed to imply. As a reporter at the *New York Post* scathingly put it, "Alba started a company selling overpriced goods to nervous people with money to spare. . . . She tells the world that she's the only one who can be trusted, implying the rest are out to harm, maim, poison and kill. The 'Honest' Company thrives on alarmism, and a false promise of safer, healthier products at a high price."[14] In 2018, the Honest Company announced that it had received $200 million to revive the brand.[15] So time will tell whether it is able to reconnect with its core values and customers, or whether it will continue to be weakened by what some people see as its use of greenwashing practices.

Another large company whose B Corp status has lapsed is the eyeglass manufacturer Warby Parker, which hit the market with an exciting concept: an affordable price point and the option to try on their frames at home. Warby Parker certified as a B Corporation soon after the company was founded. Among other initiatives, its production and distribution processes are carbon-neutral, and for every pair of glasses the company sells, it gives another to someone in need in the developing world. Additionally, the employee culture at Warby Parker is focused on professional and personal growth through speaker series and "Lunch and Learn" programs. Its social mission and employee-focused workplace have led to high employee attraction and retention rates. And yet Warby Parker let its B Corp certification lapse when it chose not to incorporate as a benefit corporation.[16]

This strikes me as a surprising turn. In 2012, I spent the day at Warby Parker's headquarters and interviewed CEO Neil Blumenthal. The B Corp logo was prominently displayed at the entrance, and it was clear that the company was passionate about its commitment to the movement. At the time, Blumenthal intimated that Warby Parker's investors were on board with the move to incorporate as a benefit corporation—the company has investors in common with fellow B Corp (and benefit corporation) Allbirds, such as Tiger Management. Further, Blumenthal was one of the CEOs who went to Wilmington to lobby the Delaware legislature to pass benefit corporation law. Given these facts, "investor resistance" may not have been the only or primary reason Warby decided not to adopt benefit corporation governance. Unfortunately, I was unable to discuss the decision with Blumenthal directly.

When I spoke to Kaki Read, Warby Parker's senior communications manager, she told me: "The process to change the legal structure at the time proved challenging, given the size and stage of Warby Parker. There's a chance we may just revisit that decision in the future.

This isn't a hard-and-fast decision on our part. It just didn't necessarily make sense at the time. If we were to form today, it would be likely that we would incorporate as a public benefit corporation, but the status didn't exist when we were founded in 2010."

Thus, part of the issue might be a matter of timing. Things have changed within the B Corp movement since Warby's decision: Natura, owner of iconic cosmetic brands the Body Shop and Avon, has had continued success as a publicly traded company, B Corp and benefit corporation Laureate had a successful IPO on the Nasdaq exchange, and many large multinationals have been actively purchasing B Corps. Perhaps in time the increasing track record of public market acceptance will persuade Warby Parker's management and investors that regaining their B Corp certification and adopting benefit corporation governance will help them withstand the pressures of short-termism, to which Whole Foods fell prey, and the pressures of profit maximization, which did such harm to Etsy.

The specific reasons behind their lapses may differ, but Etsy, the Honest Company, and Warby Parker illustrate that the path of the B Corp movement is not necessarily a straight line; it includes many forks and alternative ways to achieve impact. Even companies with missions and values that clearly resonate with the B Lab founders' intentions may not be able to fully and consistently commit to the B brand. That doesn't mean they can't derive positive outcomes from the movement, and it also doesn't mean that they aren't supportive of its goals. Read quickly pointed out to me: "We really are super supportive of what they're doing. So we just want to make sure that that continues to remain well known and we may revisit our decision at some point."

While the loss of Etsy, the Honest Company, and Warby Parker was keenly felt, it also brings into stark relief the fact that the two elements of the B Lab model (accountability and legal structure) could be decoupled and refined separately to bring more companies into the movement. There are approximately 125 million businesses in the world and all of them can make a difference. When one of them chooses to align its business interests with those of society, when it at least begins to act like a B Corp, managing its impacts with as much rigor as its profits, then it is participating in the change, whether it ultimately seeks certification and reincorporates or not. As Andrew Kassoy emphasizes, the B Corp movement isn't an "in-club." "It's a theory of change," he says, that is directed at "an ever-larger portion of the economy." As Coen Gilbert puts it, "If we wanted to grow at a larger scale and if our objective is to redefine success in business, we're not going to get there simply by certifying more companies."

Boston-based Dancing Deer Baking Company provides reason for hope. The first time I taught the Harvard Business School case study I published on B Lab in 2010, I invited the B Lab leaders and several current and prospective B Corps to class. One of the latter was represented by Trish Karter, chair, former CEO, and cofounder of Dancing Deer, who at the time had tried unsuccessfully to convince her board to adopt B Corp certification. The company eventually overcame its concerns, and Dancing Deer became not only a certified B Corp but one of the first companies in Massachusetts to register as a benefit corporation after the law was passed in 2012.

As Andrew Kassoy emphasizes, a key way for B Lab to "widen the funnel" and get more businesses involved in the movement is to share some of its tools that promote impact management broadly. Even companies on the outskirts of the B Corp community can gain a great deal from the work to overthrow shareholder primacy. There are a number of current initiatives that scale the accountability aspect of the B Lab model and work toward the creation of a "B Economy" by encouraging all businesses to be a force for good. These include initiatives to spread the measurement of social and environmental factors, and an important partnership with the United Nations to make that organization's Sustainable Development Goals (SDGs) more measurable and traceable at the business level. The different components that make up the B Economy—B Corporations, benefit corporations, B impact management tools, the B Analytics platform, and the various B Lab partnerships—are all working together to upend shareholder primacy and achieve a greater impact for both businesses and society.

Spreading Impact beyond B Corps

Bart Houlahan reflects that "every company in the world can and should participate in this movement, to be part of the 'B Economy' in some way." When companies that aren't aiming for certification use the B Impact Assessment, it becomes a learning tool. They can see what's possible for their business, and it becomes easier for them to adopt certain practices when the pressure of committing to full certification is removed.

Some of these companies may ultimately become B Corporations. Solberg Manufacturing, for example, is a Chicago-based manufacturer of filtration, separation, and silencing products. Bart Houlahan told me that initially, the family-owned business's leaders weren't sure they could become a B Corp. A competitor had certified, and although Solberg believed in the movement, the company didn't think it could hit the certification benchmark. Its leaders began using the B Impact Assessment simply to improve themselves, thinking, "We're building a better business, and we [will] use these tools to systematically help us get there." In 2011, the company became a certified B Corp, but even if that hadn't been the outcome, it used the assessment tools in exactly the way the B Lab team intended.

Measuring What Matters

B Lab launched its "Measure What Matters" campaign in 2014 to make the BIA accessible to companies of all sizes across all industries. Involving multiple partnerships among investors, supply chain managers, and cities and municipalities, its mission is to use the powerful data platform B Analytics to make impact management the norm.[17] A member of the Measure What Matters team pointed out to me that giving companies the opportunity to see how they're doing relative to others in their industry and how they can improve is one of the most useful aspects of the B Analytics platform, not just for companies but investors. Investors may ask companies to go through the BIA process so they can see where they are excelling and how they can get all of the companies in their portfolios above a certain level. This can be helpful in marketing. For instance, an investment company might say, "All of our companies have grown in jobs by 5 percent annually, which is higher than the average."

Another useful feature of the B Analytics platform is its ability to measure and track impact trends. "A lot of what we are collecting here is inputs and outputs," I was told, "and people want to get to that outcomes part." In other words, the B Analytics platform draws companies' attention to things they might not have been thinking about. Portfolio managers could realize that a company is missing an opportunity; on the flip side, they can leverage a company's successful practices across the rest of their portfolio. B Lab describes the platform as both a monitoring and a learning and improvement tool.

The B Analytics team constantly considers the different ways that people want to interact with the information the platform can compile. The team begins by building generic dashboards that are available to anyone. From there, companies and investors can zero in on their key areas of impact and use filters to set benchmarks. For example, if you were an investor and had permission to view a certified

B Corp's data, you would first see its BIA score and the different underlying dimensions. You would see aggregate data for its peer universe and could then drill down into the company line by line to benchmark against the peer group's BIA results. The introductory version is the standard view that everyone sees, and then customized views are built for every user, based specifically on what that user wants to be looking at. As of 2018, there were over seventy thousand users of the BIA. B Lab has also partnered with more than fifty companies, supply chain managers, and governments to introduce them to impact measurement.[18]

At the 2015 Davos Conference, Natura cofounder and B Team leader Guilherme Leal announced that Virgin Group founder Sir Richard Branson would be partnering with B Lab to help develop a more sustainable economic model for the world. Two crucial programs to expand usage of B Lab's tools were introduced—driving impact through supply chains and a challenge for all companies to be "The Best."[19]

Driving Impact through Supply Chains

Many companies outside of the B Corp movement have begun to reexamine their supply chains. Nike, for example, has prescribed a code of conduct that covers child labor, forced labor, and compensation, and it requires its suppliers to use vendors that meet its standards as well. The company works to continually evaluate and improve its supply chain management system, carrying out audits to ensure compliance. In this way, Nike is pushing social responsibility outward and creating, quite literally, a global impact.[20]

This is precisely the type of impact that B Lab wants all companies, whether certified B Corps or not, to work toward, and it is asking more companies to encourage or require their suppliers to complete the BIA, or a pared-down version of it. Seventh Generation has been a leader in this effort. The company has set a goal to purchase only from companies that qualify for B Corp certification by 2020. Other B Corporations, including King Arthur Flour and COOK, have committed to similar goals. These B Corps are working together, sharing best practices, and problem solving as they attempt to reframe the typical supply chain compliance regime into a more rewarding program that will encourage their suppliers to join them in using their businesses as a force for good.[21]

Similarly, BAMA Companies requires its suppliers to take a sustainability survey, and the company is working to get its top twenty-five suppliers to complete a pared-down BIA. The company has hosted several seminars with the B Lab team to educate suppliers about the process. As Kim Owens, BAMA's director of community relations, explains, "We very much want to infiltrate this into our supply base." Cabot has a team of employees working closely with co-op farmers (because Cabot is a supplier-owned cooperative, these are both its suppliers and its owners) to improve their practices, and it has developed a sustainability tool for their use.[22]

Since becoming a B Corp, the Italian olive oil company Fratelli Carli has created a set of guidelines—called the "Codici"—for its suppliers to ensure that all of the company's products are sustainable, and has been conducting regular quality assurance reviews with suppliers. In addition to better protecting the environment, the ecosystem, the farmers, and the company's workers, this has led to a shorter and more efficient production chain. Bringing the B into the supply chain has led many suppliers to improve their own standards and impact; some have become B Corps themselves.[23]

Natura created an electronic bidding system for its suppliers that is based on B Corp values. This system screens suppliers based on their capacity, performance, and, most recently, their credibility. Natura asks suppliers for information on their nonfinancial performance as well as their social and ecological footprint to ensure that their values are in line with Natura's. Their suppliers' loyalty is also rated and evaluated biannually to gauge their satisfaction and willingness to recommend Natura to others.[24]

Focusing on supply chains substantially scales social and environmental impact. Moyee Coffee, a certified B Corporation since 2014, offers a great example of what this looks like on the ground. The vast majority of coffee beans come from South American and African countries in what is known as the "coffee belt." These countries are underdeveloped and rely on extensive aid from countries such as the United States. How could that be when they produce and export a commodity that almost everyone in the developed world keeps in the cupboard? Big coffee corporations might source their beans from these countries, but they roast them in the developed world, which ultimately means fewer job opportunities and profits for Colombia, Ethiopia, and the other major coffee-producing countries.

Guido van Staveren van Dijk, a Dutch entrepreneur and investor, founded Moyee Coffee with the express purpose of sourcing *and* roasting Arabica beans in Ethiopia. This innovative supply chain process is named FairChain, Moyee Coffee's motto. FairChain guarantees that more jobs and profits stay within the beans' home countries. By keeping the roasting process in the coffee belt, Moyee has improved working conditions, increased wages, and had a positive effect on local communities.[25]

Celebrating the Best

Celebrating the good work of community members has always been an important element of B Lab's work. In 2013 the team introduced the first annual Best for the World list, which captures the top 10 percent of B Corps according to their BIA scores in several categories: overall, community, environment, workers, governance, and customers. In 2018, 203 B Corps were so honored.

In 2014, B Lab partnered with the New York City Economic Development Corporation (NYCEDC) to inspire and equip the city's two hundred thousand small businesses to compete to be the best for the city's workers and neighborhoods. About two thousand companies participated during the first three months of the multiyear program. Their impacts were evaluated via a twenty-minute survey adapted from the B Impact Assessment. "Best for NYC challenges local companies to give back, create opportunities, and do what is best for the city," says NYCEDC president Kyle Kimball.[26] In 2017, the program expanded to Colorado, the first certified B Corp hotspot. The nonprofit that runs the Best for Colorado challenge, Alliance Center, sets up networking events, one-on-one mentor opportunities, and workshops with the goal of encouraging local businesses to improve their practices.[27]

Since the inception of the Best for NYC challenge, over thirty cities across the globe have expressed interest in running similar campaigns. Programs like these give the B Lab team opportunities to expand organically. "Going out and trying to talk to hundreds of businesses individually about using this tool [the BIA] is a bad exercise," Kassoy explains. Instead, they can harness the power of existing B corporations or partners in a city or state to "create a network effect."

In Scotland, the Best for Cities initiative inspired a partnership between B Lab UK and CAN DO, an organization focused on fostering innovation and entrepreneurship in Scotland. Scotland CAN B supports businesses by hosting online and in-person classes, workshops, and discussions on impact management, offering group and one-on-one mentoring and much more, all with the goal of getting them to use the BIA to increase their impacts.[28] Rio+B is a program that Sistema B runs for the city of Rio de Janeiro. The project works in partnership with Rio de Janeiro's city hall, the Ellen MacArthur

Foundation, and others. After assessing and understanding their impact, companies can work with Rio+B to improve their engagement with social and environmental issues.[29]

Integration with United Nations
Sustainable Development Goals

Just as the B Corp movement was really picking up speed, the United Nations released its Sustainable Development Goals. The first official year the SDGs were implemented was 2016, with the aim of achieving them by 2030. They are:

Goal   1: No poverty;

Goal   2: Zero hunger;

Goal   3: Good health and well-being;

Goal   4: Quality education;

Goal   5: Gender equality;

Goal   6: Clean water and sanitation;

Goal   7: Affordable and clean energy;

Goal   8: Decent work and economic growth;

Goal   9: Industry, innovation, and infrastructure;

Goal 10: Reduced inequality;

Goal 11: Sustainable cities and communities;

Goal 12: Responsible consumption and production;

Goal 13: Climate action;

Goal 14: Life below water;

Goal 15: Life on land;

Goal 16: Peace and justice strong institutions;

Goal 17: Partnerships to achieve the goal.[30]

Recognizing that the SDG framework could bring tremendous scale to the movement, the B Lab team began to incorporate the UN's goals into the BIA, encouraging certified B Corporations and benefit corporations to embrace them. Mapping the BIA to the SDGs, the team bundled existing BIA metrics into each relevant SDG, then added additional ones to fill identified gaps. Such a partnership is truly a win-win. Aligning with the SDGs gives B Lab greater leverage in the movement to overthrow shareholder primacy. At the same time, this connection helps scale the SDGs through quantifiable metrics, the tools that B Lab has created to measure the metrics, and, most important, the vast community of interconnected companies, nonprofits, government organizations, and individuals working together to create true, sustainable change. As Max Mintz, the chief investment officer of the wealth management firm Common Interests put it, "This platform will give us and others the next step: tools to align our mission with the SDGs and report back to our stakeholders. We don't have the infrastructure to develop this kind of platform on our own, so we rely on B Lab to provide these kinds of tools."[31]

In 2019, B Lab and the United Nations Global Compact (UNGC), an effort launched in 2000 to guide companies to align their strategic decisions and business operations with ten universal principles regarding human rights, labor, the environment, and anticorruption, joined forces to develop an online platform that will allow companies to estimate and assess their impact in terms of the SDGs. Known as the SDG Action Manager, this free web-based impact management tool went live in early 2020.[32]

Lorna Davis, global ambassador for Danone, thinks that "the world has finally realized that we need to work together," and that is why the UN SDGs have gained so much traction. Businesses in particular seem to have realized that "governments are not going to solve their problems for them and they need to help." However, she points outs that the SDGs are not very operational, which is where the B Corp community and the B Lab team come in. Combining the broad SDGs with the B Lab's focus on corporate accountability provides a potent combination to scale the movement, and at the same time help the world achieve the SDGs.[33]

Numerous certified B Corporations have been working with the SDGs. Bridges Fund Management has made an explicit commitment to use the SDGs as a guide for where to invest its capital. Bridges's understanding is echoed among the rest of the B Corp movement. This isn't about one company achieving one goal; it is about all companies coming together under the umbrella of the SDGs to achieve all of them.[34] Mightybytes, a digital marketing agency based in Chicago, addresses SDGs 1, 2, and 8 via paying a living wage and offering optimal employee benefits. As an LGBTQ-owned company, it also has an advisory committee consisting of women and people from diverse cultures, supporting SDGs 5 and 10.[35] Similarly, by providing jobs to underemployed populations, John's Crazy Socks addresses two SDGs at the same time: 8 and 10.[36]

In November 2017, the first B Corp "Hackathon," focused on developing innovative ways to use SDG 12 to ensure sustainable consumption and production patterns, was held in London. DAME, an organic tampon delivery service, got support and advice during the Hackathon for its efforts to reduce the waste from the 9 billion plastic applicators per year produced by disposable menstrual products. Kresse Wresling of Elvis and Kresse, a manufacturer of fashion accessories made from recycled materials, explained that while she did not start her business with SDG 12 in mind, the human waste consumption problem was an issue that needed resolving.[37] Her business has recently formed a partnership with Burberry to begin confronting the eight hundred thousand tons of waste produced every year by the leather industry.[38]

In the fall of 2018, Danone's Emmanuel Faber and Andrew Kassoy hosted a conversation in Amsterdam on the partnership between the

B Corp movement and the SDGs. Many in the audience asked how any one person could help create such widespread change. Faber responded, "We do not know how fast things will proceed, but if we don't try, we will not succeed." He emphasized that, although the work to be done is daunting, it's important to embrace that fear and push forward.[39]

Again, the goal is not just to enlist B Corps but to change the entire economy, moving it away from the pitfalls of traditional shareholder-focused capitalism and toward creating long-lasting impact. The B Lab team's tools and resources can aid any company to become a force of good, and now, working alongside the United Nations, the movement has the potential to scale even more rapidly.

10

Big Isn't Always Bad

On April 12, 2018, Danone's North American organization held an event in Manhattan to celebrate several recent achievements. Hosted by the company's CEO, Mariano Lozano, the event would be viewed, either in real time or as a recording, by Danoners around the world. The energy in the room was palpable. It was the company's first birthday—it had come into being the year before as a merger of Danone's North American Dairy business and WhiteWave Foods, the producer of such well-known health-focused brands as Horizon Organic, Silk, and Earthbound Farm. It was the company's first anniversary as a benefit corporation as well. And, Lozano announced, it had just achieved B Corp certification, two years ahead of its planned schedule. This officially made Danone NA, with its $6 billion in sales, the largest certified B Corp in the world by a factor of two. Roughly two dozen of the more than 150 people who played a role in Danone NA's B Corp certification traveled to New York to participate.[1]

The panelists provided an in-depth account of the process of B Corp certification for a big company. Emmanuel Faber, CEO of Danone's parent company, emphasized the importance of the teams that completed the process and elaborated on why he and others have focused so much of Danone's time and resources on becoming a B Corp. "Finance should serve the economy, and the economy should serve society," Faber stated, maintaining that companies have a choice to make: they can resist and use their power, size, and market share to support the traditional model, or they can accept the disruption and serve the revolution that's already happening. Faber later announced that the global organization had set a goal to achieve certification by 2030.

Certification for such a huge multinational, a Fortune 500 company with more than $30 billion in revenues and scores of distinct business units, will be an unprecedented challenge. Danone NA had faced a daunting process itself. While a typical BIA consists of roughly 250 questions, Danone NA had to answer over 1,500 for its five stand-alone business units, which are separate legal subsidiaries within the Danone NA legal structure. The path to certification for Danone's global organization will be many times harder.

Danone's efforts have prompted significant questions for B Lab. How can the system that B Lab set up to certify mostly smaller and medium-size organizations be improved and refined to enable larger organizations to join the B Corp movement? How can the lessons from Danone NA's experience be best applied? The logistical process of assessing a large company is one of the biggest obstacles to the widespread growth of the B Corp movement. As Danone's experience shows, it takes a significant amount of time and effort for a complex multinational to be certified, though perhaps not as much time as one may think when the company has the drive that Danone does. We are potentially at the tipping point of this movement, and it is crucial that multinational companies and public market investors are brought on board. For that to happen, changes must be made to the BIA assessment process to accommodate their breadth and scale—while at the same ensuring that standards are not diluted.

A related obstacle that larger companies and B Lab will have to overcome is the effects on the smaller companies in the B Lab universe. Those larger companies are already swallowing them whole. When B Lab certifies a local bookstore that provides for its community, the

B helps it thrive . . . until B Lab also certifies Amazon. Many B Lab proponents also worry about the broader effects on B Lab's integrity. Would B Lab successfully change Walmart, for example, or would Walmart change the B Corp movement?

Consumers are justifiably wary of large corporations. Their intentions are often questioned, and their errors in judgment quickly go viral. Their social or environmental initiatives are often met with raised eyebrows and disbelief, and rightly so. But if the global economy is to be revolutionized, if shareholder primacy is to be overthrown, if B Lab is to achieve its overall mission—that "one day, all companies compete to be the best for the world"—it must recruit large, public, multinational companies. The B Corp movement can't just be about small, "cute" social businesses.

The question then becomes how can the B Lab team devise a system that works for large companies, stands up to public scrutiny, maintains the team's standards, and strikes an acceptable balance between the large scale of these companies and the values that make the movement work? B Lab's Multinationals and Public Markets Advisory Committee (MPMAC) is working closely with a number of multinationals, including Danone, Unilever, and Natura, to do just that. Big need not be bad: B Corp certification may be possible for some of the biggest companies in world.

Danone as the Vanguard

Emmanuel Faber and Danone's interest in alternative corporate governance models is long-standing. In 2006, the company partnered with the microfinance pioneer Grameen Bank to create Grameen Danone Foods, a social business focused on providing daily nutrition to the poor in Bangladesh that became B Corp certified in 2018. The company followed the progress of the community interest corporation in the United Kingdom and low-profit limited liability companies in the United States. Marcello Palazzi, cofounder of B Lab Europe, recalls receiving an email from Faber in 2015: "He said, 'hey, what is this B Corp idea? I'm very interested in what I've been seeing and reading. It's amazing. Let's meet.' I went to Paris a few days later, and we spent the whole afternoon together." Palazzi remembers that Faber told him, "We have been looking for our tribe." Danone has always believed that "big companies can drive big changes. . . . With our scale, we have the power to join forces with other B Corps and to inspire non-B Corps and our large network of suppliers and partners to join the collective mission to use business as a force for good."[2]

In December 2015, Danone signed an agreement with B Lab that required two major commitments. First, Danone would pilot the BIA tool with some of its subsidiaries, including its North American one. Second, it would help B Lab adapt the BIA to large companies, test it on itself when it became available, and help introduce it to others. This partnership, which led to the certification of Danone NA and the goal of certification for the global Danone organization, was crucial to the progress of B Lab Europe and is now a key stepping-stone for the B Corp movement at large.

The biggest challenge Danone NA faced during its certification stemmed from the sheer number of people working on the process. Creating a clearly outlined process for 150 people to follow was not easy. Even something as mundane as log-in accounts had to be rethought: a limited number of log-in accounts could be used for the assessment, and there were far more people actually working on it. This limited Danone NA's ability to track who was inputting what information. Houlahan notes that B Lab was a pretty decentralized organization at the time, and "without a single point of contact, we were difficult to work with. We were structured without the ability to deal with the demand of an organization of that scale," he admits, "but we've changed." Today, B Lab appoints an account manager who not only brings a new company in but manages its engagement with the process.

Part of certification includes a disclosure questionnaire that has no impact on the score but considers possible negatives that may outweigh the positives assessed by the BIA—sensitive practices, fines, sanctions on the company or its partnerships, and so on. B Lab usually administers the disclosure questionnaire at the very end of the process, after the company has scored 80 on the BIA. But, as Houlahan says, "It's a pretty massive list for a company of [Danone's] scale and leaving it for the back end created enormous anxiety for everybody. So we decided to pull that forward to the front end of the process." B Lab also discovered that it needed to determine the scope of the assessment with large multinationals up front—how many assessments they had to complete, when the legal portion needed to be completed, and so on. As Houlahan explains, all of these aspects came together as one big lesson for B Lab: "What it meant was that we're bringing forward a pre-scoping process. We're bringing forward the disclosure questionnaire and background check so that we can at least mitigate and control what we can control in terms of that uncertainty."

For Danone NA, the specifics were grueling, and the nine-month process was intense. The B Lab team began by figuring out which entities would be in the scope of Danone's certification and what the best approach would be for each of them. For some companies, the various entities and subsidiaries could be consolidated and reported together. Christina Forwood of B Lab explains that this broke down into the following types of questions: "Do they have the same board, or do the subsidiaries have their own board of directors? We look at their management, their policies, whether they're set by the same management teams or they have different management teams and therefore different policies. Their geography is also taken into account. And finally, we look at their industry, because the impact assessment has a few industry agendas that need to be assessed separately." Subsidiaries vary more frequently on their legal than their operational structures, so often this process involves just trying to aggregate operational entities under one assessment.

In total, Danone NA had to complete BIAs for its core Danone dairy business, Earthbound Farm, Alpro (the European business), and two smaller entities. The B Lab team set up regularly scheduled touch points and a detailed project management structure to offer as much support as possible—which it continues to improve as it does more work with large multinationals.

Developing Pathways for Large Companies

As larger companies began to express interest in becoming B Corps, B Lab worked to develop new pathways toward certification based on their size and complexity. In April 2019, the MPMAC unveiled its new assessment and verification process for companies with over $5 billion in revenue. The geographic location or complexity of the company does not play a role—the MPMAC structured the additional requirements and assessments around the scale of the company and nothing else.[3]

The MPMAC team started with questions about the rigor and breadth of the standards for a large multinational, considering if the traditional B Corp legal requirement should still be included. The team members quickly aligned on the idea that the standards needed to be even more rigorous to match the scope of large companies' impacts on society and the environment. And they also doubled down on the fact that public companies must meet the legal requirements in the same way that other B Corps have, recognizing that public market firms have the most pressure around short-term earnings.

An important new step for large companies is an additional prescreening process verifying that the company has met some baseline requirements. For instance, the company must provide a materiality assessment and develop an associated stakeholder engagement process that is transparent and conducted at least every other year. Next, companies must provide management strategies that include specific performance goals—goals that have been assessed by their boards of directors and made available to all of their stakeholders. A disclosure statement on the company's approach to government affairs and tax philosophy must be prepared by the board of directors as well as a human rights policy that either commits the company to certain human rights agreements or identifies issues that are relevant to the business. Finally, companies must prepare annual impact reports using third-party standards that are made available to the public.

In the scoping process, B Lab also requires an overview of the company's structure and management, which helps establish the number of BIAs that must be completed for full certification. Kara Peck, B Lab's director of business development, shared with me that this is sometimes easier said than done. "In many cases it's a lot more complicated than just saying, 'Well, here's one chunk of business, we can draw a circle around it, we know exactly what it's doing.' For instance, the company may have a brand that is operating in the U.S., but their international operations are integrated into the parent company. So the same brand, but different employees, different manufacturing facilities, and different practices. The reality is that ways large companies work make it a challenge to divide them into neat parts." The importance of this scoping, which ensures that every aspect of the company is acting in the spirit of the B Corp community and that the company's BIA score reflects all of its various business units, cannot be overstated.

The next step—assessment and verification—is the most grueling. This is when the company completes its multiple B Impact Assessments, working toward a minimum score of 80. Large companies must complete a "Global Headquarters" version of the BIA, which focuses on best practices in governance, before they complete the BIAs for each of their various subsidiaries and operations. The scores are then aggregated to calculate a final, overall BIA score.

The certification progress is significantly more difficult and rigorous for big companies, but it ensures that they are assessed in detail. At least 95 percent of their overall operations must pass the BIA for the company to become certified. If the overall company achieves at least an 80 but for some reason a subsidiary does not, then the company becomes certified but the subsidiary is limited with regard to B logo branding and marketing. These subsidiaries must improve their individual scores or the whole certification will be at risk. After achieving a score of 80, companies have two years to amend their corporate governance to legally require the consideration of all stakeholders or else they will lose their certification.

Certifying subsidiaries is the main way larger companies have been so far engaging with the B Corp movement. B Lab's website lists numerous examples of large companies with certified B Corp subsidiaries, covering a variety of industries. Many of their names are familiar: Unilever (Ben & Jerry's, Seventh Generation), Danone (Happy Family, Danone NA), and Procter & Gamble (New Chapter). The MPMAC has recommended that B Lab should "create separate 'global' and 'subsidiary' versions of the B Impact Assessment that can be distributed and combined, allowing the entire organization to be assessed comprehensively and efficiently."[4]

Danone was the first "house of brands" that B Lab certified, and although the company wanted to use the B Lab logo on all of its products, the B Lab team realized the necessity to differentiate where and how it could be used. To do that, B Lab established a minimum performance requirement for each brand: each must score an 80 or higher on the BIA to use the B Corp logo. As Houlahan explains, "Imagine if Danone had a wonderful yogurt business and, on the side, they had a coal business. They had this great Danone coal business and they wanted to stamp the B on the side of every lump of coal. I think we would all be concerned about the message that would send." For instance, International Delight, Danone's coffee creamer brand, could not use the certified B Corporation logo until late 2018, after it had achieved non-GMO verification and pushed its BIA score above 80.

Laureate Education: The First Publicly Traded Benefit Corporation

Laureate Education was established in 1999 with the goal of providing quality higher education that is accessible and affordable to underserved populations. By 2018, more than a million students were enrolled at its eighty-eight institutions in twenty-eight countries. Many of those institutions are in emerging markets, and account for 80 percent of corporate revenue. Recently, Laureate announced that in the future it will be narrowing its geographic focus mostly to Chile, Peru, Mexico, and Brazil, although it will still have operations in Australia and New Zealand.[5] Smaller institutions will likely be leaving the network, and Laureate hopes this will allow the company to concentrate on areas most in need of help. Adam Morse, Laureate's senior vice president of corporate finance and global treasurer, explains that this is more aligned with the "core mission of Laureate—to provide quality higher education where there is an imbalance between the quality of supply and demand, largely in emerging markets."

Laureate has worked hard to dispel the poor reputation of the for-profit education sector. In 2015, it became a certified B Corp and registered in Delaware as a benefit corporation. By 2017, it had completed an initial public offering, making it the first benefit corporation to go public. In some countries, Laureate actually owns the educational institutions. In others, because of legislation or how the government is set up, Laureate has partnerships with local institutions. While the company needed only the combined and weighted BIA scores across its subsidiaries to be over the 80 points required to achieve certification, it ensured that *all* of their institutions met that benchmark.

The most recent certification, which Laureate Education underwent in 2017, highlighted some key aspects of its business. Almost half of Laureate's students come from underserved groups; all the company's institutions have Corporate Citizenship programs focused on volunteering, community development, pro bono work, and the like; and more than 70 percent of its institutions have environmental management systems. With a new CEO at its helm, Laureate has made a number of changes, but these have not affected its dedication to creating long-lasting impact.

Tackling the Complex Certification Process

At the time of its initial certification, Laureate had over eighty institutions grouped into more than fifty subsidiaries, so its certification process was complex and onerous. Emal Dusst, who at the time was head of strategy and chief of staff under founder Doug Becker, explains that while many people think that certification can occur in the background of a company's regular operations, Laureate essentially "dropped everything to get this done." The process went from top to bottom: Dusst briefed the CEOs in each region, who then worked with the CEOs of each institution. Materials, resources, and guidelines were distributed through this chain of executives. "Then we just made sure that all of them were on biweekly calls with headquarters to keep them on track," Dusst says. Each institution was responsible for collecting all of the relevant data and documentation for its assessment. Todd Wegner, at the time senior manager of global public affairs and B Corp program manager, worked on the corporate assessment and helped coordinate the institutional assessments, and

B Lab chose five institutions to audit with on-site visits. As Wegner notes, "It was very rigorous."

In some cases, institutions faced difficulties because the BIA asked for things that hadn't been tracked. "Going forward, we now have a [tracking] system in place," Dusst says. Some of the situations they had to deal with were counterintuitive. For example, Dusst expected a newer institution in a brand-new building to be rewarded for being "green," but instead it lost points because the BIA has a bias toward using existing buildings. Part of the learning curve, as this example points out, was understanding how the standards were set up.

Morse points out, "The advantage we had was that a lot of the things we were asked about through the certification process were things we were already doing. The B Corp mindset was already well ingrained in our organization. Maybe we had to change the way we managed and tracked them, but we weren't starting from zero." Wegner reflects on what they learned throughout the certification process: "We really spent a lot of time dissecting all the data and understanding where we could improve on the assessment in a way that was authentic and made sense for our business while also positively impacting our stakeholders."

One of the changes Laureate made after certification was to its global code of ethics, borrowing language from the BIA to solidify and strengthen it. A big takeaway for Laureate was that key focus areas on the assessment may be different depending on what country an institution is based in, but what remained consistent was its focus on the quality of education provided to its students. Therefore, it's more effective to implement improvements important to particular institutions rather than just enacting blanket policy changes. As Wegner points out, "It's important for a global company to create policies that are flexible enough to be applicable in all countries, but also specific enough to meet some of the criteria in the assessment."

Before the BIA, Laureate had never had a centralized data set that allowed its leaders to visualize their constituents on a global scale. Having one has changed their business in many ways—they now understand their clientele better and can strongly state, "We're doing this, and this is who we're trying to reach." On the environmental side of things, Laureate has become much more aware of what components need to be taken into account during construction, for example. The effects of becoming certified and being on board with the B Corp movement have been huge. The company is more in tune with its actions, its externalities, and its impact. Certification has also made a difference in the lives of the millions of people—students, staff, faculty, employees—who are members of the Laureate community.

Bringing Investors on Board

Laureate was able to get its board of directors and mainstream private equity investors like KKR on board prior to its IPO. But its leaders worried that other mainstream investors would hesitate to take part in the stock offering. Morse recalls company leaders asking, "How do you articulate to investors, when they have a natural bias against for-profit education, that for-profit education is good, it's needed, and it's doing really good things for the world?" The B Corp movement provided the answer. Laureate could point to a host of highly successful and profitable companies that were already on board.

When company executives were conducting a road show to introduce investors to the company, Becker recalls that investors would ask, " 'What is a public benefit corp? What does that mean?' The initial perception most people had is, 'Wow, this must be a tax planning strategy.' " But then Laureate would dedicate five minutes of its presentation to explaining the B Corp movement, reminding investors that Laureate's slogan is "Here for Good," which carries a double meaning: Laureate is a company doing good work for the benefit of society, and it is a company that plans to stick around.

The presenters emphasized the importance of long-term planning and long-term returns rather than the traditional short-term returns achieved through shareholder primacy. Morse reflects, "Our 'Here for Good' philosophy is one of both purpose and permanence. We realize that decisions can't be made with just a short-term focus on the next quarter, especially if that is to the detriment of what happens two years from now." Esther Benjamin, former chief benefit officer and senior vice president of global public affairs for Laureate International Universities, emphasized the investment Laureate made in this effort to bring investors on board; she told Coen Gilbert that the process of raising investor awareness about benefit corporations and certification took almost two years.[6]

In the letter to potential investors that was included in the company's SEC security registration document (also known as an S-1), Becker wrote, "Balancing the needs of our constituents has been instrumental to our success and longevity, allowing us to grow even in challenging economic times. For a long time, we didn't have an easy way to explain the idea of a for-profit company with such a deep commitment to benefitting society." This is why the B Corp movement caught his attention, he explained. "We watched this concept carefully as it swept the nation, . . . this new class of corporation, which commits itself to high standards of corporate purpose, accountability, and transparency."[7] Before the IPO, Laureate decided to reincorporate in Delaware, which had the most up-to-date benefit corporation law on the books.

In October 2015, Laureate became the first benefit corporation to file an S-1 with the SEC. Morse recalls that one of the most common questions he received was, "Does this mean that if something is beneficial to shareholders, you're not going to do it?" He explains it like this: "It means that we just need to take into consideration that stated public purpose or benefit of the company when making decisions." A prime example of this would be with a capital investment project. Morse explains, "As part of that proposal, where someone says, 'I want to spend money on a new campus,' or 'I want to do this type of investment in this type of project,' the investment proposal that gets reviewed has to incorporate a report which measures how this project aligns with our B Corp checklist that we've internally developed." Rather than focus on just one thing when making decisions, he tells investors, the company needs to focus on different components and make a more complex and more beneficial decision. In the end, Laureate didn't encounter too much pushback from investors, who were already aware of the company's commitment to a strong social mission and core values.

Seeking Continual Improvement at Natura and Danone

In December 2014, Natura, Brazil's top cosmetic and personal hygiene products manufacturer, announced that it had committed to adopt new sustainability guidelines by 2020. This spurred the company's pursuit of B Corp certification, which it achieved later that year, becoming the first B Corporation traded on a major national public stock exchange (São Paulo), as well as the largest certified B Corp at the time.[8] With nearly seven thousand employees and operations across Europe and Latin America (including the UK-based natural cosmetics pioneer the Body Shop, which it acquired), Natura generated more than $3 billion in net sales as of 2019. Natura has also won B Lab's Best for Environment award in 2015, 2016, and 2017. In May 2019, Natura announced that it had agreed to buy Avon for $2 billion, making it the world's fourth-largest beauty company. This is significant because it was the first time that the directors of a publicly traded

American company voted to adopt a corporate structure focused on all stakeholders.[9]

Like Avon, Natura has a direct sales model; its network of 1.6 million people, mostly women, sell the company's products in several countries. Natura also supports thirty-one hundred family-run businesses by using them as suppliers. Its salespeople are trained extensively, and about three-quarters of them participate in the company's profit-sharing plan.[10] Natura's core mission is to build a better world through its "commitment to transparency, sustainability, and well-being." True to its tagline "Well Being Well," Natura's sustainability initiatives include its efforts to preserve the Amazon region by establishing new demand for ingredients from its forests, such as newly discovered oils and fruits that can be incorporated into the company's manufacturing processes.[11]

In 2013, Natura became one of the first companies in the world to publish an integrated annual report that offered insight into the company's performance and strategy across not just financial but also social and environmental metrics, covering financial capital, manufactured capital, human capital, social capital, natural capital, and intellectual capital. This allows the company to better define its values while surfacing any improvements that need to be made.[12]

This is also the case with Danone NA. After the BIA set a baseline, firm leaders committed to continually improve, internally and externally, to prepare for the next assessment. Deb Eschmeyer, who joined Danone NA in May 2017 as vice president of communications and community affairs after serving as executive director of Michelle Obama's Let's Move campaign and as a senior advisor for nutrition policy in the White House, recalls the day the company achieved certification: "We gave ourselves, like, two hours to celebrate. And then we were like, 'Okay, we just got this great score of 85, but we know we can do better—what does that look like?' "

Deanna Bratter, Danone North America's senior director of public benefit and sustainable development, points out that as a first step the company mapped progress on the BIA by a color-coded system. "Green was where we thought we were strong and we had information to back it up; yellow was, we think we have information, we think we're okay; red is an area where we don't have information or we think we have a potential weakness; and black is to signify the things where we know the data doesn't exist, and that we couldn't answer on our first go." Danone's next step was examining the yellow category, "where we know we've got some work going, but we might not necessarily have the system or data to track and prove it." This is the major focus of the company's improvement strategy and its road map moving forward. However, she emphasizes, the focus will always be on "living the ideals of a B Corp" rather than the BIA score per se.

While 2030 is Danone's target for the certification of its global operation, the B Corp community director at Danone, Blandine Stefani, explains that the company has "actually received a very large number of requests from different Danone businesses to go through the B Corp certification process." Danone leaders are currently working with B Lab to determine if all areas of the Danone global family are qualified for certification; once that's established, they have to create a system to handle the "global" aspect, including the global brand, global procurement, and international operations. Danone also plans to test the new version of the BIA built for multinationals. Over time, as the BIA is integrated into Danone's internal reporting system, this will become easier.

Building a Movement That Welcomes Large Public Companies

B Lab is moving through the early stages of raising awareness among large corporations quickly and efficiently. Since Danone NA certified in 2018, at least seven other multinationals have reached out to Danone to ask about the process. Bratter reflects, "With size comes an opportunity to really be part of a tipping point where large corporations and large multinationals are operating with public benefit, with society, environment, and human rights top of mind. That's when we'll really start to change the system as a whole, creating the long-term value, and start eliminating some of the short-term risk."

The B Lab team has also been asking deeper questions on what it means for a large multinational company to not just adopt CSR practices and talk about corporate purpose, but to truly align the company around these ideals. Interested companies tell them, "Our vision says that we should be the kind of company that creates value for stakeholders, for our employees, and for our communities. We know that's where we need to go, but we need help in figuring out how to get there." Kara Peck told me that B Lab's response used to be, "This is not our job. Our job is to certify you when you get here. The BIA is your tool to learn about the standards and to adopt best practices."

B Lab now understands that there are three key barriers that stand in the way of large companies certifying. One is the need for a road map. Where do they start? How can they begin to move in the direction of being more like a B Corp? Simply using the BIA, or even the MPMAC process, isn't practical for this work. Companies need a framework. The second barrier, which is related to the first, is the need to connect with peers. Multinationals are constantly asking, "Who else is doing this? Can you connect us?" The third, which is definitely the most challenging and probably the most important, is the hurdle of getting shareholders on board and pursuing the idea of actually making the legal transition to a benefit corporation.

To address these issues, B Lab had to revisit its core principles and ask, "What is the B Corp movement?" It has always been inclusive of B Corporations, of course, but thinking more deeply about the goal of overthrowing shareholder primacy, B Lab's leaders came to realize they should create a broader community. As a result, they came up with its B Movement Builders program, which articulates six principles. If a big company commits to adopting them and takes tangible steps to demonstrate that it is doing so in a way that's rigorous and meets the spirit of the B Corp community, then it's helping to build the B Corp movement.

B Lab anticipates enrolling about ten companies in the program during its first years. The six principles are going to sound familiar. First, of course, the companies must make a strong commitment to the movement by signing the Declaration of Interdependence. The next revolves around assessment and verification. B Movement Builders must immediately begin assessing parts of their businesses, identifying key areas where improvement is needed, and then acting on that information. This can occur over time—at first assessing a single business unit, for example, and increasing the scope of the assessments every year. Improvement is a key part of being a member of the B Corp community, and it's no different for Movement Builders. The third principle is to work on goals that address the UN's SDGs.

The next two principles address the importance of impact and transparency. Movement Builders commit to working with their peers and the larger B Corp community to create widespread impact. Transparency is a foundational aspect of B Lab's work and of the B Corp movement, so all B Movement Builders must publicly share their annual impact reports.

The last principle—and for some the most important—is that of stakeholder governance. Movement Builders are asked to sign and release a public letter that demands the necessary changes in corporate leadership, capital markets, and policy to create governance structures that will lead to an economy that focuses on all stakeholders, rather than just shareholders.

Why should a company that isn't ready to take the leap and become a B Corps join the B Movement Builders? In many ways, the framework of this book—the various points I've highlighted and outlined—provides all the reasons. A company may be interested in increasing employee engagement and retention, attracting positive press attention, and, of course, building trust and brand value with the general public. B Corps reap all those benefits. So will Movement Builders. Many companies are interested in aligning their investors with long-term values and overcoming short-termism in the capital markets. The B Movement Builder program will allow them to do just that.

Lorna Davis, senior advisor to Danone's CEO, has become a global ambassador for B Lab. She shared with me her belief that in twenty years, people will look at non–B Corps and say, "Well, that's kind of ridiculous that you're not certified because that's how you run a business, for goodness' sake!" In a broad sense, *this* is the reason why companies should, and will, join the B Movement Builders program. In her capacity as global ambassador, Davis is leading the charge to expand the movement. She described her outreach efforts to me. "I say at the beginning that the reason we chose this particular certification is because it has three elements that are critical. It has a legal framework, and the transformation of the legal system is really important, and big corporations need to play a role in that. Secondly, the certification is hard, it's competitive, but there's a real benefit, from a strategic point of view and also from an achievement point of view. And thirdly, because it's a movement, it's very young, it's kind of hip." However, she is quick to add, "I think there's going to be an elite small group of early movers that are brave enough. Over time, a bunch of other people will come along." Many of these early movers have emerged already—Danone and Unilever being prime examples—and now, with the B Movement Builders program, many more will join in.

11

Convincing Consumers to Care

As the B Corp movement has grown, a large-scale challenge has persisted, especially for consumer products companies: consumers don't know about B Lab or B Corporations. In 2017, an internal study by B Lab pegged general consumer awareness at just 7 percent in the United States. Some might say that given the fact that B Lab had never done any consumer-facing marketing of the B Corp brand and does not require B Corps to use the logo, 7 percent awareness is actually a surprisingly good baseline. Nevertheless, the average consumer is unaware of B Corporations, what they stand for, and what the movement is accomplishing. While many may be buying their products, they don't know about the certification that links them together. Propelling the movement forward requires consumers to understand that their choices can provide support for the development of a new model of sustainable capitalism that creates higher-quality jobs, improves the quality of life, and preserves our natural environment. Absent this brand awareness, many of the leaders of B Corps whom I interviewed expressed their fear that the movement will eventually stall.

The issue has in fact been a long-standing concern. In 2010, Coen Gilbert told me that when he tries to convince companies to be part of the movement, most ask about brand equity. In those early days of the movement, B Lab could not promise that becoming a B Corp or a benefit corporation would translate into improved sales. But B Lab's founders had reason to hope. In their initial market research, they discovered that over "95 percent of people had a positive reaction to the B Corp concept and about two-thirds said they would look for B Corp products the next time they shopped."

There are key challenges to convincing consumers to care, but this is essential to achieve the movement's objective, and B Lab is currently working to turn a corner on this issue. Millennials and the generation that follows them are highly engaged consumers who care about equity and sustainability. As they come into positions of greater responsibility and their purchasing power increases, they will have a large effect. But the movement won't tip until all consumers know about it.

Part of the reason for B Corp's poor brand awareness is the inaction of some of the movement's actors, and part of it is because it is difficult to properly express the complexity of the B brand.

Challenges with Consumer Awareness

Many companies that I interviewed told me there are inherent challenges in creating awareness of the B logo. While companies can increase their market value by clearly identifying with specific causes that their consumers care about, B Corp certification encompasses a wide array of social and environmental measurements, so it is harder for consumers to see the relevance. For example, outdoor company Patagonia's focus is on the environment, and that is made apparent to its customers in every aspect of its branding and marketing. Step into a Patagonia store and you are confronted with beautiful photos of mountain landscapes. For a long time, Patagonia's catalogues featured more photos of the outdoors than of its products. But the B Corp movement is more holistic: its logo doesn't tell the customer whether a company is particularly strong on environmental issues, governance, employee programs, or something else. Paula Marshall, CEO of BAMA Companies, believes there needs to be a clearer explanation of where the movement fits: "The confusion is, well, where do I put this in? Do I call this sustainability or B Corp sustainability? Or do I change the whole name of what I'm doing from corporate sustainability to something else?"

Companies I talked to also believe there is a challenge in helping customers distinguish between a benefit corporation and a certified B Corp. Both share similar accountability and transparency requirements—as well as similar names, which is where much of the confusion might emerge. But benefit corporations and B Corps differ drastically in terms of how they demonstrate their performance. The former self-report their progress; the latter must earn a minimum verified score on the BIA, and their progress is tracked. They differ in availability (benefit corporations exist in thirty-five U.S. states and Italy, Colombia, Ecuador, and British Columbia; B Corps are all over the world) and cost (a B Corp certification can cost significantly more than becoming a benefit corporation). Regarding this potential confusion, a B Lab staff member I talked to likened this situation to the case of organic products: "There's tons of different versions of organic. We're hopefully showing the market that the premier version is the certified B Corp." It's difficult to substantiate how much this confusion plays into consumer awareness. However, it threatens to become even more prevalent as consumer awareness grows.

To add to the challenge, the whole idea of for-profit social mission companies is relatively new. A 2017 study in the *Journal of Consumer Research* found that only a quarter of consumers were aware of the existence of for-profit social ventures (FPSV).[1] It also found that the discovery of companies' profit orientation depressed consumer support, meaning that FPSVs need to clearly disclose their for-profit orientation up front or risk consumer backlash. B Corporations and other mission-driven businesses are emerging from an environment that has been rife with empty corporate social responsibility initiatives and greenwashed sustainability goals, so consumers are understandably wary of "faux-responsible" businesses. But on the flip side, the systemic problems laid bare by the coronavirus, growing income inequality, and environmental concerns all suggest the time is ripe for these types of businesses.

All of these challenges point to huge opportunities. "Greenwashing" and empty corporate promises have become a major concern for consumers. Every day, it seems, a major corporation is exposed for telling lies. Consumers are wary of corporate claims about sustainability and equity. The B Corp movement, in particular its certification process, directly addresses this. The B Impact Assessment is rigorous and all-encompassing—once consumers recognize its strength in assessing a company's impact, they can begin to trust the company. A recent study revealed some promising findings on this point. Experimenters showed participants pictures of Ben & Jerry's ice cream tubs with and without the B Corp logo. Importantly, the pictures included not just the logo but also an explanation of what it means. Under these conditions, there was a positive effect of the certification on consumers' purchase intentions, willingness to pay a premium price, and trust of the brand.[2]

We know that consumers want to shop in responsible and conscious ways and are willing to pay more to do so. The B logo represents what conscious consumers are looking for—they just need to know about it and what it means.

Why Consumers Should Care

An article in *Inc.* magazine titled "Market Like Patagonia, Warby Parker, and Tom's Shoes—Your Social Values Can Be a Boon to Your Brand—and Your Revenue" encourages companies to market their missions and values ahead of everything else. It highlights Patagonia's focus on ecological commitments which, in 2010, the company wrote into its vendor standards. By 2011, its revenues increased by 30 percent and it had to open a dozen new stores to meet demand.[3]

This story suggests that there is much that B Lab can build on to increase consumer awareness. In 2016, marketing leaders from a number of B Corps, including Cabot Creamery, A to Z Wines, and Plum Organics, formed a committee to understand how they can improve consumer awareness of the B brand. One of the conclusions was that it was important that consumers recognize that the B represents more than sustainability and the environment; it encompasses many other things that are important to the average American consumer, including fair wages, access to jobs, and diversity. It represents benefits, community and personal development, and safe workplaces, not to mention good working conditions and improved quality of life. As Cabot's Amy Levine puts it, "There's a much bigger, wider, long-term play here to get a much broader swath of citizens connecting with B Corp." She says Cabot Creamery wants to push its consumers to ask themselves, "Do you want to align your vote—whether that's a dollar vote or the businesses you'd work with or where you have a job—with companies that follow these values?" The push for consumer awareness must be grounded in what people care about.

Many trends suggest that consumers are headed in the right direction; conscious consumerism is on an upswing. A 2017 survey released by Good.Must.Grow found that 61 percent of Americans surveyed said that they believe that buying products from socially responsible companies is important. However, 40 percent of respondents also said that they don't know where to find these products or how to identify if a company is socially responsible.[4]

Convincing consumers to care is closely related to the UN's Sustainable Development Goal 12, which focuses on ensuring sustainable consumption and production patterns.[5] As this goal highlights, we must reframe our consumption and production patterns because, as it stands today, our planet will be unable to sustain us by 2050. If the Earth's population grows as projected and we stick to the same patterns of production and consumption, the resources of four Earths will be needed to sustain the human race.[6] Beyond what is right and what is good, it is a matter of existential importance that we change.

Demographics play a big role in trends that suggest a growing awareness in the future. For instance, 73 percent of millennials across the globe are willing to pay extra for products they believe are sustainable and that come from businesses that are focused on doing good. Driven by a desire to create an impact in the world, they are actively looking for the right products that will allow them to do so. Millennials are the largest retail demographic and have $200 billion in annual buying power. Respondents under twenty years of age are equally interested in sustainability.[7] A 2010 study of millennials' purchasing decisions investigated the difference between them and Generation X in making ethical decisions and found that millennials give higher priority and attention to corporate conduct and mission.[8] Millennials are an important force propelling the B Corp movement, and they are also driving the movement toward responsible business as a whole.

A 2015 study also found that millennials have a strong intention to purchase products associated with eco-friendliness and positive health effects. Grace Farraj, senior vice president of public development and sustainability at Nielsen, predicts, "Brands that establish a reputation for social responsibility and environmental stewardship among today's youngest consumers have an opportunity to not only grow market share but build loyalty among the power-spending Millennials of tomorrow, too."[9]

Millennials are also encouraging companies to work toward increased awareness and internal improvement in different ways. Younger generations embrace competitiveness within the B Corp community, and this encourages everyone to be more proactive.

Many young employees are learning about the movement and encouraging their companies to pursue certification.

Every year since 2010, I have taught my students about B Corporations and have sponsored events on campus to host the B Lab founders and have them discuss their work. When I invited the B Lab trio to the first such event in 2010, only a handful of students attended, but since 2016, these events have been standing room only.

My experience isn't isolated. John Pepper, founder of Boloco, noticed a shift in awareness as well when he recently interacted with millennials on a college campus. During a lecture at Emerson University in Boston, he mentioned B Corps during his presentation, expecting no one to know what they were. A student jumped in with "Wait! Boloco is a B Corp?" That student, along with a couple of others in the classroom, began to describe the movement for their peers' benefit and, as Pepper put it, "all of a sudden, there's a spark." In that classroom, on that day, students swore off Boloco's competition.

Micha Mador, engagement manager at the Foundry Group in Boulder, says that when Foundry was undergoing certification, a University of Colorado MBA student reached out to the firm after hearing about the movement, learned about the BIA, and then helped the company achieve certification. Every year, the City of Boulder has a "Start Up Week." Mador recalls that in 2016, the B Corp session attracted about 50 people. Two years later, 250 people crowded into the panel on B Corps. The spike in interest and awareness over such a short period of time is simply astounding. It certainly proves that the world is hungry for change and improvement.

Shifts in the Great Logo Debate

It's a catch-22: consumer awareness can't grow without more B logos on product packaging, but many B Corps are reluctant to devote space on their product labels to the logo because they believe consumers won't know what it signifies. Real estate on packaging is extremely valuable, and many companies feel that there isn't room to include both the B Corp logo and the needed explanation of what it stands for. Most B Corps create products that are certified in other ways—as Fair Trade, organic, or energy efficient, for example—and each certification has its own logo. As Kyle Garner, the CEO of Organic India, maker of Tulsi tea and organic herbal supplements, put it: "We've got organic, we've got non-GMO; everyone knows what those are." Rebecca Magee at EILEEN FISHER explains that there are several types of certifications that her company is trying to communicate to consumers in its stores. Adding the B Corp certification story to the mix would result in "a sensory overload situation," she says.

Early in the movement, companies placed the B Corp logo on their products as an act of leadership in the sector. King Arthur Flour placed the logo on its packaging as soon as the company was certified in 2006. As co-CEO Ralph Carlton told me when I asked him why the logo and B Lab introduction occupied an entire side panel of the companies' flour sacks, "It's there because it's the right thing to do." Cabot Creamery also put the logo on its packaging "as a sign of good faith," explains Amy Levine. Similarly, Mascoma Bank displays the B logo across much of its marketing material. As its CEO Clayton Adams told me, "There's low awareness and we have to help build it. All B Corps have an obligation to do that."

Some of the largest recently certified companies such as Athleta, an athletic wear brand owned by Gap, and Danone NA have taken a number of important steps to let their customers know about their B Corp certification. At Athleta, the leadership team debated whether to advertise its certification status to its employees or to its customers, and "we decided to go forward with both," says Emily Allbritten, Athleta's manager of strategic initiatives, adding, "It's really paid off more than we expected." Athleta displays the logo prominently on its storefronts and has posters explaining the B Corp movement in its stores. The Athleta team even went as far as putting the logo on product hangtags.

Danone has also accepted a big role in increasing consumer awareness—as its products become certified, it adds the B Corp logo to their packaging. As Deanna Bratter points out, the company's reach will be massive: "There are 900 million consumers of Danone products; that's a lot of people." As of late 2018, the B Corp logo was displayed on Vega, Silk, and So Delicious products, and Danone NA is looking to add it to other products through 2019. Deb Eschmeyer reflected, "You want to make sure that a consumer has not only awareness, but a full understanding and education of what . . . [the B logo] means. This is where there's a lot of opportunity for us at Danone North America. That's where we're taking this on as a really great opportunity to bring greater awareness to B Corps."[10]

This large public commitment from more recently certified B Corps is surely turning the tide. Andrew Fyfe, who works on business development at B Lab, says: "With more committed large-scale companies, the better the benefit will be to smaller companies, either for business development opportunities or being able to kind of ride the coattails of that brand awareness." Organic India's Kyle Garner says that his company has reversed course on its decision not to feature the logo. When I met him in the summer of 2018, he said, "Now that the B Corps are up to about twenty-five hundred worldwide, it seems to be catching on more. I'm more confident that it'll keep going in that direction." As of September 2018, Organic India had put the B Corp logo on the back of all its packaging and found room for it on the front of the packaging for three products. Ashley Orgain, director of mission advocacy and outreach for Seventh Generation, also sees a shift: "I think consumers are demanding more from companies, whether it's transparency or actual ingredients and materials for the packaging." As a result, Seventh Generation is "feeling that we're needing to disrupt in entirely new ways because . . . our approach is becoming mainstream."

New Belgium Brewing also recently added the B logo to its products. It can be found on Fat Tire beer bottles and on the exterior packaging for other products. The team at New Belgium has also begun organizing in-store marketing promotions that highlight other B Corps. For example, if you buy multiple B Corp products, you get a discount.

But there are still some important companies that haven't come aboard. Early and well-known B Corps like Ben & Jerry's and Patagonia continue to shy away from including the B logo on their packaging. Ben & Jerry's Rob Michalak says that the company looks for other ways to get the B in front of consumers, such as its website, social media, and advertising. Patagonia often highlights its various environmentally focused certifications in its marketing, yet the B Corp logo has yet to make its way into its messaging. In an encouraging sign, Ben & Jerry's did recently add the logo to the side of a recently launched novelty product called Slices. Michalak explains, "We've started to tiptoe into using the B and we're realizing that's something maybe we can dial up a little bit more because that's how people become aware of the movement."

While we may not have reached the tipping point on these issues yet, perhaps we are getting close to the edge that will propel the movement into the next phase. Consistent with the findings of the study mentioned above—that when the B logo was presented with an explanation, purchase intention increased—we are at a point where consumers are beginning to understand the importance of the logo. But for the movement to continue to grow, there is a distinct need for leading B Corps such as Patagonia, Ben & Jerry's, and others to catch up to newer B Corps like Athleta and Danone and begin using their widespread influence to help build consumer awareness. As early movers, they may be stuck in the mindset that placing the logo on their packages is solely an act of leadership, not realizing that the B Corp brand is clearly beginning to pay dividends.

The Power of Accountability and Authenticity

An important dimension of what B Corp certification brings to a company is credibility. It signifies that the company is the real deal and is not greenwashing. This is clearly one aspect of the value large companies like Athleta and Danone NA see in the logo—it differentiates them from their competitors. Coen Gilbert shared a sentiment he has heard often from B Corps leaders and his fellow B Lab team members: "People are hungry for the tools to make it easier for them to make good decisions. They trust themselves more than anybody else, and if you're giving them a tool to go dive deeper in transparency standards and say, 'Okay, now I know what backs up the claim that this company is better,' that's a huge public service." The B logo helps consumers identify the real deal.

Other forms of certification are growing, underscoring consumers' desire and demand for accountability to standards. Research on Fair Trade certification has found that 75 percent of millennials consider it when purchasing, and they are willing to pay over 20 percent more for products with that certification. Millennials have also said that they look for proof when a company claims a social or environmental mission—they don't just take its word.[11]

Customer Impact: Reputation and Loyalty

Consumer loyalty is another important consideration. When Ben & Jerry's conducted a study to better understand existing consumer resonance and loyalty, it discovered that its customers are two and a half times more loyal to its brand than other ice cream consumers are to different brands. The study revealed that their loyalty is so high because they believe the company stands for something and is authentic about it.

At Preserve, Eric Hudson points out that the B logo leads customers to think, "This is another reason that Preserve is different, that Preserve is in that bucket of companies that are pushing the envelope." Preserve believes that building recognition of the B and what it stands for among its existing customers and, eventually, mass-market consumers is a way to "serve the B Corp movement." Green Mountain Power feels similarly, as Amanda Beraldi explained. "Our customers expect us to be good at all of the things B Lab expects us to be good at. Vermonters, for example, have set a goal to have 90 percent renewable energy by 2050 and GMP aims to exceed those expectations—we have announced we will have a 100 percent carbon-free energy supply by 2025, and be 100 percent renewable by 2030." When B Corps highlight their commitment to the B Corp mission as well as their wider commitments, consumers, especially younger consumers, are more likely to be loyal to their brand.

As Ben & Jerry's learned, a company's social mission and responsible business practices resonate with consumers, leading to increased loyalty. Nielsen released a study in 2015 that examined the effect of a company's commitment to sustainability on its consumers. Brand trust topped the list. Nearly two-thirds of consumers across the globe say that their trust in a brand's name and reputation influences their purchasing choices. Trust and loyalty work hand in hand, and it only makes sense to build that up around the B.[12]

Having a social mission enhances a company's image and reputation, which means customers will refer their friends to the company. The Nielsen study found that 66 percent of respondents said they'd pay more for sustainable goods. A decade ago, sustainable and responsible business choices were largely being made by wealthier people; today, the support for sustainability is consistent across all income levels. In fact, the study found that those earning less money are more willing to pay more for products from companies that have a focus on social and environmental impact.[13]

There's also a strong correlation between social mission, consumer awareness, and firm value. A recent journal article showed that as social and community-based contributions are incorporated into companies' DNA, the purchase intentions of their consumers increase.[14] This suggests that when consumers recognize what the B represents, they will *intentionally* purchase more of the company's products.

Finding and Inspiring Community Jo(e)s

Fair Trade, USDA Organic, Made in USA, and Rainforest Alliance certifications all impact consumer opinions and shopping preferences. But who is influenced by the B? What kinds of shoppers care the most about B Corps' products and can help promote them? Obviously, millennials are key. But B Lab's consumer awareness study suggests that there is an additional group of shoppers, whom they label "Community Jo(e)s," who also may find B Corp messaging appealing.

Community Jo(e)s are people who are naturally involved in social causes. They look for certifications, do research on them, and talk about them, and their grassroots, word-of-mouth recommendations are worth more than you might think in this social media–driven world. Learning about the things these consumers care about and mapping them onto the B Corp marketing strategy could be highly effective.[15] These are typically people who support their local businesses, their communities, and their neighborhoods. They are usually connected and engaged by promotions such as Small Business Saturday. They are individuals who would strongly agree with these statements:

1. I make an effort to shop at the independent local businesses in my community.
2. I go out of my way to shop at businesses that have fair hiring practices and/or pay a living wage.
3. I'm willing to pay more for brands that demonstrate a commitment to sustainability.
4. I buy environmentally friendly brands whenever possible.
5. I am willing to pay more for brands that do good in the world.

Studies have suggested this demographic makes up as much as one-third of all U.S. primary grocery shoppers. They are highly educated, have higher than average incomes, and most of them (two-thirds) are women. They are more likely to have kids in the household than not, and they skew a little toward the millennial generation. Community Jo(e)s are invested in racial equality, access to education, and fair wages. Global warming and clean water initiatives are also incredibly important to them. They are politically active, donate to charity, and participate in fund-raisers. When Community Jo(e)s believe in a product, they advocate strongly for it—41 percent of them will go out of their way to purchase products with certifications, and 44 percent will recommend them.[16]

Finding and reaching out to Community Jo(e)s can help to create a market. Marcello Palazzi explains that "companies create their market; the market is not something that is static. Basically, it's a relationship—it's how you communicate to your customers, potential customers, and how they respond back to you. So companies have a huge power to actually proclaim that they stand for certain values and principles and that they are walking the talk. This results in a different kind of consumer." Palazzi calls it a self-selecting system and sees it as the best way to build consumer awareness of the B Corp movement.

Media Outreach

Recently B Lab has developed a strategy that uses the power of social media to reach all those Community Jo(e)s and increase awareness of its movement. Coen Gilbert explains that it has to be a "constant drumbeat." Marketing on social media must be relentless and consistent to build a brand.

Being at the nexus of so many important trends is helping B Lab garner attention in traditional media as well. The team often gets phone calls asking for comments on a story about, say, green ESOPs, women-run companies that alleviate poverty, or any number of other things that are perfectly reflected in the B Corp community. Business writers are in touch with and writing about the B Lab team and the B Corp movement. The combination, as Houlahan puts it, of "a rich community across lots of different geographies, industries, and impact areas," coupled with the rise of benefit corporations and the fact that B Corps are "willing to be accountable to that new way of doing business," has led to great press.

With Your Purchases, You Vote Every Day

On November 12, 2018, the day after the U.S.'s midterm elections, B Lab launched an important two-year marketing campaign called "Vote Every Day."[17] The goal is to increase engagement with the B Corp brand and encourage participants to "buy from, do business with, and work for" B Corporations—in essence, encouraging people to cast their votes in favor of the B Corp movement. Anthea Kelsick, B Lab's chief marketing officer, says, "The campaign was born out of the insight that our movement aligns with the values of a good chunk of the U.S. population. But, despite that, awareness has been low."[18]

The idea of "voting with your dollars" has been gaining popularity among conscious consumers in recent years. The Vote Every Day initiative educates consumers on how business affects the aspects of the world that they want to change and then encourages them to take part in that endeavor by buying from companies committed to making that change happen.

B Lab built a comprehensive website to go along with the campaign, which invites participants to take part in a simple one-minute quiz. The quiz asks about their daily habits and then sends them an email suggesting how they can cast a vote for change. For example, if someone indicates that he or she starts each day with coffee or tea, the generated response suggests that that individual buy from certified B Corp coffee or tea companies.[19] The idea is to make it easier for consumers to see the connection between their values and their purchases. As Kelsick elaborates, "Where you're buying from, working for or doing business with: Those are all opportunities to make daily choices as a way of voting for your values."[20] Often consumers don't realize how much purchasing power they have. Something as simple as changing the brand of coffee they drink can have a significant impact when considered annually or over a lifetime.

This campaign, of course, also helps encourage and improve consumer awareness. As Kelsick points out, "So many people share our beliefs and values. If they only knew about B Corps and understood that engaging with them was a way to express those values, then we would grow our movement exponentially." She adds, "The journey has just begun. We need many more people who have not yet heard about B Corps to join us. And we intend to keep raising the volume so we can build advocates for our global movement."[21]

The recent experience of B Corps research suggests that the tide is finally turning, and for companies like Ben & Jerry's, including the certification on ice cream tubs will make a difference. In addition to more leading B Corps including the certification on products, now is the time for B Lab to double down on its branding, marketing, and overall awareness work. The only way to increase understanding of what the B represents is to increase awareness and visibility of the B.

Within a few years, the majority of the workforce and the majority of consumers will be members of younger generations, who expect more from the world and from business. As they begin to grasp the idea of externalities and why—if we are to build a more sustainable and resilient economy—we must consider them as interdependencies, they will shift their purchasing power toward companies, such as B Corps, that think in the same way.

Conclusion: An Age of Interdependence

In 1995, Eric Hobsbawm published the final book in a series that covered the eighteenth, nineteenth, and twentieth centuries. His books were acclaimed as groundbreaking studies of the modern world, and Hobsbawm was widely considered to be "our greatest living historian."[1] *Age of Extremes: The Short Twentieth Century, 1914–1991* was deeply pessimistic. Hobsbawm dismissed the popular notion that free market capitalism would benefit and improve developing countries by bringing them industrialization and increasing international trade, predicting instead many of the crises we are now facing, from extreme economic inequality to the destruction of the environment, from unjust working conditions to a rise in ethnic hatred and nationalism, as well as "consumer egoism." Even as the Soviet Union collapsed, he held that capitalism's seeming triumph was a mirage—the system, he said, would not hold. Capitalism would continue to be subject to booms and busts and eventually fail altogether.[2]

In the final section of his book, Hobsbawm recapped the events of the last two decades—1973 to 1991—in which, he said, the world had witnessed the collapse of "most things." Looking ahead, he described a future in which science moves from triumph to triumph but politicians are ever more complacent and evasive, and multinational corporations grow ever bigger and more rapacious. In the book's closing pages, Hobsbawm focused on the humanitarian issues that he anticipated. Mass population growth and political and environmental catastrophes in the southern half of the globe, he said, would lead to increased disparities of wealth, widespread poverty, and mass migration. Today it seems like he was downright prescient. Not only that, but he correctly diagnosed the problem—capitalism's sole focus on profit maximization.

This book also paints a picture of our current age and examines what we can achieve in the future. The world we live in is dangerous and in flux, but our times (and this book) also offer reasons for hope. Hobsbawm's jaundiced view of capitalism is being echoed in the voices of the millennial generation and subsequent ones. Back in 2006, when three American businessmen decided that enough was enough, a revolution began. B Lab is changing the processes and standards of traditional business and of capitalism itself. The late twentieth century saw the rise of shareholder primacy and the pursuit of profits. Those practices have brought us to a turning point today, heightened by the economic effects of the coronavirus pandemic. B Lab is working to change the system in the hope that our global economy can be diverted onto a different and better path. The B Corp revolution demands that companies take responsibility for their decisions that affect consumers, employees, local communities, and the planet. It recognizes that we can only truly thrive when we recognize the interdependencies between business, society, and the environment.

Before the B Corp movement began, there were calls for a more conscious capitalism and various efforts toward corporate social responsibility. But such initiatives or commitments don't do enough and are a fundamentally flawed way to create lasting and systemic change. Why? Because they ask leaders to be heroic in a system that punishes heroism; they vest too much faith in leadership and corporate culture and not enough in material verified changes in performance and true legal accountability to balance purpose and profit. Too many companies are "all talk, no action," offering greenwashing instead of fundamental change. As Anand Giridharadas argued in his book *Winners Take All*, businesses often jump on bandwagons without doing the actual work, just so that they can appease their customers. We can't look to businesses for answers, he said, because they have been fundamentally co-opted. While I agree with him that policy corrections are needed, I think he missed a critical point. Business *can* and *must* play a crucial role in capitalism's reform, but to do so it must build on a strong and authentic foundation of transparency, accountability, and stakeholder-focused corporate governance.

The processes and systems that B Lab has put into place have created a movement that is enacting real change every day. As we've seen through the various stories shared by certified B Corporations, the BIA is not only rigorous and all encompassing, it encourages and, in some ways, demands improvement from the companies it assesses. Every B Corp I spoke to told me that it was aiming for an improved score the next time it completed the BIA, and a better score can be achieved only by improving social and environmental policies. The creation of other tools, including B Analytics, has allowed companies across the globe to pursue a B Corp mindset, even if they aren't B Corps themselves. This is, perhaps, one of the most important points to make— that the B Corp movement is not just about B Corps. Its goal is not to certify every company as a B Corporation, but rather to encourage every company to function more like a B Corp, so that the regime of shareholder primacy can be overthrown.

B Lab created a new corporate form—the benefit corporation— that encodes social and environmental benefits into corporations' DNA. This innovative and world-changing initiative is being supported by politicians on both sides of the aisle in the United States and around the world.

The B Corp movement has gone through ups and downs, but progress has been made. The interdependencies that link our world together—connections between the very basic aspects of people, profit, and planet—are what we must focus on and what we must look to improve. Most important of all, however, is the grassroots story that exists here, in this movement. The B Lab founders themselves had no idea that things would happen the way they did—they underestimated the world's need for change. Looking back on the past decade, one can see that many of those interdependent networks that make the B Corp movement what it is emerged organically and with minimal input—just maximum support—from B Lab. The connections and partnerships among certified B Corps and benefit corporations allow more and more people to engage with the movement. Whole industries are changing the way they function to accommodate the need for sustainability, the investment world is rapidly shifting toward impact investing, and the effects of the B Corp movement on communities and the environment are palpable.

Moving forward, the biggest challenge that B Lab faces is the need to continue to scale the movement. The founders of B Lab are Americans, but the movement has become a global phenomenon. They have to be prepared to adapt to new markets and industries, to different countries and customs. But they also have to shift their attention away from tending to the networks—which are thriving on their own—and toward the inclusion of public firms and multinationals, increasing consumer awareness, and upending shareholder primacy not only in our laws and markets but in people's minds.

I believe that we are on the brink of unprecedented change for the better. Whether you're an employer, an employee, a consumer, a student, or a leader—or a combination of these things—I hope that this book has convinced you to rally behind the B Corp movement and help push it past the tipping point into full-fledged global expansion.

Notes

Preface

1. Peggie Pelosi, "Millennials Want Workplaces with Social Purpose. How Does Your Company Measure Up?" *Talent Economy,* February 20, 2018, https://www. chieflearningofficer.com/2018/02/20/millennials-want-workplaces-social-purpose-company-measure/.

2. Cinantyan Prapatti, "Chateau Maris, a Winery That Saves the Planet." *Impakter,* October 16, 2017, https://impakter.com/chateau-maris-winery-save-planet/.

Introduction

1. Simon Leadbetter, "We Are Stealing the Future, Selling It in the Present, and Calling It GDP," *Blue & Green Tomorrow,* October 10, 2013, https://blueandgreen tomorrow.com/category/energy/.

2. Trucost Plc, *Natural Capital at Risk: The Top 100 Externalities of Business,* April 2013, https://www.trucost.com/wp-content/uploads/2016/04/TEEB-Final-Report-web-SPv2.pdf.

3. Olivia Solon, "Uber Fires More Than 20 Employees after Sexual Harassment Investigation," *Guardian,* June 7, 2017, https://www.theguardian.com/technol ogy/2017/jun/06/uber-fires-employees-sexual-harassment-investigation; Mythili Sampathkumar, "New York's Lawsuit against Harvey Weinstein's Company Reveals Details of Sexual Harassment Scandal," *Independent,* February 12, 2018, https://www. independent.co.uk/news/world/americas/new-york-harvey-weinstein-company-sexual-harassment-employees-details-attorney-general-a8206976.html.

4. Sarah Butler, "HSBC Pay Gap Reveals Men Being Paid Twice as Much as Women," *Guardian,* March 15, 2018, https://www.theguardian.com/business/2018/ mar/15/hsbc-pay-gap-reveals-men-being-paid-twice-as-much-as-women.

5. The Economy of Francesco website, accessed December 30, 2019, https:// francescoeconomy.org.

6. B Lab UK, "Over 500 B Corps around the World Commit to Net Zero at COP25," *Medium,* December 12, 2019, https://medium.com/reinventing-business/over-500-b-corps-around-the-world-commit-to-net-zero-at-cop25-375e74b0fb83.

7. Barbara Spector, "Cascading Force for Good," *Family Business,* January/February 2018, https://www.familybusinessmagazine.com/cascading-force-good.

8. Spector, "Cascading."

9. Terry Macalister and Eleanor Cross, "BP Rebrands on a Global Scale," *Guardian,* July 25, 2000, https://www.theguardian.com/business/2000/jul/25/bp.

10. Rosemary Westwood, "Mutated Fish Still Haunt Louisiana's Fishermen after the BP Oil Spill," *VICE,* February 10, 2017, https://www.vice.com/en_us/article/z4gbb4/bp-oil-spill-louisiana-fishermen-deepwater-horizon; Jackie Tiffany, "Health Effects from British Petroleum Oil Spill," *Teach the Earth,* last modified March 7, 2018, https://serc.carleton.edu/68785.

11. Adam Vaughan, "Lightweight PR and Greenwash—BP's Low-Carbon Plan Dismissed," *Guardian,* April 16, 2018, https://www.theguardian.com/business/2018/apr/16/lightweight-pr-greenwash-bp-low-carbon-plan-dismissed-environmentalists.

12. Jessica Assaf, "The Ugly Truth about Lush," *Beauty Lies Truth,* May 25, 2015, http://www.beautyliestruth.com/blog/2015/5/the-ugly-truth-about-lush.

13. Lush website, accessed September 19, 2019, https://www.lush.com/.

14. Arash Massoudi, James Fontanella-Khan, and Bryce Elder, "Unilever Rejects $143bn Kraft Heinz Takeover Bid," *Financial Times,* February 18, 2017, https://www.ft.com/content/e4afc504-f47e-11e6-8758-687615182126.

15. Andrew Edgecliffe-Johnson, "Unilever Chief Admits Kraft Heinz Bid Forced Compromises," *Financial Times,* February 28, 2018, https://www.ft.com/content/ea0218ce-1be0-11e8-aaca-4574d7dabfb6.

16. Allana Akhtar, "Warren Buffett Says He Eats McDonald's 3 Times a Week and Pounds Cokes because He's Not 'Bothered' by Death," *Entrepreneur Asia Pacific,* April 26, 2019, https://www.entrepreneur.com/article/332881.

17. Jo Confino, "Unilever's Paul Polman: Challenging the Corporate Status Quo," *Guardian,* April 24, 2012, https://www.theguardian.com/sustainable-business/paul-polman-unilever-sustainable-living-plan.

18. Unilever, "Unilever's Sustainable Living Plan Continues to Fuel Growth," October 5, 2018, https://www.unilever.com/news/press-releases/2018/unilevers-sustainable-living-plan-continues-to-fuel-growth.html.

19. Eillie Anzilotti, "Young People Are Really over Capitalism," *Fast Company,* December 8, 2017, https://www.fastcompany.com/40505017/young-people-are-really-over-capitalism.

20. Justin Worland, "Global CO2 Concentration Passes Threshold of 400 PPM—and That's Bad for the Climate," *Time*, October 24, 2016, https://time.com/4542889/carbon-dioxide-400-ppm-global-warming/.

21. Eddie Lou, "Why Millennials Want More Than Just Work: The Importance of Your 'Double Bottom Line,'" *Forbes*, June 9, 2017, https://www.forbes.com/sites/theyec/2017/06/09/why-millennials-want-more-than-just-work-the-importance-of-your-double-bottom-line/; "The Deloitte Global Millennial Survey 2019," Deloitte, accessed December 31, 2019, https://www2.deloitte.com/global/en/pages/about-deloitte/articles/millennialsurvey.html.

22. Alex Buerkle, Max Storto, and Kylee Chang, *Just Good Business: An Investor's Guide to B Corps,* Yale Center for Business and the Environment, Patagonia, Inc., and Caprock, accessed September 17, 2019, https://cbey.yale.edu/sites/default/files/Just%20Good%20Business_An%20Investor%27s%20Guide%20to%20B%20Corps_March%202018.pdf.

23. Christie Smith and Stephanie Turner, "The Millennial Majority Is Transforming Your Culture," Deloitte, accessed December 31, 2019, https://www2.deloitte.com/content/dam/Deloitte/us/Documents/about-deloitte/us-millennial-majority-will-transform-your-culture.pdf.

24. "Survey of Young Americans' Attitudes toward Politics and Public Service, 29th Edition: March 18–April 3, 2016," Harvard University Institute of Politics, accessed December 31, 2019, https://iop.harvard.edu/sites/default/files/content/160423_Harvard%20IOP_Spring%202016_TOPLINE_u.pdf.

25. Morley Winograd and Michael Hais, "How Millennials Could Upend Wall Street and Corporate America," *Governance Studies at Brookings,* May 2014, https://www.brookings.edu/wp-content/uploads/2016/06/Brookings_Winogradfinal.pdf.

26. "Larry Fink's 2019 Letter to CEOs Purpose & Profit," BlackRock, accessed December 31, 2019, https://www.blackrock.com/corporate/investor-relations/larry-fink-ceo-letter.

27. "Political Typology Reveals Deep Fissures on the Right and Left," Pew Research Center, October 24, 2017, https://www.people-press.org/2017/10/24/political-typology-reveals-deep-fissures-on-the-right-and-left/.

28. Megan Brenan, "More Still Disapprove Than Approve of 2017 Tax Cuts," Gallup, October 10, 2018, https://news.gallup.com/poll/243611/disapprove-approve-2017-tax-cuts.aspx.

29. Michelle Goldberg, "No Wonder Millennials Hate Capitalism," *New York Times,* December 4, 2017, https://www.nytimes.com/2017/12/04/opinion/millennials-hate-capitalism.html.

30. Julie Creswell, "Indra Nooyi, PepsiCo C.E.O. Who Pushed for Healthier Products, to Step Down," *New York Times,* August 6, 2018, https://www.nytimes.com/2018/08/06/business/indra-nooyi-pepsi.html.

31. David Rutz, "Deval Patrick Supports Democrats Impeaching Trump if They Take House," *Washington Free Beacon,* August 5, 2018, https://freebeacon.com/politics/deval-patrick-supports-democrats-impeaching-trump/; "Deval Patrick and Richelieu Dennis Have Proven You Don't Have to Trade Return for Impact," ICIC, accessed December 31, 2019, http://icic.org/blog/deval-patrick-richelieu-dennis-proven-dont-trade-return-impact/.

32. Elizabeth Warren, "Companies Shouldn't Be Accountable Only to Shareholders," *Wall Street Journal,* August 14, 2018, https://www.wsj.com/articles/companies-shouldnt-be-accountable-only-to-shareholders-1534287687.

33. Marco Rubio, "American Investment in the 21st Century," Office of Senator Marco Rubio, May 15, 2019, 3–4, https://www.rubio.senate.gov/public/_cache/files/9f25139a-6039-465a-9cf1-feb5567aebb7/4526E9620A9A7DB74267ABEA58810 22F.5.15.2019.-final-project-report-american-investment.pdf.

34. George Bradt, "How the New Perspective on the Purpose of a Corporation Impacts You," *Forbes,* August 22, 2019, https://www.forbes.com/sites/georgebradt/2019/08/22/how-the-new-perspective-on-the-purpose-of-a-corporation-impacts-you/#331f303c94f1.

Chapter 1. Focusing on Interdependencies, Not Externalities

1. Ryan Honeyman, "How Did the B Corp Movement Start?" *LIFT Economy,* April 28, 2019, https://www.lifteconomy.com/blog/2019/4/28/how-did-the-b-corp-movement-start.

2. Christopher Marquis, Andrew Klaber, and Bobbi Thomason, "B Lab: Building a New Sector of the Economy," Harvard Business School Case 411047, revised September 28, 2011, 4, https://www.sistemab.org/wp-content/uploads/2016/01/B-Lab-Case-Study.pdf.

3. Milton Friedman, "The Social Responsibility of Business Is to Increase Its Profits," *New York Times Magazine,* September 13, 1970, https://www.nytimes.com/1970/09/13/archives/a-friedman-doctrine-the-social-responsibility-of-business-is-to.html.

4. William G. Roy, *Socializing Capital: The Rise of the Large Industrial Corporation in America* (Princeton: Princeton University Press, 1999).

5. Adolf A. Berle and Gardiner C. Means, *The Modern Corporation and Private Property* (New Brunswick, NJ: Transaction, 1932).

6. Andrew Baskin, "Jay Coen Gilbert: How B Corps Help Fix the Source Code Error in the DNA of Business," *B the Change*, June 19, 2018, https://bthechange.com/jay-coen-gilbert-how-b-corps-help-fix-the-source-code-error-in-the-dna-of-business-c66e001fce5e.

7. Lynn A. Stout, "The Shareholder Value Myth," Cornell Law Faculty Publications Paper 771, April 19, 2013, 1–10; Lynn A. Stout, *The Shareholder Value Myth: How Putting Shareholders First Harms Investors, Corporations, and the Public* (Oakland, CA: Berrett-Koehler, 2012), https://scholarship.law.cornell.edu/cgi/viewcontent.cgi?articl e=2311&context=facpub.

8. B Lab, "Shareholder Primacy Myths and Truths," accessed December 31, 2019, https://docs.google.com/presentation/d/1MTqxQRnWeZ3hNkX3SqHOErAKnC8-e43Eg9-xJosafmk/edit#slide=id.g1cc9265712_0_0.

9. Jay Coen Gilbert, "Why a Delaware Corporate Lawyer Went from Business-with-Purpose Skeptic to Full-Time Legal Advocate," *Forbes*, October 16, 2017, https://www.forbes.com/sites/jaycoengilbert/2017/10/16/why-a-delaware-corporate-lawyer-went-from-business-with-purpose-skeptic-to-full-time-legal-advocate/#425b8ff840b1.

10. Trucost Plc, *Natural Capital at Risk: The Top 100 Externalities of Business*, April 2013, https://www.trucost.com/wp-content/uploads/2016/04/TEEB-Final-Report-web-SPv2.pdf.

11. Garrett Camp, "Uber's Path Forward," *Medium*, June 21, 2017, https://medium.com/@gc/ubers-path-forward-b59ec9bd4ef6; Aditya Gupta, "Gig Economy & the Future of Work," *Medium*, July 2, 2019, https://medium.com/swlh/gig-economy-the-future-of-work-885354c39ad0; Paul Davidson, "The Job Juggle Is Real. Many Americans Are Balancing Two, Even Three Gigs," *USA Today*, October 17, 2016, https://www.usatoday.com/story/money/2016/10/17/job-juggle-real-many-americans-balancing-two-even-three-gigs/92072068/.

12. Elizabeth Bauer, "SEC Commissioner Warns: A Retirement Crisis 'Tsunami' Is Approaching," *Forbes*, October 18, 2018, https://www.forbes.com/sites/ebauer/2018/10/18/sec-commissioner-warns-a-retirement-crisis-tsunami-is-approaching/#4176f4501ac7.

13. Chris Isidore, "What's Killing Sears? Its Own Retirees, the CEO Says," *Cable News Network*, September 14, 2018, https://money.cnn.com/2018/09/14/news/companies/sears-pension-retirees/index.html; Steven R. Strahler, "Will Sears Retirees See Their Pensions?" *Crain's Chicago Business*, October 11, 2018, https://www.chicago business.com/retail/will-sears-retirees-see-their-pensions.

14. Catherine Clifford, "Whole Foods Turns 38: How a College Dropout Turned His Grocery Store into a Business Amazon Bought for $13.7 Billion," *CNBC Make It*,

September 20, 2018, https://www.cnbc.com/2018/09/20/how-john-mackey-started-whole-foods-which-amazon-bought-for-billions.html.

15. Conscious Capitalism, "Welcome to Conscious Capitalism," accessed December 31, 2019, https://www.consciouscapitalism.org; John Mackey and Rajendra Sisodia, *Conscious Capitalism: Liberating the Heroic Spirit of Business* (Cambridge, MA: Harvard Business Review Press, 2013).

16. Alex Morrell, "The Hedge Fund That Turned Whole Foods into a Takeover Target for Amazon Is Walking Away with $300 Million," *Business Insider,* July 20, 2017, https://www.businessinsider.com/jana-partners-makes-300-million-return-amazon-whole-foods-deal-2017-7; John Mackey, *B Inspired Talk 2017,* interview by Jay Coen Gilbert, B Inspired Toronto, YouTube, October 26, 2018, https://www.youtube.com/watch?v=q8U-6McdL5k.

17. Jay Coen Gilbert, "Panera Bread CEO and Cofounder Ron Shaich Resigns to Join the Conscious Capitalism Movement," *Forbes,* December 13, 2017, https://www.forbes.com/sites/jaycoengilbert/2017/12/13/boy-oh-boy-oh-boy-another-conscious-capitalist-joins-the-fight-against-short-termism/#4f08b4a773cd.

18. Mackey, *B Inspired Talk 2017.*

19. Leo E. Strine Jr., "The Dangers of Denial: The Need for a Clear-Eyed Understanding of the Power and Accountability Structure Established by the Delaware General Corporation Law," *Wake Forest Law Review* 50 (2015): 9, https://papers.ssrn.com/sol3/papers.cfm?abstract_id=2576389##.

20. Ken Bertsch, "Council of Institutional Investors Responds to Business Roundtable Statement on Corporate Purpose," Council of Institutional Investors, August 19, 2019, https://www.cii.org/aug19_brt_response.

21. Strine, "The Dangers of Denial," 9.

22. Ryan Bradley, "The Woman Driving Patagonia to Be (Even More) Radical," *Fortune,* September 14, 2015, https://fortune.com/2015/09/14/rose-marcario-patagonia/.

23. Jeff Beer, "Exclusive: 'Patagonia Is in Business to Save Our Home Planet,'" *Fast Company,* December 13, 2018, https://www.fastcompany.com/90280950/exclusive-patagonia-is-in-business-to-save-our-home-planet; Sandra Stewart, "Thinkshift Joins Patagonia and Other Sustainability Leaders in Becoming California's First Benefit Corporations," *Thinkshift,* January 3, 2012, https://thinkshiftcom.com/thinkshift-joins-patagonia-and-other-sustainability-leaders-in-becoming-californias-first-benefit-corporations/.

24. Bradley, "Woman Driving Patagonia."

25. Patagonia, "B Lab," accessed December 31, 2019, https://www.patagonia.com/b-lab.html.

26. Patagonia, 2017 Annual Benefit Corporation Report, accessed December 31, 2019, https://www.patagonia.com/static/on/demandware.static/-/Library-Sites-PatagoniaShared/default/dw824facof/PDF-US/2017-BCORP-pages_022218.pdf.

27. Karim Abouelnaga, "3 Reasons to Consider Converting a Nonprofit to a For-Profit," *Entrepreneur Asia Pacific,* July 5, 2017, https://www.entrepreneur.com/article/295533.

28. Deborah Dsouza, "The Green New Deal Explained," *Investopedia,* October 28, 2019, https://www.investopedia.com/the-green-new-deal-explained-4588463.

29. Jessica Glenza, "Tobacco Companies Interfere with Health Regulations, WHO Reports," *Guardian,* July 19, 2017, https://www.theguardian.com/world/2017/jul/19/tobacco-industry-government-policy-interference-regulations; Aditya Kalra, Paritosh Bansal, Duff Wilson, and Tom Lasseter, "Inside Philip Morris' Campaign to Subvert the Global Anti-smoking Treaty," Reuters, July 13, 2017, https://www.reuters.com/investigates/special-report/pmi-who-fctc/.

30. Anand Giridharadas, *Winners Take All: The Elite Charade of Changing the World* (New York: Vintage, 2019); Jay Coen Gilbert, "Can Stakeholder Capitalism Spur Talk into Action?" *B the Change,* September 5, 2018, https://bthechange.com/can-stakeholder-capitalism-spur-talk-into-action-97fc6ee10489; " 'B Corps'—For-Benefit Corporations (Rather Than Only For-Profit)—Are Proving Their Worth," The Alternative UK, February 1, 2019, https://www.thealternative.org.uk/dailyalternative/2019/2/2/b-corps-for-benefit.

31. Coen Gilbert, "Can Stakeholder Capitalism Spur Talk into Action?"

32. Just Capital website, accessed September 19, 2019, https://justcapital.com/rankings/.

33. Just Capital, "2018 Overall Rankings," accessed December 31, 2019, https://justcapital.com/past-rankings/2018-rankings/.

34. Ian Lecklitner, "What's in This? Mountain Dew," *MEL Magazine,* accessed September 19, 2019, https://melmagazine.com/en-us/story/whats-in-this-mountain-dew; Michael Moss, "The Extraordinary Science of Addictive Junk Food," *New York Times Magazine,* February 20, 2013, https://www.nytimes.com/2013/02/24/magazine/the-extraordinary-science-of-junk-food.html.

35. Cam Simpson, "American Chipmakers Had a Toxic Problem. Then They Out-sourced It," *Bloomberg,* June 15, 2017, https://www.bloomberg.com/news/features/2017–06–15/american-chipmakers-had-a-toxic-problem-so-they-outsourced-it.

36. Just Capital, "2018 Overall Rankings"; "Just Capital, 2019 Overall Rank-ings," accessed December 31, 2019, https://justcapital.com/past-rankings/2019-rankings/; Glassdoor, "Texas Instruments Reviews," accessed September 18, 2019,

https://www.glassdoor.com/Reviews/Texas-Instruments-profit-sharing-Reviews-EI_
IE651.0,17_KH18,32_IP5.htm.

37. Douglas Rushkoff, "Just Capitalism: Can Billionaires Gamify Social Good?"
Medium, September 19, 2018, https://medium.com/team-human/just-capitalism-
billionaires-social-good-1099efad5008.

38. Rushkoff, "Just Capitalism."

39. "Larry Fink's Annual Letter to CEOs: A Sense of Purpose," BlackRock, accessed December 31, 2019, https://www.blackrock.com/hk/en/insights/larry-fink-
ceo-letter.

40. "Larry Fink's 2019 Letter to CEOs: Purpose & Profit," BlackRock, accessed
December 31, 2019, https://www.blackrock.com/corporate/investor-relations/larry-
fink-ceo-letter.

41. Greyston Bakery, "Center for Open Hiring," accessed September 19, 2019,
https://greyston.org/the-center-for-open-hiring-at-greyston-sight-visit/.

42. Lucius Couloute and Daniel Kopf, "Out of Prison & out of Work: Unemployment among Formerly Incarcerated People," *Prison Policy Initiative,* July 2018,
https://www.prisonpolicy.org/reports/outofwork.html.

43. Sentencing Project, "Criminal Justice Facts," accessed December 31, 2019,
https://www.sentencingproject.org/criminal-justice-facts/.

44. Lillian M. Ortiz, "Using Business as a Force for Good," *Shelterforce,* October
20, 2016, https://shelterforce.org/2016/10/20/using-business-as-a-force-for-good-2/.

45. Greyston Bakery, "About Greyston," accessed December 31, 2019, https://
greystonbakery.com/pages/about-greyston.

46. Boloco website, accessed December 31, 2019, http://www.boloco.com.

47. Allison Engel, "Inside Patagonia's Operation to Keep Clothing out of Landfills," *Washington Post,* September 1, 2018, https://www.washingtonpost.com/business/
inside-patagonias-operation-to-keep-you-from-buying-new-gear/2018/08/31/d3d
1fab4-ac8c-11e8-b1da-ff7faa680710_story.html.

48. Josh Hunter, "Last Chair: Yvon Chouinard," *SKI,* updated December 13, 2016,
https://www.skimag.com/ski-resort-life/last-chair-yvon-chouinard.

49. Ryan Grenoble, "Patagonia Takes a Stand against Companies That Aren't
Working to Better the Environment," *HuffPost,* April 3, 2019, https://www.huffpost.
com/entry/patagonia-co-brand-vest-program_n_5ca4c058e4b07982402592ae?gucco
unter=1&guce_referrer=aHR0cHM6Ly93d3cuZ29vZ2xlLmNvbvbS8&guce_referrer_
sig=AQAAABaMUk6T50RtSxwnpf-S-M4sxRw4oGvyxysUSjL1LB-oggBtCJGZhw
DmX3WjT7dJdvLwV_cisN16qVsiTMIugp1_lmf2u-XOfmvPfRSE8xX3-jwm3O
QzXGW1qycbMW4s7sfAfQ5ToPede5L5gkr4pt5TxVyrXICPErnVsAeJ9S3X.

50. Allbirds website, accessed September 19, 2019, https://www.allbirds.com/pages/our-matcrials-sugar.

51. Jay Coen Gilbert, "The Best Way to Fight Climate Change Is to Treat It Like a Business," *Quartz,* May 29, 2019, https://qz.com/work/1626563/b-corps-should-declare-a-climate-change-emergency/.

52. Jay Coen Gilbert, "Allbirds' Reported Billion-Dollar Valuation: What Makes These Strange Birds Fly," *Forbes,* January 9, 2019, https://www.forbes.com/sites/jaycoengilbert/2019/01/09/allbirds-reported-billion-dollar-valuation-what-makes-these-strange-birds-fly/#3fb469237d38.

53. Cassie Werber, "The Extraordinary Story of the Only B Corp in Afghanistan," *Quartz at Work,* December 12, 2019, https://qz.com/work/1765329/roshan-the-extraordinary-story-of-the-only-b-corp-in-afghanistan/; Roshan, "Roshan Honored as a 'Best for the World' Company by B Corp for Creating Most Overall Social and Community Impact," accessed December 31, 2019, https://www.roshan.af/en/personal/about/media/roshan-honored-as-a-best-for-the-world-company-by-b-corp-for-creating-most-overall-social-and-community-impact/.

Chapter 2. Interdependence Day

1. Deanna Wylie Mayer, "How to B Good," *Pacific Standard,* updated June 14, 2017, https://psmag.com/economics/how-to-b-good-4166.

2. Rob Wherry, "Hip, Hop, Hot," *Forbes,* December 27, 1999, https://www.forbes.com/forbes/1999/1227/6415060a.html#3bcc15bdd1af; Alexander Wolff, "The Other Basketball," *Sports Illustrated,* June 13, 2005, https://www.si.com/vault/2005/06/13/8263082/the-other-basketball.

3. Larry Hamermesh et al., "A Conversation with B Lab," *Seattle University Law Review* 40, no. 2 (April 2017): 323, https://digitalcommons.law.seattleu.edu/cgi/viewcontent.cgi?article=2392&context=sulr.

4. Jay Coen Gilbert, "Ring the Bell: Bringing My Whole Self to Work and the Origin Story of the B Corp Movement" (unpublished manuscript, July 5, 2017), 84.

5. Ralph Warner, Angel Diaz, and Jose Martinez, "The Oral History of the AND1 Mixtape Tour," *Complex,* September 3, 2013, https://www.complex.com/sports/2013/09/and1-mixtape-tour-oral-history/the-hype.

6. Coen Gilbert, "Ring the Bell," 23.

7. Coen Gilbert, "Ring the Bell," 24.

8. Hamermesh et al., "A Conversation with B Lab," 324.

9. Coen Gilbert, "Ring the Bell," 55.

10. Coen Gilbert, "Ring the Bell," 55-56.

11. Coen Gilbert, "Ring the Bell," 48.

12. Andrew Kassoy, "Reconciling Profit and Purpose: A Declaration of Interdependence" (Wealth & Giving Forum Seminar, New York, March, 2007).

13. Coen Gilbert, "Ring the Bell," 56.

14. Coen Gilbert, "Ring the Bell," 56–57.

15. Coen Gilbert, "Ring the Bell," 57.

16. Coen Gilbert, "Ring the Bell," 46–48.

17. Coen Gilbert, "Ring the Bell," 89.

18. Coen Gilbert, "Ring the Bell," 88.

19. Coen Gilbert, "Ring the Bell," 59.

20. Coen Gilbert, "Ring the Bell," 88.

21. Coen Gilbert, "Ring the Bell," 88.

22. Coen Gilbert, "Ring the Bell," 89.

Chapter 3. Putting the Spotlight on Interdependencies

1. Jay Coen Gilbert, "Ring the Bell: Bringing My Whole Self to Work and the Origin Story of the B Corp Movement" (unpublished manuscript, July 5, 2017), 95.

2. Russell Hotten, "Volkswagen: The Scandal Explained," *BBC News,* December 10, 2015, https://www.bbc.com/news/business-34324772.

3. Arwa Lodhi, "Brands You Think Are Eco Friendly . . . but Really Aren't," *Eluxe Magazine,* November 15, 2019, https://eluxemagazine.com/magazine/5-brands-you-think-are-eco-but-really-arent/.

4. Coen Gilbert, "Ring the Bell," 93.

5. Coen Gilbert, "Ring the Bell," 94.

6. B. Cohen and M. Warwick, *Values-Driven Business: How to Change the World, Make Money, and Have Fun* (Oakland, CA: Berrett-Koehler, 2006).

7. Larry Hamermesh et al., "A Conversation with B Lab," *Seattle University Law Review* 40, no. 2 (April 2017): 338, https://digitalcommons.law.seattleu.edu/cgi/viewcontent.cgi?article=2392&context=sulr.

8. Hamermesh et al., "A Conversation with B Lab," 334.

9. B Lab, "Measure What Matters," *Medium,* April 10, 2015, https://medium.com/@bthechange/measure-what-matters-c2bf7e8f5560.

10. Coen Gilbert, "Ring the Bell," 96.

11. Hamermesh et al., "A Conversation with B Lab," 335, 344.

12. Dan Osusky, "Measuring Impact versus Measuring Practices: How the B Impact Assessment's Dual Objectives Require a Balance," *B the Change,* November 15,

2018, https://bthechange.com/measuring-impact-versus-measuring-practices-how-the-b-impact-assessments-dual-objectives-require-9e44821e9c6b.

13. Jeffrey Hollender, *What Matters Most: How a Small Group of Pioneers Is Teaching Social Responsibility to Big Business, and Why Big Business Is Listening* (New York: Basic Books, 2006).

14. Christopher Marquis, Andrew Klaber, and Bobbi Thomason, "B Lab: Building a New Sector of the Economy," Harvard Business School Case 411047, revised September 28, 2011, 5, https://www.sistemab.org/wp-content/uploads/2016/01/B-Lab-Case-Study.pdf.

15. Issie Lapowsky, "What to Do When You're Fired from the Company You Started," *Inc. Magazine*, July/August 2011, https://www.inc.com/magazine/201107/how-i-did-it-jeffrey-hollender-seventh-generation.html.

16. Coen Gilbert, "Ring the Bell," 99.

17. Coen Gilbert, "Ring the Bell," 99.

18. Coen Gilbert, "Ring the Bell," 100.

19. Coen Gilbert, "Ring the Bell," 102.

20. Coen Gilbert, "Ring the Bell," 103.

21. Marquis, Klaber, and Thomason, "B Lab," 5.

22. Coen Gilbert, "Ring the Bell," 103.

Chapter 4. Getting the Law on the Stakeholders' Side

1. Jay Coen Gilbert, "Sen. Elizabeth Warren, Republicans, CEOs & BlackRock's Fink Unite around 'Accountable Capitalism,' " *Forbes*, August 15, 2018, https://www.forbes.com/sites/jaycoengilbert/2018/08/15/sen-elizabeth-warren-republicans-ceos-blackrocks-fink-unite-around-accountable-capitalism/#4270b98e51d9.

2. "Dodge v. Ford Motor Co," *Casebriefs*, accessed December 31, 2019, https://www.casebriefs.com/blog/law/corporations/corporations-keyed-to-klein/the-nature-of-the-corporation/dodge-v-ford-motor-co/.

3. Chancellor Chandler, "eBay Domestic Holdings Inc v. Craigslist, Inc., Nominal Defendant," *FindLaw*, accessed December 31, 2019, https://caselaw.findlaw.com/de-supreme-court/1558886.html.

4. Christopher Marquis, Andrew Klaber, and Bobbi Thomason, "B Lab: Building a New Sector of the Economy," Harvard Business School Case 411047, revised September 28, 2011, 10, https://www.sistemab.org/wp-content/uploads/2016/01/B-Lab-Case-Study.pdf.

5. Jay Coen Gilbert, "Ring the Bell: Bringing My Whole Self to Work and the Origin Story of the B Corp Movement" (unpublished manuscript, July 5, 2017), 106.

6. Marquis, Klaber, and Thomason, "B Lab," 10.

7. Alison Klein, "An Epic Tale: The Birth of the Benefit Corporation," *RoundPeg*, May 25, 2016, https://www.roundpegcomm.com/epic-tale-birth-benefit-corporation/.

8. Benefit Corporation, "What Is a Benefit Corporation?" accessed January 1, 2020, https://benefitcorp.net/what-is-a-benefit-corporation.

9. Lynn A. Stout, "The Shareholder Value Myth," Cornell Law Faculty Publications Paper 771, April 19, 2013, 4, https://scholarship.law.cornell.edu/cgi/view content.cgi?article=2311&context=facpub; Lynn A. Stout, *The Shareholder Value Myth: How Putting Shareholders First Harms Investors, Corporations, and the Public* (Oakland, CA: Berrett-Koehler, 2012).

10. Lynn A. Stout, "The Shareholder Value Myth," *European Financial Review*, April 30, 2013, https://www.europeanfinancialreview.com/the-shareholder-value-myth/.

11. Marc Gunther, "B Corps: Sustainability Will Be Shaped by the Market, Not Corporate Law," *Guardian*, August 12, 2013, https://www.theguardian.com/sustainable-business/b-corps-markets-corporate-law.

12. Leo E. Strine Jr., "The Dangers of Denial: The Need for a Clear-Eyed Understanding of the Power and Accountability Structure Established by the Delaware General Corporation Law," *Wake Forest Law Review* 50 (2015): 8, https://papers.ssrn.com/sol3/papers.cfm?abstract_id=2576389##.

13. Marquis, Klaber, and Thomason, "B Lab," 11.

14. Larry Hamermesh et al., "A Conversation with B Lab," *Seattle University Law Review* 40, no. 2 (April 2017): 327, https://digitalcommons.law.seattleu.edu/cgi/viewcontent.cgi?article=2392&context=sulr.

15. Jay Coen Gilbert, "Why a Delaware Corporate Lawyer Went from Business-with-Purpose Skeptic to Full-Time Legal Advocate," *Forbes*, October 16, 2017, https://www.forbes.com/sites/jaycoengilbert/2017/10/16/why-a-delaware-corporate-lawyer-went-from-business-with-purpose-skeptic-to-full-time-legal-advocate/#4540253040b1.

16. Hamermesh et al., "A Conversation with B Lab," 332.

17. Kendall Cox Park, "B the Change: Social Companies, B Corps, and Benefit Corporations" (PhD diss., Princeton University, 2018), 24–25.

18. J. Haskell Murray, "Understanding and Improving Benefit Corporation Reporting," American Bar Association, July 20, 2016, https://www.americanbar.org/groups/business_law/publications/blt/2016/07/04_murray/.

19. J. Haskell Murray, "Elizabeth Warren's Accountable Capitalism Act and Benefit Corporations," *Law Professor Blogs*, August 16, 2018, https://lawprofessors.

typepad.com/business_law/2018/08/elizabeth-warrens-accountable-capitalism-act-and-benefit-corporations.html.

20. Murray, "Understanding and Improving Benefit Corporation Reporting."

21. Social Impact Investment Taskforce Mission Alignment Working Group, *Profit-with-Purpose Businesses,* September 2014, https://www.scrt.scot/wp-content/uploads/2019/03/G8-Social-Impact-Taskforce-Mission-Alignment-Report.pdf.

22. Julia Sherbakov, "Italy Became a 'Lamp Shining a Light' for Other Countries to Pursue Better Business," *B the Change,* May 31, 2017, https://bthechange.com/italy-became-a-lamp-shining-a-light-for-other-countries-to-pursue-better-business-e35141a7ce43.

Chapter 5. Investing for Impact

1. Marjorie Kelly, *The Divine Right of Capital: Dethroning the Corporate Aristocracy* (Oakland, CA: Berrett-Koehler, 2001); Marjorie Kelly, *Owning Our Future: The Emerging Ownership Revolution* (Oakland, CA: Berrett-Koehler, 2012).

2. William Donovan, "The Origins of Socially Responsible Investing," *Balance,* updated October 24, 2019, https://www.thebalance.com/a-short-history-of-socially-responsible-investing-3025578.

3. Saadia Madsbjerg, "Bringing Scale to the Impact Investing Industry," Rockefeller Foundation, August 15, 2018, https://www.rockefellerfoundation.org/blog/bringing-scale-impact-investing-industry/.

4. B Lab, "Funders & Finances," accessed January 3, 2020, https://bcorporation.net/about-b-lab/funders-and-finances.

5. Global Impact Investing Network, "About the GIIN," accessed January 3, 2020, https://thegiin.org/about/.

6. B Analytics, "Overall Impact Business Model and Overall Operations Ratings," accessed January 3, 2020, https://b-analytics.net/content/giirs-fund-rating-methodology.

7. "Profile: Sir Ronald Cohen: Midas with a Mission—to Make Gordon King," *Sunday Times,* January 23, 2005, https://archive.is/20110604030107/http:/www.timesonline.co.uk/article/0,,2088–1452226,00.html.

8. "The Compassionate Capitalist," *Economist,* August 4, 2005, https://www.economist.com/business/2005/08/04/the-compassionate-capitalist.

9. Sorenson Impact, "From Refugee to Venture Capitalist to Social Impact Pioneer," *Forbes,* July 30, 2018, https://www.forbes.com/sites/sorensonimpact/2018/07/30/from-refugee-to-venture-capitalist-to-social-impact-pioneer/#69b683176886.

10. Bridges Ventures, "To B or Not to B: An Investor's Guide to B Corps," September 2015, https://www.bridgesfundmanagement.com/wp-content/uploads/2017/08/Bridges-To-B-or-Not-To-B-screen.pdf.

11. Bridges Ventures, "To B or Not to B."

12. Laura Colby, "J. B. Hunt Majority Backs LGBT Protection, Activist Investor Says," *Bloomberg,* April 22, 2016, https://www.bloomberg.com/news/articles/2016–04–21/j-b-hunt-majority-backs-lgbt-protection-activist-investor-says.

13. Jon Herskovitz, "Global Investors Warn Texas to Withdraw Transgender Restroom Legislation," Reuters, February 22, 2017, https://www.reuters.com/article/us-texas-lgbt-idUSKBN16025P.

14. jimmy-guterman, "A Venture Capital Firm Goes B Corp," *Newco Shift,* May 24, 2016, https://shift.newco.co/2016/05/24/a-venture-capital-firm-goes-b-corp/.

15. Shelley Alpern, "When B Corp Met Wall Street," *Clean Yield,* March 18, 2015, https://www.cleanyield.com/when-b-corp-met-wall-street/.

16. John Cassidy, "Trump University: It's Worse Than You Think," *New Yorker,* June 2, 2016, https://www.newyorker.com/news/john-cassidy/trump-university-its-worse-than-you-think.

17. Brad Edmondson, "The First Benefit Corporation IPO Is Coming, and That's a Big Deal," *TriplePundit,* February 4, 2016, https://www.triplepundit.com/story/2016/first-benefit-corporation-ipo-coming-and-thats-big-deal/28586.

18. Jay Coen Gilbert, "Allbirds Quickly Soars to Success as It Aims to 'Make Better Things in a Better Way,' " *B the Change,* January 14, 2019, https://bthechange.com/allbirds-quickly-soars-to-success-as-it-aims-to-make-better-things-in-a-better-way-dffae809b14e.

19. Susan Price, "This Entrepreneur Takes Her Company's Commitment to Transparency to a New Level with Its Latest Product," *Forbes,* March 1, 2016, https://www.forbes.com/sites/susanprice/2016/03/01/this-entrepreneur-takes-her-companys-commitment-to-transparency-to-a-new-level-with-its-latest-product/#31db7452471c.

20. "Happy Family's Shazi Visram and Danone's Lorna Davis on How Going Big Doesn't Have to Mean Selling Out," *B the Change,* December 8, 2016, https://bthechange.com/happy-familys-shazi-visram-and-danone-s-lorna-davis-on-how-going-big-doesn-t-have-to-mean-selling-132f5fdc409e.

21. Danone, "Our Vision," accessed January 3, 2020, https://www.danone.com/about-danone/sustainable-value-creation/our-vision.html.

22. Keith Nunes, "Danone's Social, Environmental Journey Continues," *Baking Business,* April 12, 2018, https://www.bakingbusiness.com/articles/45925-danone-s-social-environmental-journey-continues.

23. David Gelles, "How the Social Mission of Ben & Jerry's Survived Being Gobbled Up," *New York Times,* August 21, 2015, https://www.nytimes.com/2015/08/23/business/how-ben-jerrys-social-mission-survived-being-gobbled-up.html.

24. Kathleen Masterson, "The Giant Corporation That Bought Ben & Jerry's Acquired Another Quirky Company from Vermont—Here's What It Was Like in the Room When It Happened," *Business Insider,* December 28, 2016, https://www.businessinsider.com/unilever-is-buying-seventh-generation-but-its-ceo-is-excited-2016–12.

25. Unilever, "Unilever to Acquire Seventh Generation, Inc," September 19, 2016, https://www.unilever.com/news/press-releases/2016/Unilever-to-acquire-Seventh-Generation-Inc.html.

26. Maddie Maynard, "Alan Jope: Who Is Unilever's New Chief Executive?" *William Reed,* November 29, 2018, https://www.thegrocer.co.uk/movers/alan-jope-who-is-unilevers-new-chief-executive/574319.article.

27. Kathleen Kim, "Green Merger: Method Bought by Ecover," *Inc.,* September 4, 2012, https://www.inc.com/kathleen-kim/method-and-ecover-join-hands-in-eco-friendly-partnership.html.

28. S. C. Johnson & Son, "SC Johnson Signs Agreement to Acquire Method and Ecover," September 14, 2017, https://www.scjohnson.com/en/press-releases/2017/september/sc-johnson-signs-agreement-to-acquire-method-and-ecover.

29. Amy Cortese, "Crowdfunded B Corps Find Success with Follow-on Funding," *B the Change,* December 13, 2018, https://bthechange.com/crowdfunded-b-corps-find-success-with-follow-on-funding-4a3c4a8ebc4b.

30. Lisa Anne Hamilton, "ESG Guidance from the Department of Labor Clarifies Fiduciary Duty," Center for International Environmental Law, May 8, 2018, https://www.ciel.org/esg-guidance-department-labor-fiduciary-duty/.

Chapter 6. Employees as the Heart of the Company

1. Evelyn Hartz, "How to Impact the Way Business Is Done," *Medium,* November 20, 2017, https://medium.com/@EvelynHartz/how-to-impact-the-way-business-is-done-and-the-story-behind-the-invention-of-cookie-dough-ice-481e7bc40709.

2. Laura Willard, "Rhino Foods Makes the Cookie Dough in Your Ice Cream. They Also Treat Their Employees Like Family," *Upworthy,* May 1, 2015, https://www.upworthy.com/rhino-foods-makes-the-cookie-dough-in-your-ice-cream-they-also-treat-their-employees-like-family.

3. Rhino Foods, "Life at Rhino," accessed January 3, 2020, https://www.rhinofoods.com/about-rhino-foods.

4. "Trusting Diversity to Make a Difference: Lessons from a Company Employing Immigrants for More Than 25 Years," *B the Change,* December 7, 2016, https://bthechange.com/sponsored-rhino-foods-trusting-diversity-to-make-a-difference-e7765d53fcd1.

5. Christiane Bode, Jasjit Singh, and Michelle Rogan, "Corporate Social Initiatives and Employee Retention," *Organization Science* 26, no. 6 (October 2015): 1702–20, https://doi.org/10.1287/orsc.2015.1006; David A. Jones, Chelsea R. Willness, and Sarah Madey, "Why Are Job Seekers Attracted by Corporate Social Performance? Experimental and Field Tests of Three Signal-Based Mechanisms," *Academy of Management Journal* 57, no. 2 (2014): 383–404, http://dx.doi.org/10.5465/amj.2011.0848; David B. Montgomery and Catherine A. Ramus, "Calibrating MBA Job Preferences for the 21st Century," *Academy of Management Learning & Education* 10, no. 1 (2011): 9–26, https://doi.org/10.5465/amle.10.1.zqr9; Donald F. Vitaliano, "Corporate Social Responsibility and Labor Turnover," *Corporate Governance* 10, no. 5 (2010): 563–73, https://doi.org/10.1108/14720701011085544; Seth Carnahan, David Kryscynski, and Daniel Olson, "When Does Corporate Social Responsibility Reduce Employee Turnover? Evidence from Attorneys before and after 9/11," *Academy of Management Journal* 60, no. 5 (2017): 1932–62, https://doi.org/10.5465/amj.2015.0032.

6. Richard Yerema and Kristina Leung, "Nature's Path Foods, Inc., Recognized as One of BC's Top Employers (2019)," Canada's Top 100 Employers, February 21, 2019, https://content.eluta.ca/top-employer-natures-path-foods.

7. Bode, Singh, and Rogan, "Corporate Social Initiatives and Employee Retention," 1702–20.

8. "Rhino Foods," *Talent Rewire,* accessed January 3, 2020, https://talentrewire.org/innovation-story/rhino-foods/.

9. W. S. Badger Company, "Badger's History & Legend," accessed January 3, 2020, https://www.badgerbalm.com/s-14-history-legend.aspx.

10. W. S. Badger Company, "Family Friendly Workplace," accessed January 3, 2020, https://www.badgerbalm.com/s-98-family-friendly-workplace.aspx.

11. New Hampshire Breastfeeding Task Force, "Breastfeeding Friendly Employer Award," accessed January 3, 2020, http://www.nhbreastfeedingtaskforce.org/employerawards.php; W. S. Badger Company, "Babies at Work Policy," accessed January 3, 2020, https://www.badgerbalm.com/s-19-babies-at-work.aspx.

12. W. S. Badger Company, "Calendula Garden Children's Center," accessed January 3, 2020, https://www.badgerbalm.com/s-89-calendula-garden-child-care.aspx.

13. Katarzyna Klimkiewicz and Victor Oltra, "Does CSR Enhance Employer Attractiveness? The Role of Millennial Job Seekers' Attitudes," *Corporate Social Respon-*

sibility and Environmental Management 24, no. 5 (February 2017): 449–63, https://doi.org/10.1002/csr.1419; Victor M. Catano and Heather Morrow Hines, "The Influence of Corporate Social Responsibility, Psychologically Healthy Workplaces, and Individual Values in Attracting Millennial Job Applicants," *Canadian Journal of Behavioural Science / Revue canadienne des sciences du comportement* 48, no. 2 (2016): 142–54, https://doi.org/10.1037/cbs0000036.

14. Annelize Botha, Mark Bussin, and Lukas De Swardt, "An Employer Brand Predictive Model for Talent Attraction and Retention: Original Research," *SA Journal of Human Resource Management* 9, no. 1 (January 2011): 1–12, https://hdl.handle.net/10520/EJC95927.

15. Helle Kryger Aggerholm, Sophie Esmann Andersen, and Christa Thomsen, "Conceptualising Employer Branding in Sustainable Organisations," *Corporate Communications: An International Journal* 16, no. 2 (May 2011): 105–23, https://doi.org/10.1108/13563281111141642.

16. James Manyika et al., *Independent Work: Choice, Necessity, and the Gig Economy,* McKinsey Global Institute, October 2016, https://www.mckinsey.com/featured-insights/employment-and-growth/independent-work-choice-necessity-and-the-gig-economy.

17. Paul Davidson, "The Job Juggle Is Real. Many Americans Are Balancing Two, Even Three Gigs," *USA Today,* October 17, 2016, https://www.usatoday.com/story/money/2016/10/17/job-juggle-real-many-americans-balancing-two-even-three-gigs/92072068/.

18. King Arthur Flour, "Our History," accessed January 3, 2020, https://www.kingarthurflour.com/about/history.

19. Claire Martin, "At King Arthur Flour, Savoring the Perks of Employee Ownership," *New York Times,* June 25, 2016, https://www.nytimes.com/2016/06/26/business/at-king-arthur-flour-savoring-the-perks-of-employee-ownership.html.

20. Jon L. Pierce, Stephen A. Rubenfeld, and Susan Morgan, "Employee Ownership: A Conceptual Model of Process and Effects," *Academy of Management Review* 16, no. 1 (January 1991): 121–44, https://doi.org/10.5465/amr.1991.4279000.

21. Marjorie Kelly and Sarah Stranahan, "Next Generation Employee Ownership Design," *Fifty by Fifty,* November 1, 2018, https://www.fiftybyfifty.org/2018/11/next-generation-employee-ownership-design/.

22. Sarah Stranahan, "Eileen Fisher: Designing for Change," *Fifty by Fifty,* August 15, 2018, https://www.fiftybyfifty.org/2018/08/eileen-fisher-designing-for-change/.

23. Kelly and Stranahan, "Next Generation Employee Ownership Design."

24. Amy Cortese, "The Many Faces of Employee Ownership," *B the Change,* April 1, 2017, https://bthechange.com/the-many-faces-of-employee-ownership-aa048ba262af.

25. Madeline Buxton, "Uber Is Facing a New Discrimination-Based Lawsuit," *Refinery 29,* October 27, 2017, https://www.refinery29.com/en-us/2017/10/178457/uber-lawsuit-women-unequal-pay.

26. Salvador Rodriguez, "Uber versus Women: A Timeline," *Inc.*, March 28, 2017, https://www.inc.com/salvador-rodriguez/uber-women-timeline.html.

27. "Yonkers, New York Population 2019," World Population Review, accessed January 3, 2020, http://worldpopulationreview.com/us-cities/yonkers-ny-population/.

28. Aaron Bence, "My Greyston Experience," Greyston Bakery, accessed September 22, 2019, https://www.greyston.org/my-greyston-experience-by-aaron-bence-unilever/; Greyston Bakery, "The Center for Open Hiring," accessed September 22, 2019, https://www.greyston.org/about/the-center-for-open-hiring/.

29. Deborah Hicks-Clarke and Paul Iles, "Climate for Diversity and Its Effects on Career and Organisational Attitudes and Perceptions," *Personnel Review* 29, no. 3 (2000): 324–45, https://doi.org/10.1108/00483480010324689; Derek R. Avery et al., "Examining the Draw of Diversity: How Diversity Climate Perceptions Affect Job-Pursuit Intentions," *Human Resource Management* 52, no. 2 (March/April 2013): 175–93, https://doi.org/10.1002/hrm.21524; Eden B. King et al., "A Multilevel Study of the Relationships between Diversity Training, Ethnic Discrimination and Satisfaction in Organizations," *Journal of Organizational Behavior* 33, no. 1 (January 2012): 5–20, https://doi.org/10.1002/job.728; Frances J. Milliken and Luis L. Martins, "Searching for Common Threads: Understanding the Multiple Effects of Diversity in Organizational Groups," *Academy of Management Review* 21, no. 2 (1996): 402–33, https://doi.org/10.5465/amr.1996.9605060217; Goce Andrevski et al., "Racial Diversity and Firm Performance: The Mediating Role of Competitive Intensity," *Journal of Management* 40, no. 3 (March 2014): 820–44, https://doi.org/10.1177/0149206311424318; Lisa H. Nishii, "The Benefits of Climate for Inclusion for Gender-Diverse Groups," *Academy of Management Journal* 56, no. 6 (2013): 1754–74, https://doi.org/10.5465/amj.2009.0823; Lynn A. Shore et al., "Inclusion and Diversity in Work Groups: A Review and Model for Future Research," *Journal of Management* 37, no. 4 (July 2011): 1262–89, https://doi.org/10.1177/0149206310385943; Suzanne T. Bell et al., "Getting Specific about Demographic Diversity Variable and Team Performance Relationships: A Meta-analysis," *Journal of Management* 37, no. 3 (May 2011): 709–43, https://doi.org/10.1177/0149206310365001.

30. David M. Kaplan, Jack W. Wiley, and Carl P. Maertz Jr., "The Role of Calculative Attachment in the Relationship between Diversity Climate and Retention," *Human Resource Management* 50, no. 2 (March/April 2011): 271–87, https://doi.org/10.1002/hrm.20413; Eden B. King et al., "Why Organizational and Community Diversity Matter: Representativeness and the Emergence of Incivility and Organizational Performance," *Academy of Management Journal* 54, no. 6 (2011): 1103–18, https://doi.org/10.5465/amj.2010.0016; Frances Bowen and Kate Blackmon, "Spirals of Silence: The Dynamic Effects of Diversity on Organizational Voice," *Journal of Management Studies* 40, no. 6 (2003): 1393–417, https://doi.org/10.1111/1467–6486.00385; Orlando Curtae' Richard et al., "The Impact of Store-Unit–Community Racial Diversity Congruence on Store-Unit Sales Performance," *Journal of Management* 43, no. 7 (September 2017): 2386–403, https://doi.org/10.1177/0149206315579511; Patrick F. McKay et al., "Does Diversity Climate Lead to Customer Satisfaction? It Depends on the Service Climate and Business Unit Demography," *Organization Science* 22, no. 3 (May/June 2011): 788–803, https://doi.org/10.1287/orsc.1100.0550; Yang Yang and Alison M. Konrad, "Understanding Diversity Management Practices: Implications of Institutional Theory and Resource-Based Theory," *Group & Organization Management* 36, no. 1 (February 2011): 6–38, https://doi.org/10.1177/1059601110390997.

31. Jay Coen Gilbert, "The Elections, the Politics of Division, and the Business of Inclusion," *Forbes*, October 30, 2018, https://www.forbes.com/sites/jaycoengilbert/2018/10/30/the-elections-the-politics-of-division-and-the-business-of-inclusion/#2370f8c31add.

32. Certified B Corporation, "Inclusive Economy Challenge 2019," accessed September 22, 2019, https://bcorporation.net/for-b-corps/inclusive-economy-challenge.

33. Mise à jour le, "TriCiclos (Chile): Encouraging Sustainable Consumption through Innovative Recycling," *BipiZ*, May 23, 2016, https://www.bipiz.org/en/csr-best-practices/triciclos-chile-encouraging-sustainable-consumption-through-innovative-recycling-.html?tmpl=component&print=1.

34. Natura, "About Us," accessed September 22, 2019, https://www.naturabrasil.fr/en-us/about-us/cosmetics-leader-in-brazil.

35. "Living Paycheck to Paycheck Is a Way of Life for Majority of U.S. Workers, According to New CareerBuilder Survey," *CareerBuilder*, August 24, 2017, http://press.careerbuilder.com/2017–08–24-Living-Paycheck-to-Paycheck-is-a-Way-of-Life-for-Majority-of-U-S-Workers-According-to-New-CareerBuilder-Survey.

36. Rhino Foods, "Rhino Foods' Income Advance Program," accessed September 22, 2019, https://www.rhinofoods.com/rhino-foods-income-advance-program.

37. Income Advance website, accessed September 22, 2019, https://www.incomeadvance.org.

38. Jay Coen Gilbert, "Distracting Trade Wars: How to Really Help American Workers," *Forbes,* September 27, 2018, https://www.forbes.com/sites/jaycoengilbert/2018/09/27/distracting-trade-wars-how-to-really-help-american-workers/#380bb29f3a8f.

Chapter 7. Finding Kindred Spirits

1. "Beyond Certification, B Corp Is about Community," *MaRS,* October 8, 2013, https://marsdd.ca/news/beyond-certification-b-corp-is-about-community/.

2. "Sharing the Power: Solar Energy, Employee Ownership, and the B Corp Community," *B the Change,* February 6, 2018, https://bthechange.com/sharing-the-power-solar-energy-employee-ownership-and-the-b-corp-community-ceea7dcc629a.

3. RSF Social Finance, "About Us—Mission," accessed September 23, 2019, https://rsfsocialfinance.org/our-story/mission-values/.

4. RSF Social Finance, "RSF Helps Launch the New Resource Bank," *CSRwire,* December 5, 2006, https://www.csrwire.com/press_releases/17152-RSF-Helps-Launch-The-New-Resource-Bank.

5. Jillian McCoy, "RSF Capital Management Is a B Corp!" RSF Social Finance, September 16, 2009, https://rsfsocialfinance.org/2009/09/16/rsf-cmi-b-corp/.

6. Jillian McCoy, "B Lab Seeds a Movement toward a New Kind of Corporation," RSF Social Finance, September 14, 2012, https://rsfsocialfinance.org/2012/09/14/b-lab-movement/.

7. Triodos Bank UK Ltd., "About Us," accessed January 3, 2020, https://www.triodos.co.uk/about-us.

8. "B Lab Partners with CESR," Leeds School of Business, September 24, 2014, https://www.colorado.edu/business/CESR/cesr-blog/b-lab-partners-cesr.

9. "Sustainability Marketplace," Leeds School of Business, January 29, 2016, https://www.colorado.edu/business/2016/01/29/sustainability-marketplace.

10. "The GrowHaus: B of Service Volunteering," Wordbank, accessed January 3, 2020, https://www.wordbank.com/us/blog/b-corp/the-growhaus-volunteering/.

11. "Los Angeles B Corporations Join Together to Form B Local LA," Falcon Water Technologies, January 1, 2016, https://falconwatertech.com/los-angeles-b-corporations-join-together-to-form-b-local-la/.

12. Kerry Vineberg, "6 Lessons from B Corp Leadership Development: Bay Area," Certified B Corporation, accessed January 3, 2020, https://bcorporation.net/news/6-lessons-b-corp-leadership-development-bay-area-0.

13. Ryan Honeyman and Tiffany Jana, *The B Corp Handbook: How You Can Use Business as a Force for Good,* 2nd ed. (Oakland, CA: Berrett-Koehler, 2019), https://bcorporation.net/news/b-corp-handbook.

14. Berrett-Koehler Publishers website, accessed January 3, 2020, https://www.bkconnection.com.

15. Numi Organic Tea, "Our Story," accessed January 3, 2020, https://numitea.com/our-story/.

16. Kristin Carlson, "GMP Becomes First Utility in the World to Receive B Corp Certification," Green Mountain Power, December 1, 2014, https://greenmountainpower.com/news/gmp-becomes-first-utility-world-receive-b-corp-certification/.

17. Andrea Kramar, "How a 25-Year-Old Turned His 'Passion Project' into a Global Business with $30 Million in Sales," *CNBC Make It,* July 3, 2018, https://www.cnbc.com/2018/07/02/how-the-founders-of-lukes-lobster-built-a-global-food-business.html.

18. "Luke's Lobster Grows Impact and Revenue by Working with Fellow B Corps," *B the Change,* August 23, 2018, https://bthechange.com/lukes-lobster-grows-impact-and-revenue-by-working-with-fellow-b-corps-893f308855e2.

19. "Luke's Lobster."

20. Greyston Bakery, "Partners," accessed January 3, 2020, https://www.greyston.org/partners/.

21. Greyston Bakery, "About Greyston," accessed January 3, 2020, https://greystonbakery.com/pages/about-greyston.

22. Will Haraway, "Rubicon Global, World Centric Join Forces to Promote Shared Sustainability Vision," GlobeNewswire, September 27, 2016, https://www.globenewswire.com/news-release/2016/09/27/874918/0/en/Rubicon-Global-World-Centric-Join-Forces-to-Promote-Shared-Sustainability-Vision.html.

23. Corey Simpson, "Patagonia Leads All B Corp Group in $35 Million Dollar Residential Solar Investment," *Patagonia Works,* March 10, 2016, http://www.patagoniaworks.com/press/2016/3/10/clbwie1mk5rnw6jn5iygmi81sn7r46.

24. Adam Fetcher, "Patagonia & Kina'ole Invest $27 Million in Solar for Hawai'i," *Patagonia Works,* October 15, 2014, http://www.patagoniaworks.com/press/2014/10/14/patagonia-kinaole-invest-27-million-in-solar-for-hawaii.

25. Rana DiOrio, "It's the Why That Matters," *AdvisoryCloud,* November 25, 2015, https://www.advisorycloud.com/board-of-directors-articles/its-the-why-that-matters.

26. "Little Pickle Press," tapbookauthor, accessed January 3, 2020, http://www.tapbookauthor.com/customers-view/customers-3/.

27. The Judge Family, "Sewn to Restore: Elegantees," *Elleanor + Indigo*, August 9, 2017, https://www.elleanorandindigo.com/ontheblog/2017/7/22/sewn-to-restore-elegantees.

28. The Community of Certified B Corporations, *Welcome to the B Hive*, February 4, 2015, YouTube, https://www.youtube.com/watch?v=tsxxM6Rakmw.

29. Kendall Cox Park, "B the Change: Social Companies, B Corps, and Benefit Corporations" (PhD diss., Princeton University, 2018), 111.

30. Alex Buerkle, Max Storto, and Kylee Chang, *Just Good Business: An Investor's Guide to B Corps,* Yale Center for Business and the Environment, Patagonia, Inc., and Caprock, accessed September 17, 2019, https://cbey.yale.edu/sites/default/files/Just%20Good%20Business_An%20Investor%27s%20Guide%20to%20B%20Corps_March%202018.pdf.

Chapter 8. Going Global

1. RP Siegel, "B Corporations to Expand 'Business for Good' Initiative Globally," *TriplePundit,* October 3, 2012, https://www.triplepundit.com/story/2012/b-corporations-expand-business-good-initiative-globally/61891.

2. Grupo Bancolombia, "Our Purpose," accessed January 3, 2020, https://www.grupobancolombia.com/wps/portal/about-us/corporate-information/financial-group.

3. Andres Felipe Perilla Rodriguez, "Bancolombia Sustainability Project," *B Analytics,* accessed January 3, 2020, https://b-analytics.net/customers/case-studies/bancolombia-sustainability-project.

4. Rodriguez, "Bancolombia Sustainability Project."

5. Academia B, *Case Studies in Innovation Purpose-Driven Companies and Sistema B in Latin America,* Inter-American Development Bank, 2017, https://sistemab.org/wp-content/uploads/2017/11/fomin_ingles_28_11_2017.pdf; Ryan Honeyman and Tiffany Jana, *The B Corp Handbook: How You Can Use Business as a Force for Good,* 2nd ed. (Oakland, CA: Berrett-Koehler, 2019), 51, https://bcorporation.net/news/b-corp-handbook.

6. "Triple Bottom Line," *Economist,* November 17, 2009, https://www.economist.com/news/2009/11/17/triple-bottom-line.

7. "ISSP Sustainability Hall of Fame," International Society of Sustainability Professionals, accessed January 3, 2020, https://www.sustainabilityprofessionals.org/issp-sustainability-hall-fame; "John Elkington," WWF-UK, accessed January 3, 2020, https://www.wwf.org.uk/council-of-ambassadors/john-elkington.

8. Ceri Witchard, "CIC Incorporations: The New Online Process," *GOV.UK blog,* March 13, 2019, https://communityinterestcompanies.blog.gov.uk/2019/03/13/cic-incorporations-the-new-online-process/.

9. B Lab, "Global Partners and Community," accessed January 3, 2020, https://bcorporation.net/about-b-lab/global-partners.

10. Alyssa Harriman, "The Making of a Movement: The Rise of the B Corp on the Global Stage" (MSc thesis, Copenhagen Business School, 2015), 90, http://academiab.org/wp-content/uploads/2015/10/Thesis-FINAL.pdf.

11. B Lab Europe, "B Corp movement in BeNeLux," accessed January 3, 2020, https://bcorporation.eu/about-b-lab/country-partner/benelux.

12. Emmanuel Faber, "To B or Not to B Corp: That Is No Longer a Question," Linkedin, April 13, 2018, https://www.linkedin.com/pulse/b-corp-longer-question-emmanuel-faber-1/.

13. "Making an Impact with B Lab Australia & New Zealand," Hub Australia, accessed January 3, 2020, https://www.hubaustralia.com/making-an-impact-with-b-lab-australia-new-zealand/.

14. Wenlei Ma, "B Corps and Social Enterprise Movement to Hit Australia," *News.com.au,* August 28, 2014, https://www.news.com.au/finance/business/b-corps-and-social-enterprise-movement-to-hit-australia/news-story/7777cbe89da7be011802ab8f11cf36b3.

15. Harriman, "The Making of a Movement," 81.

16. Sara Parrott, "Social Impact Investing Discussion Paper," *Treasury,* March 20, 2017, https://static.treasury.gov.au/uploads/sites/1/2017/08/c2017-183167-Suncorp.pdf.

17. Jim Antonopoulos, "Profit and Responsibility," *Medium,* September 13, 2018, https://medium.com/meaningful-work/profit-and-responsibility-88f807b02757.

18. Gayertree Subramania, "The Low Down: B Corp Champions Retreat Alice Springs," Linkedin, May 17, 2017, https://www.linkedin.com/pulse/b-corp-champions-retreat-alice-springs-gayertree-subramaniam/.

19. B Lab Taiwan, *His Excellency Ma Ying-jeou—B Corp Asia Forum 2016 Keynote,* YouTube, July 12, 2017, https://www.youtube.com/watch?v=ahrAbKjoOaw.

20. Certified B Corporation, "B Impact Report Education for Good CIC Ltd.," accessed January 3, 2020, https://bcorporation.net/directory/education-good-cic-ltd.

21. "Donghsu (Jaff) ShenGlobal," Philanthropy Forum, accessed January 3, 2020, https://philanthropyforum.org/people/donghsu-jaff-shen/.

22. Larry Hamermesh et al., "A Conversation with B Lab," *Seattle University Law Review* 40, no. 2 (April 2017): 365, https://digitalcommons.law.seattleu.edu/cgi/viewcontent.cgi?article=2392&context=sulr.

23. B Lab, "Global Partners and Community."

Chapter 9. Widening the Funnel

1. Ruth Reader, "A Brief History of Etsy, from 2005 Brooklyn Launch to 2015 IPO," *VentureBeat,* March 5, 2015, https://venturebeat.com/2015/03/05/a-brief-history-of-etsy-from-2005-brooklyn-launch-to-2015-ipo/.

2. Brady Dale, "Over Etsy's B Corp Status, Who Will Bend: B Lab or Etsy?" *Technical.ly Brooklyn,* March 16, 2015, https://technical.ly/brooklyn/2015/03/16/etsy-ipo-b-corp-status/.

3. Chad Dickerson, "Etsy's Next Chapter: Reimagining Commerce as a Public Company," *Etsy,* April 16, 2015, https://blog.etsy.com/news/2015/etsys-next-chapter-reimagining-commerce-as-a-public-company/.

4. David Gelles, "Inside the Revolution at Etsy," *New York Times,* November 25, 2017, https://www.nytimes.com/2017/11/25/business/etsy-josh-silverman.html.

5. Max Chafkin and Jing Cao, "The Barbarians Are at Etsy's Hand-Hewn, Responsibly Sourced Gates," *Bloomberg,* May 18, 2017, https://www.bloomberg.com/news/features/2017-05-18/the-barbarians-are-at-etsy-s-hand-hewn-responsibly-sourced-gates.

6. black-and-white Capital LP, Letter to the Board of Directors of Etsy, Inc., March 13, 2017, https://www.bw-etsy.com/assets/BW-Letter-to-ETSY-Board_FINAL-3.13.17.pdf, accessed January 4, 2020.

7. "black-and-white Capital Calls for Change at Etsy," *Business Wire,* May 2, 2017, https://www.businesswire.com/news/home/20170502005999/en/black-and-white-Capital-Calls-Change-Etsy.

8. Catherine Shu, "Etsy Will Cut 15 Percent of Its Workforce in a New Round of Layoffs," TechCrunch, June 22, 2017, https://techcrunch.com/2017/06/21/etsy-will-cut-15-percent-of-its-workforce-in-a-new-round-of-layoffs/.

9. Ina Steiner, "Etsy Gives Up B Corp Status to Maintain Corporate Structure," EcommerceBytes, November 30, 2017, https://www.ecommercebytes.com/2017/11/30/etsy-gives-b-corp-status-maintain-corporate-structure/.

10. Jay Coen Gilbert, "B Lab Responds to Etsy," Westaway, December 1, 2017, https://westaway.co/b-lab-responds-etsy/.

11. "Jessica Alba Talks Honest Beauty and Why She Loves Target," A Bullseye View, March 22, 2017, https://corporate.target.com/article/2017/03/honest-beauty;

Madeline Stone, "Go Inside the Gorgeous Offices of Jessica Alba's Diaper Company, Which Reportedly Just Raised $100 Million at a $1.7 Billion Valuation," *Business Insider*, August 14, 2015, https://www.businessinsider.com/inside-the-offices-of-jessica-albas-honest-company-2015-08.

12. Dan Schawbel, "Jessica Alba on Becoming an Entrepreneur," *Forbes*, August 27, 2012, https://www.forbes.com/sites/danschawbel/2012/08/27/exclusive-jessica-alba-on-becoming-an-entrepreneur/#709cfceb2700.

13. Jason Del, "Jessica Alba's Honest Company Is Replacing Its CEO after a Sale to Unilever Fell Through," *Vox*, March 16, 2017, https://www.vox.com/2017/3/16/14951098/new-honest-company-ceo-change-nick-vlahos.

14. Julie Gunlock, "The 'Toxic' Lies behind Jessica Alba's Booming Baby Business," *New York Post*, June 17, 2015, https://nypost.com/2015/06/17/the-toxic-lies-behind-jessica-albas-booming-baby-business/.

15. Shwanika Narayan, "Honest Company Receives $200 Million Investment," *Los Angeles Business Journal*, June 6, 2018, https://labusinessjournal.com/news/2018/jun/06/honest-co-receives-200-million-investment/.

16. James Surowiecki, "Companies with Benefits," *New Yorker*, July 28, 2014, https://www.newyorker.com/magazine/2014/08/04/companies-benefits.

17. B Analytics, "Measure What Matters Initiative Launches," accessed January 4, 2020, https://b-analytics.net/articles/measure-what-matters-initiative-launches.

18. Dan Osusky, "The B Impact Assessment's Commitment to Continuous Improvement: Public Comment of New Version Happening Now," *B the Change*, October 23, 2018, https://bthechange.com/the-b-impact-assessments-commitment-to-continuous-improvement-public-comment-of-new-version-a25b651caa4e.

19. Jo Confino, "Will Unilever Become the World's Largest Publicly Traded B Corp?" *Guardian*, January 23, 2015, https://www.theguardian.com/sustainable-business/2015/jan/23/benefit-corporations-bcorps-business-social-responsibility.

20. Abhijeet Pratap, "Nike Supply Chain Management," notesmatic, last updated September 26, 2019, https://notesmatic.com/2018/02/nike-supply-chain-management/.

21. B Analytics, "Measure What Matters Initiative Launches."

22. Francesca Rheannon, "Practicing Deep Sustainability: Cabot Creamery & Context Based Sustainability Metrics," *CSRwire*, August 30, 2012, https://www.csrwire.com/blog/posts/522-practicing-deep-sustainability-cabot-creamery-context-based-sustainability-metrics.

23. Marco Scuri, "Certified B Corps in Italy: Organization, Motivations and Change after the Certification" (master's thesis, Università Commerciale Luigi Bocconi, 2016/17), 57.

24. Natura, 2016 Annual Report, accessed January 4, 2020, https://natu.infoinvest.com.br/enu/6049/natura_annual_report_2016.pdf.

25. Moyee Coffee, "About Us," accessed January 4, 2020, https://moyeecoffee.ie/pages/story; Moyee Coffee, "A Radically Transparent Impact Report, 2017," accessed January 4, 2020, http://impact.moyeecoffee.com/impact-report-2017#!/home-copy-copy-copy-copy-2.

26. NYCEDC, "NYCEDC Announces Launch of Best for NYC Business Campaign to Inspire and Equip Businesses with Resources to Improve Job Quality, Invest in Communities, and Preserve a Healthier Urban Environment," March 11, 2015, https://edc.nyc/press-release/nycedc-announces-launch-best-nyc-business-campaign-inspire-and-equip-businesses.

27. Megan Anthony, "The Alliance Center Wants to See More Sustainable Companies in Colorado," 5280, October 3, 2018, https://www.5280.com/2018/10/the-alliance-center-wants-to-see-more-sustainable-companies-in-colorado/.

28. Scotland CAN B website, accessed January 4, 2020, https://canb.scot.

29. RIO+B, "O QUE É O RIO+B?" accessed September 24, 2019, http://www.riomaisb.org.br/#what.

30. United Nations, "About the Sustainable Development Goals," accessed January 4, 2020, https://www.un.org/sustainabledevelopment/sustainable-development-goals/.

31. "How the Sustainable Development Goals Provide a Framework for Impact-Minded Businesses," B the Change, July 31, 2019, https://bthechange.com/how-the-sustainable-development-goals-provide-a-framework-for-impact-minded-businesses-eae3f3506937.

32. Susmita Kamath, "FAQ: How the B Impact Assessment and SDG Action Manager Can Help Businesses Plan and Measure Progress," B the Change, November 13, 2019, https://bthechange.com/faq-how-the-b-impact-assessment-and-sdg-action-manager-can-help-businesses-plan-and-measure-5aad2d1e0b96.

33. Larry Hamermesh et al., "A Conversation with B Lab," Seattle University Law Review 40, no. 2 (April 2017): 339, https://digitalcommons.law.seattleu.edu/cgi/viewcontent.cgi?article=2392&context=sulr.

34. Michelle Meagher and Fran van Dijk, "B Corps Unite to Hack One Sustainable Development Goal: Responsible Consumption and Production," B the Change, December 8, 2017, https://bthechange.com/b-corps-unite-to-hack-one-sustainable-development-goal-responsible-production-and-consumption-b8537a3d7c2c.

35. Tim Frick, "Aligning Your Organization with U.N. Sustainable Development Goals," Mightybytes, September 24, 2018, https://www.mightybytes.com/blog/aligning-un-sustainable-development-goals/.

36. "How the Sustainable Development Goals Provide a Framework."

37. Meagher and van Dijk, "B Corps Unite."

38. "The Burberry Foundation Partners with Elvis & Kresse to Tackle Waste Created by the Leather Goods Industry," Elvis & Kresse, October 16, 2017, https://www.elvisandkresse.com/blogs/news/the-burberry-foundation-partners-with-elvis-kresse.

39. B Lab, *A Conversation with Emmanuel Faber & Andrew Kassoy,* YouTube, November 28, 2018, https://www.youtube.com/watch?v=P-ofxmInWwU.

Chapter 10. Big Isn't Always Bad

1. Christopher Marquis and Effie Sapuridis, "Danone North America: The World's Largest B Corporation," Harvard Kennedy School Case 2156.0, April 26, 2019, 15, https://casc.hks.harvard.edu/danone-north-america-the-worlds-largest-b-corporation/.

2. "The World's Largest B Corp on the Future of Business," *B the Change,* April 13, 2018, https://bthechange.com/the-worlds-largest-b-corp-on-the-future-of-business-673bccda1d54.

3. Certified B Corporation, "Large Companies," accessed January 3, 2020, https://bcorporation.net/certification/large-companies.

4. Elizabeth Freeburg, "Advisory Council Seeks Feedback on Recommendations for Multinational Certification," Certified B Corporation, accessed January 3, 2020, https://bcorporation.net/news/advisory-council-seeks-feedback-recommendations-multinational-certification.

5. Laureate Education, Inc., SEC Form 10-Q Quarterly Report for the Quarterly Period Ended March 31, 2019, May 9, 2019, https://www.sec.gov/Archives/edgar/data/912766/000162828019006341/laur3312019-10xq.htm.

6. Jay Coen Gilbert, "For-Profit Higher Education: Yes, Like This Please," *Forbes,* January 4, 2018, https://www.forbes.com/sites/jaycoengilbert/2018/01/04/for-profit-higher-education-yes-like-this-please/#78e20bea7937.

7. Laureate Education, Inc., SEC Form S-1 Registration Statement under the Securities Act of 1933, December 15, 2016, https://www.sec.gov/Archives/edgar/data/912766/000104746916017211/a2228849zs-1a.htm.

8. Anderson Antunes, "Brazil's Natura, the Largest Cosmetics Maker in Latin America, Becomes a B Corp," *Forbes,* December, 16, 2014, https://www.forbes.com/sites/andersonantunes/2014/12/16/brazils-natura-the-largest-cosmetics-maker-in-latin-america-becomes-a-b-corp/#eaa3b5225a2e.

9. Jay Coen Gilbert, "New Business Trend: An Authentic Commitment to Purpose," *Forbes,* July 18, 2019, https://www.forbes.com/sites/jaycoengilbert/2019/07/18/new-business-trend-an-authentic-commitment-to-purpose/#749232e6324d.

10. Leon Kaye, "Brazil's Natura Cosmetics Now the World's Largest B Corp," *TriplePundit,* December 29, 2014, https://www.triplepundit.com/story/2014/brazils-natura-cosmetics-now-worlds-largest-b-corp/38231.

11. Oliver Balch, "Natura Commits to Sourcing Sustainably from Amazon," *Guardian,* March 18, 2013, https://www.theguardian.com/sustainable-business/natura-sourcing-sustainably-from-amazon.

12. Meghan French Dunbar, "How Natura Became the World's Largest B Corp—and How It's Helping," *Conscious Company,* January 5, 2016, https://consciouscompanymedia.com/sustainable-business/how-natura-became-the-worlds-largest-b-corp-and-how-its-helping/.

Chapter 11. Convincing Consumers to Care

1. Saerom Lee, Lisa E. Bolton, and Karen P. Winterich, "To Profit or Not to Profit? The Role of Greed Perceptions in Consumer Support for Social Ventures," *Journal of Consumer Research* 44, no. 4 (May 2017): 876, https://academic.oup.com/jcr/article-abstract/44/4/853/3835623.

2. Albena Ivanova et al., "Moderating Factors on the Impact of B Corporation Certification on Purchasing Intention, Willingness to Pay a Price Premium and Consumer Trust," *Atlantic Marketing Journal* 7, no. 2 (2018): 17–35, https://digitalcommons.kennesaw.edu/amj/vol7/iss2/2.

3. Jeff Hoffman, "Market Like Patagonia, Warby Parker, and Tom's Shoes—Your Social Values Can Be a Boon to Your Brand—and Your Revenue. Here Is How," *Inc.,* April 18, 2013, https://www.inc.com/jeff-hoffman/marketing-values-patagonia-warby-parker-toms-shoes.html.

4. "Stress of Current Events Is Generating Apathy among Americans, Says Fifth Annual Conscious Consumer Spending Index (#CCSIndex)," Good.Must. Grow., accessed January 3, 2020, https://goodmustgrow.com/cms/resources/ccsi/ccsindexrelease2017.pdf.

5. United Nations, "Goal 12: Ensure Sustainable Consumption and Production Patterns," accessed January 3, 2020, https://www.un.org/sustainabledevelopment/sustainable-consumption-production/.

6. Quadia, "Why Sustainable Production and Consumption Matters: A Perspective from Quadia Impact Finance," accessed January 3, 2020, http://www.quadia.ch/uploads/images/commitment/Quadia%20Impact%20Briefing.pdf.

7. "Consumer-Goods' Brands That Demonstrate Commitment to Sustainability Outperform Those That Don't," *Nielsen,* December 10, 2015, https://www.nielsen.com/us/en/press-releases/2015/consumer-goods-brands-that-demonstrate-commitment-to-sustainability-outperform/.

8. David Boyd, "Ethical Determinants for Generations X and Y," *Journal of Business Ethics* 93, no. 3 (May 2010): 465–69, https://doi.org/10.1007/s10551–009–0233–7.

9. "Consumer-Goods' Brands."

10. Christopher Marquis and Effie Sapuridis, "Danone North America: The World's Largest B Corporation," Harvard Kennedy School Case 2156.0, April 26, 2019, 15, https://case.hks.harvard.edu/danone-north-america-the-worlds-largest-b-corporation/.

11. Fair Trade Certified, "Consumer Insights," accessed January 3, 2020, https://www.fairtradecertified.org/business/consumer-insights.

12. "Green Generation: Millennials Say Sustainability Is a Shopping Priority," *Nielsen,* November 5, 2015, https://www.nielsen.com/ie/en/insights/article/2015/green-generation-millennials-say-sustainability-is-a-shopping-priority/.

13. "Green Generation."

14. Ki-Hoon Lee and Dongyoung Shin, "Consumers' Responses to CSR Activities: The Linkage between Increased Awareness and Purchase Intention," *Public Relations Review* 36, no. 2 (June 2010): 193–95, https://doi.org/10.1016/j.pubrev.2009.10.014.

15. BrandIQ, "Benchmark Awareness Report," April 2017, unpublished PowerPoint presentation.

16. BrandIQ, "Benchmark Awareness Report."

17. "Your Chance to Vote Doesn't End on Election Day—Use Your Vote Every Day," *B the Change,* November 12, 2018, https://bthechange.com/your-chance-to-vote-doesnt-end-on-election-day-use-your-vote-every-day-18d19934b1e9.

18. Anne Field, "Boosting Awareness of B Corps by Linking Them to Voting," *Forbes,* November 27, 2018, https://www.forbes.com/sites/annefield/2018/11/27/boosting-awareness-of-b-corps-by-linking-them-to-voting/#1932eb9c6a70.

19. Certified B Corporation, "Vote Every Day. Vote B Corp," accessed January 3, 2020, https://bcorporation.net/vote.

20. Field, "Boosting Awareness of B Corps."

21. Anthea Kelsick, "Vote Every Day—Empowering a Movement to Take Action," *B the Change,* November 12, 2018, https://bthechange.com/vote-every-day-empowering-a-movement-to-take-action-3802434d7068.

Conclusion

1. Michael Moynihan, "How a True Believer Keeps the Faith," *Wall Street Journal,* August 20, 2011, https://www.wsj.com/articles/SB10001424053111903480904576 512722707621288.

2. Eric J. Hobsbawm and Marion Cumming, *Age of Extremes: The Short Twentieth Century, 1914–1991* (London: Abacus, 1995).

Acknowledgments

My research on the B Corp movement now spans over a decade, and so there are many people to acknowledge for their help and support along the way. First, thanks are due to B Lab, particularly its founders, Jay Coen Gilbert, Bart Houlahan, and Andrew Kassoy. From my first call with Jay in the summer of 2009 until today, they have all been incredibly generous with their time and insights. And I am especially grateful for the many times they have journeyed to my classes at Harvard and Cornell to share their experiences directly with students. They have been willing and engaged participants in my pursuit to understand this movement; all three did not hesitate to open their doors and tell their stories not only for this book, but also for the case studies I previously published through Harvard Business School and Harvard Kennedy School. It has been refreshing to work with individuals who are not only innovative and dedicated, but who also actively seek feedback focused on improvement. I want to give a special thanks to Jay Coen Gilbert for sharing his personal reflections with me in an unpublished manuscript titled "Ring the Bell: Bringing My Whole Self to Work and the Origin Story of the B Corp Movement" and allowing me to quote it in this book.

I would like to thank other B Lab staff I have gotten to know over the years, including Rick Alexander, Holly Ensign Barstow, Christina Forwood, Andy Fyfe, Dan Osukusy, and Emma Schned. They have all been generous in discussing their respective work. A special recognition goes to Laura Velez Villa, who now manages B Lab's work with the UN on the Sustainable Development Goals. Her first job after college graduation was as my research assistant, and her passion for Warby Parker resulted in a coauthored case study that was influential in my research of the B Corp movement. Finally, among B Lab's global partners I greatly appreciate the help and connections I received from Marcello Palazzi in Europe and the United Kingdom.

One lesson I have learned from my research is that entrepreneurs are a potent engine of change in the world. While B Lab and academics like myself can propose new ideas, we would still be at square one without the hard work of entrepreneurs implementing these systems and creating their own innovations. I am grateful to the scores of entrepreneurs whom I have met and interviewed—many whose companies were either already a B Corp or considering becoming one. It was an honor to learn from them, and I am grateful for the time many of them took to discuss their work. Special thanks to the individuals at the six different B Corps that were the focus of several Harvard case studies I previously published: Warby Parker (Neil Blumenthal and Kaki Read), New Resource Bank (Vince Siciliano), sweetriot (Sarah Endline), VeeV (Courtney and Carter Reum), First Respond (Min Ko), and Danone NA (Michael Neuwirth, Lorna Davis, and Deanna Bratter). For this book specifically, I also interviewed over sixty additional B Corp leaders from a wide range of B Corps around the world. While I don't have the space to thank all of them individually, I hope that you will get to know them all from their cited contributions throughout this book; I greatly appreciate the time and insights they shared with me.

My journey in the social impact space has been shaped by many other scholars and institutions. My initial exposure to the power of business in this sphere was thanks to one of my dissertation chairs, Jerry Davis, and for his influence I am enduringly grateful. My career at Harvard—ten years at Harvard Business School and one and a half at the Harvard Kennedy School—has impacted and shaped this journey immensely. Dutch Leonard and Kash Rangan supported my early teaching in this area, which resulted in many case studies that deepened my understanding and put me in touch with many great students, entrepreneurs, and organizations. Other colleagues who were also fellow travelers on this path and whose insights and friendship I appreciate include Julie Battilana, Alnoor Ebrahim, Johanna Mair, and Cristian Seelos. I also thank the coauthors of a number of my B Lab or B Corp case studies, including John Almandoz, Donna Khalife, Andrew Klaber, Matthew Lee, Joshua Margolis, and Bobbi Thomason. My biggest takeaway from my time at Harvard, aside from the relationships gained among peers and students, is the value of writing a book and engaging the general public in ideas that we, as academics, sometimes keep to ourselves.

Cornell has been an engaging intellectual home for me since I moved there in 2015. In particular, I value how its students are particularly focused on social and environmental issues. The Center for Sustainable Global Enterprise provides a unique rallying point for truly engaged scholarship, and I have been inspired by its work; thanks to Cornell faculty members Glen Dowell and Mark Milstein for their support and friendship. I also appreciate the excellent graduate students I have worked with at Cornell, especially Kunyuan Qiao and Qi Li, whose research assistance has been invaluable.

Writing a book has been a very different experience than the production of academic articles and case studies, and there are many people to thank for helping me take on this challenge. Andras Tilcsik, a former student of mine who coauthored the engaging book *Meltdown*, provided me with valuable advice and was gracious enough to read some of my early chapters. I also greatly appreciate the support and guidance of Jim Levine and his literary agency, and I thank Adam

Grant for introducing me to Jim. I am also grateful to the team at Yale, especially Seth Ditchik, for making this book a reality. Special thanks also to Effie Sapuridis for her excellent research assistance, clear writing, and coauthoring the Harvard Kennedy School case study "Danone NA: The World's Largest B Corporation." Thanks too to Tandy Wu and Fangmei Lu for their research assistance. Joan Friedman greatly helped me understand the process of writing books and helped tame some awkward academic prose. And I greatly appreciate Arthur Goldswag's insightful commentary and edits. Finally, I appreciate the Bark Media team, especially James Duft and Jennifer Kongs, for ideas, help, and support on how to best communicate the messages in this book.

I also have many personal debts of gratitude. My parents Maggie and Chuck Setler have been incredibly generous, letting me stay at their home in Sewickley, Pennsylvania, sometimes for weeks on end, while spending time with my amazing children, Alex and Ava, both of whom provide inspiration for a better tomorrow. I would be remiss if I didn't thank the staff at the Sewickley Starbucks for putting up with my many hours of lingering in their store. Starbucks, while not a B Corp, has many admirable practices. They have always provided benefits even to part-time employees, they are leaders in sustainable sourcing, and their stores contribute to the communities in which they operate. They are an example of a company that is resisting the worst of shareholder capitalism that more companies should follow.

Index

INDEX

B Analytics, 194, 195

B Corp certification: accountability as key factor, 17–20, 29, 193, 202, 216; community and, 148–65; consumer awareness of, 223–39; employee recruitment and, 128–47; founding of B Lab and, 19, 54–63; global expansion of, 166–86; impact investing and, 107–27; large companies and, 204–22; legal framework and, 83–106. *See also* BIA

B Corp China, 180

The B Corp Handbook (Honeyman & Jana), 154

B Corp Leadership Development, 154

B Corps Champions Retreat, 145

B Hive, 151, 162–63

B Holdings, 57–58, 61

B Impact Assessment. *See* BIA

B Lab: accountability as focus for, 17–20, 29, 193, 202, 216; B Corp community and, 148–65; certifications by, 3; consumer awareness of, 223–39; employee recruitment and, 128–47; founding of, 19, 54–63; global expansion of, 166–86; growth and expansion of, 64–82; impact investing and, 107–27; large companies and, 204–22; legal framework and, 83–106. *See also* BIA

B Lab Asia, 180–83

B Lab Australia and New Zealand, 179–80

B Lab East Africa, 186

B Lab Europe, 177–79

B Lab Japan, 180

B Lab Taiwan, 180–81

B Lab UK, 174–76, 199

B Local Colorado, 153

B Movement Builders, 221–22

B Multipliers, 172

B Work (job board), 136–37

Babies at Work program (W. S. Badger Co.), 134

Badger Balm, 133–35

Baker, Susan, 116–17

BALLE (Business Alliance for Local Living Economies), 80

BAMA Companies, 133, 197, 224

Bancolombia, 172, 173–74

Bangladesh: Grameen Danone Foods in, 206; refugees from, 129

Bare Foods, 14

Barnum, Gregor, 75–76

Becker, Doug, 120, 121, 213

Belmont University, 104

Ben & Jerry's: B Corp community and, 78, 155, 156, 159–60; as B Corp example, 7, 58, 211; BIA for, 72; consumer awareness of B Corp certification for, 226, 232; customer loyalty for, 233–34; Greyston Bakery as supplier for, 42, 159; impact investing and, 121; Unilever purchase of, 10, 61–62, 84, 124–25, 211

benchmarking, 115, 116

Beneficial State Bank, 154, 160

benefit corporations: challenges with legislation adoption and implementation, 102–4; creation of, 20; impact investing and, 116; legal framework for, xi, 32, 33–34, 83–106; shareholder primacy and, 30, 85–86

Benjamin, Esther, 216

Beraldi, Amanda, 234

Berett-Koehler Publishers, 154–55

Berger, Seth, 47

B Analytics, 194, 195

B Corp certification: accountability as key factor, 17–20, 29, 193, 202, 216; community and, 148–65; consumer awareness of, 223–39; employee recruitment and, 128–47; founding of B Lab and, 19, 54–63; global expansion of, 166–86; impact investing and, 107–27; large companies and, 204–22; legal framework and, 83–106. *See also* BIA

B Corp China, 180

The B Corp Handbook (Honeyman & Jana), 154

B Corp Leadership Development, 154

B Corps Champions Retreat, 145

B Hive, 151, 162–63

B Holdings, 57–58, 61

B Impact Assessment. *See* BIA

B Lab: accountability as focus for, 17–20, 29, 193, 202, 216; B Corp community and, 148–65; certifications by, 3; consumer awareness of, 223–39; employee recruitment and, 128–47; founding of, 19, 54–63; global expansion of, 166–86; growth and expansion of, 64–82; impact investing and, 107–27; large companies and, 204–22; legal framework and, 83–106. *See also* BIA

B Lab Asia, 180–83

B Lab Australia and New Zealand, 179–80

B Lab East Africa, 186

B Lab Europe, 177–79

B Lab Japan, 180

B Lab Taiwan, 180–81

B Lab UK, 174–76, 199

B Local Colorado, 153

B Movement Builders, 221–22

B Multipliers, 172

B Work (job board), 136–37

Babies at Work program (W. S. Badger Co.), 134

Badger Balm, 133–35

Baker, Susan, 116–17

BALLE (Business Alliance for Local Living Economies), 80

BAMA Companies, 133, 197, 224

Bancolombia, 172, 173–74

Bangladesh: Grameen Danone Foods in, 206; refugees from, 129

Bare Foods, 14

Barnum, Gregor, 75–76

Becker, Doug, 120, 121, 213

Belmont University, 104

Ben & Jerry's: B Corp community and, 78, 155, 156, 159–60; as B Corp example, 7, 58, 211; BIA for, 72; consumer awareness of B Corp certification for, 226, 232; customer loyalty for, 233–34; Greyston Bakery as supplier for, 42, 159; impact investing and, 121; Unilever purchase of, 10, 61–62, 84, 124–25, 211

benchmarking, 115, 116

Beneficial State Bank, 154, 160

benefit corporations: challenges with legislation adoption and implementation, 102–4; creation of, 20; impact investing and, 116; legal framework for, xi, 32, 33–34, 83–106; shareholder primacy and, 30, 85–86

Benjamin, Esther, 216

Beraldi, Amanda, 234

Berett-Koehler Publishers, 154–55

Berger, Seth, 47

280